Summer Adventures

Other Books by Curtis Casewit

Colorado: Off the Beaten Path
Freelance Writing
Freelance Photography
How to Make Money from Travel Writing
Making a Living in the Fine Arts
Strategies to Get the Job You Want Now
Skier's Guide to Colorado

Summer Adventures

Curtis Casewit

Collier Books
Macmillan Publishing Company
New York

Maxwell Macmillan Canada
Toronto

Maxwell Macmillan International
New York Oxford Singapore Sydney

Collier Books
Macmillan Publishing Company
866 Third Avenue
New York, NY 10022

Maxwell Macmillan Canada, Inc.
1200 Eglinton Avenue East, Suite 200
Don Mills, Ontario M3C 3N1

Macmillan Publishing Company is part of the Maxwell Communication Group of Companies.

Library of Congress Cataloging-in-Publication Data
Casewit, Curtis W.
Summer adventures / Curtis Casewit. 1st Collier Books ed.
p. cm.
Includes index.
ISBN 0-02-079331-6
1. Volunteer workers recreation.   2. Summer employment.   3. Vacations.   I. Title.
GV166.C37   1993
790'.023—dc20   93-33298
CIP

Macmillan books are available at special discounts for bulk purchases for sales promotions, premiums, fund-raising, or educational use. For details, contact:
Special Sales Director
Macmillan Publishing Company
866 Third Avenue
New York, NY 10022

First Collier Books Edition 1994
10 9 8 7 6 5 4 3 2 1
Printed in the United States of America

Contents

Part III: Travel Adventures

Acknowledgments

Along the highways and byways of researching this book, the author was assisted by numerous people.

Special thanks go to Eric Buhlmann, Director of Swiss National Tourist Offices; Peggy Mahoney, Continental Airlines, for researching flights in the U.S. and to France and Great Britain; Sol Leftin, frequent traveler to Israel; Jodi Johnson, American Adventure Expeditions; Annette Tiffany, Washington Apple Commission; Joy Adans, Boise Cascade Timber; M. D. Gempler, Washington Growers League; Nancy Schwartz, Public Affairs, Peace Corps; Laura Otterbourg and David R. Morris, Cunard Lines; Joe Lain, Lifeguard Supervisor, City of Clearwater, Florida; Meg Maiden, Maine Windjammer Association; Alex Safos, The American Language Center, Fez, Morocco; Sue Hayes, Agricultural Extension Service, University of California at Berkeley; John Gardiner, Gardiner Tennis Ranches; Dennis Van der Meer, Tennis University, Hilton Head; Alan Lovejoy, personnel expert; Chip Dennis, Alaska worker; Dennis Burke, Idaho sheep farmer; Phil Clayberg, National Park Service; Brimstone Hill Vineyard; Colonel H. Bentegeat, Military Attaché, French Embassy; Dan Solomon, E & J

Acknowledgments

Gallo Winery; Debby Price, Weyerhaeuser Company; Rich Bell, Crow Canyon Archaeological Center; Neil Smart, Department of Parks and Recreation, City of Healdsburg, California; Rohn Engh, Photosource International; Jeanne Rogers, Florida Department of Commerce; Claudia Winkler, Volunteers for Outdoor Colorado; Maura Staker, EPA International Internships; Kristine Meyer, Beaver Village Condominiums, Winter Park; Barb Jennings, Steamboat Resort; James and Joleen Firestine, Pacific Northwest harvesters; Barb Horn and Lori Martin, Colorado Division of Wildlife; Robert Phillips, The Peach Council; Christy Metz, National Park Service; and C.E.C.S. Wordprocessing, for a job well done.

Summer Adventures was greatly enriched by the additional research of Kristine Bittner and Helen Evans.

Lastly, thanks to Niccolo Casewit, for sharing your many volunteering experiences, and to Stephen Casewit, for slaving away in Alaskan waters, French vineyards, and Swiss dairy farms and for your long letters and diary entries about other adventures.

Curtis Casewit
Denver, Colorado

Introduction

The lure of adventure! New friends, new sights, new directions! You'll find all of this in *Summer Adventures*.

Summer Adventures is designed for the person who wants to do something *different* with his or her summer. It lists a number of suggestions and encourages you to develop new ideas. I've tried to include a broad range of options in these pages, from volunteer activities to paid work to study and travel—all with a touch of adventure in them, all sure to lead to an unforgettable summer.

For instance, you can volunteer in the U.S. Forest Service, assist in a national park, or lend a hand in a state park. Or maybe you'll want to apply for a tennis instructor's job at a resort, a lifeguard position on an exotic beach, or join the crew of a cruise ship. For more adventure, try taking painting classes in Mexico, leading a rock climb in Colorado, or picking grapes in California or France.

Want to expand your knowledge this summer? You can use the time to take cooking classes or learn how to photograph the outdoors; find excitement on an archaeological dig or catch salmon on an Alaskan fishing boat; try your hand as a wrangler at a Western dude ranch or as a fire look-out in a state forest. Inside these pages you'll find ideas ranging from golf caddying in the Rockies to biking in New Zealand to learning Arabic in Morocco. Whatever course you choose to follow, you're sure to have one of the most memorable summers ever.

A lot of hands-on research went into these pages. Through journals, diaries, and interviews with people who have actually participated in the adventures, you'll get first-hand descriptions of working conditions, realistic expectations on costs or pay checks, and advice on how and when best to apply.

I've included additional names and addresses in all the chapters, giving you plenty of opportunity to research your own ideas further. While I've tried to provide a wide sampling of adventures, this book is not intended to be an exhaustive listing of every opportunity but rather a menu of possibilities. I encourage you to share your own ideas and experiences with me, so that I can include them in future editions.

The adventures in these pages are aimed at men and women ages 16 to 22, although in some cases I've stretched that range a bit in order to include particularly worthwhile trips or activities. And though we generally think of summer falling during the months of June through August, *Summer Adventures* does include some action occurring as early as April and May, or as late as October.

So keep reading; something is bound to fill your bill. And above all, enjoy yourself this summer!

Part I

Learning
Adventures

1

The Great Outdoors

Join a Mountain Club

Dawn. Your feet strike out. They carry you through a meadow; then you're in the forest, still dark and mysterious at this hour. Pine needles muffle your steps. You breathe deeply: Conifers, ferns, the bark of aspen trees. The trail now leads you upward, up a staircase of rocks, higher and higher to a sun-drenched ridge. The breeze touches your nostrils, cools your brow, stirs your mind. The mountain weaves up and flows into the sky.

You're on a week-long backpacking expedition with ten other members of a mountain club, carrying your own tent and supplies and experiencing the outdoors in a way few people do. Each day you hike from ten to twelve miles, set up camp, hungrily eat dinner around a campfire with your fellow mountain club members, and watch the dying embers as the sun sets. Then you crawl into your sleeping bag, exhausted. But you awake amazingly refreshed early the next morning to the sound of bird calls.

Mountain clubs run the gamut from giants with ambitious conservation programs, club rooms, book and magazine publishing programs, and wilderness outings of every description, to tiny fifty-people groups. A few clubs set up major expeditions. Some clubs are chiefly interested in hiking. The majority of groups organize outings. Most go for trail building or trail maintenance. By and large, all clubs are safety-conscious, and offer a splendid opportunity to spend the summer in the mountains in the company of other enthusiasts.

For Further Information

The coast-to-coast roster of mountain clubs listed below is not a complete one, but offers a number of possibilities for would-be hiking leaders and for other unpaid leadership positions, as well as for volunteer trail workers and other volunteer positions (see pages 000 and 000). The clubs are listed in approximate order of importance in terms of reputation, size, and/or activities.

The American Hiking Society
P.O. Box 20160
Washington, DC 20160

American Hiking Society Volunteer Vacations
P.O. Box 86
North Scituate, MA 02060

Appalachian Mountain Club
2 Joy Street
Boston, MA 02108
One of the oldest clubs. Well respected.

Colorado Mountain Club
710 10th Street, #200
Golden, CO 80401
Lots of outings.

MIT Outing Club
77 Massachusetts Avenue
Cambridge, MA 02139
Gobbles up volunteers.

Sierra Club
National Headquarters
730 Polk Street
San Francisco, CA 94109
*Daily trips. Environmentally conscious. The Sierra Club has
750,000 members. It is superbly well organized and charges more
than other groups.*

Adirondack Mountain Club
Volunteer Trails Program
Box 867
Lake Placid, NY 12946

Tahoe Rim Trail
P.O. Box 10156
South Lake Tahoe, CA 95731

Colorado Trail Foundation
548 Pine Song Trail
Golden, CO 80401
*In addition, willing hands are sought by the National Outdoor
Volunteer Network. It consists of the following outdoor-minded
groups:*

Florida Trail Association (FTA)
P.O. Box 13708
Gainsville, FL 32604
Brochure available.

The Trail Center
Los Altos, CA 94022

Volunteers for Outdoor Allegheny (VOA)
500 Seavey Road
Pittsburgh, PA 15209
Well organized.

Volunteers for Outdoor Colorado (VOC)
1410 Grant Street
Denver, CO 80203

Volunteers for Outdoor Washington (VOW)
4516 University Way, NE
Seattle, WA 98105-4511

Volunteers for the Outdoors (VFO)
P.O. Box 36246
Albuquerque, NM 87176

Be a Volunteer Hiking Leader

You're a volunteer hiking leader on a typical one-day hike. You're leading a group of twenty adults up a winding trail with sweeping views of
mountains, forests, and meadows of wildflowers. It is you who decides
the pace: not too slow, not too fast; no racing. Hikers must conserve
energy to complete the twelve-mile outing. The "rear guard" brings up
the slowpokes. You wait until everyone is in sight.

As a volunteer hiking leader, you have the pleasure of sharing the
outdoors with other people and of making the wilderness accessible
to them. You'll teach environmental awareness to hikers by avoiding
off-trail travel (which causes erosion) and you'll prevent the picking of
wildflowers. The group will expect you to have some savvy about wild-

flowers, birds, geological formations, and the history of an area. And you must be able to stay calm in crisis situations. In short, you carry total authority and responsibility for the outing.

What You Need to Know

Participants Most mountain clubs require leaders to be at least eighteen years old, although some allow sixteen and seventeen year olds. In some cases you need to be a member of the club to lead, and generally, a Red Cross First Aid card and CPR certification are required. You must be knowledgeable about the dangers of lightning (for it is you who decides if the party has to turn back in a storm), and backcountry knowledge is essential. A nice personality helps, too. *Duration* A typical hike can range from a couple of hours to a full week. *Facilities* Some mountain clubs supply meals, which are complimentary for the leader. In others, members bring their own food. Shelter can be a hut, a tent, a campground, or the outdoors. *Cost* There is no cost to the leader; members pay nominal fees, from a few dollars for a brief hike to several hundred, depending on the group and the outing location and length.

For Further Information

Contact mountain clubs listed above.

Join a Trail Building or Trail Maintenance Crew

Most mountain clubs and other outdoor organizations encourage volunteer trail crews. That means you could be part of trail construction or trail maintenance. For example, volunteers for the American Hiking Society helped build a suspension bridge in Yellowstone National Park. A veritable army of volunteers carved out the five-hundred-mile-long Colorado Trail connecting Denver with Durango along the Continental Divide.

Cleanup volunteers carrying large plastic bags are a common sight in the Appalachians, the Adirondacks, the Smoky Mountains, and the Rockies. You can spot them on the steep trails of Mt. Rainier, Mount Hood, Longs Peak, and dozens of other mountains clearing away beer cans and other trash left by careless tourists. Cleanup crews often work with the National Park Service or the U.S. Forest Service. The various coast-to-coast Sierra Club chapters are especially handy at this volunteer action.

Much of the other trail work is routine and includes removing rocks, handsawing tree stumps, cutting brush, and reconstructing steps. Volunteers also erect and repair stone retaining walls that help keep the trails intact.

Trail people stay out for a day, a weekend, or often for a full week. Some trips involve backpacking; others actually use South American llamas, horses, or burros to carry duffel bags and the week's food supplies.

Trail building pits you against obstacles galore. Crews sometimes labor in pouring rain, and it's not uncommon to ford a raging, ice-cold mountain stream or to find the right route along deer tracks, past trout lakes, and through thick evergreen forests. Some projects take place above eleven thousand feet, a fairly high altitude, which can make a newcomer dizzy or nauseous. What's more, the summit can be dangerous and electrical thunderstorms with lightning are not uncommon there.

It's important to be in good physical condition and to be able to maintain a cool head. An American Hiking Society bulletin advises trail crews heading for California's Plumas National Forest that "Bears and rattlesnakes will be seen; precautions will be taken to avoid confrontations. . . ." Juneau, Alaska volunteers are warned that the "cutting and clearing of trees felled by the wind and removal of brush from the trail is demanding work." Some crews wear hard hats and use picks, shovels, axes, handsaws, and McCloud rakes.

Yet the experience is rewarding and can mean an almost free or very cheap vacation with like-minded folks. Whatever the length of the trip, you get acquainted with a lot of other outdoor people, which can result in long-term relationships. After-hours volunteers fish, take pictures, hike, or just hang out. The work may be hard, but the rewards are there too: beautiful scenery and unforgettable nighttime campfires!

What You Need to Know

Participants Teams usually consist of ten to twelve volunteers plus an experienced, unpaid crew leader. The average age is from twenty-two to twenty-five, though many clubs accept workers as young as sixteen years old. *Duration* The workday lasts about five sweaty hours. You can volunteer for a single trip or several in a season. *Facilities* Food is generally free. One mountain club packs frozen gourmet beef stew, homemade Italian sausage, ingredients for stir-fry, and even turkey Stroganoff, all to be cooked on special three-burner stoves. You will usually bring your own tent for sleeping under the stars. *Cost* Costs are usually modest, ranging from completely free to a $25 fee.

For Further Information

Contact mountain clubs listed above.

Be an Outdoor Scientist

As though leading hikes, building and maintaining trails, and heading trail cleanup crews were not enough, you can also spend your summer vacation doing some fascinating outdoor science work. Volunteers are always needed throughout the U.S. to test river, stream, and lake waters.

Waters are tested for heavy metals like lead and mercury and for other toxic substances. There is often lab work involved. In one western state the program involves four-hundred high school students. Every summer they check the metal and oxygen content and the hardness of fifty-three rivers. The young people learn a lot and get some exercise at the same time.

These "monitoring" programs exist in forty states and the nature of the work varies. In Montana, for instance, the young scientists test rivers for acid rain and the effects of mining. In Groton, Connecticut, volunteers probe to evaluate shellfish and finfish health. The Delaware program examines streams for salinity and oxygen. A Louisiana "beach-sweep" catalogues the litter found on various beaches. In Massachusetts, there's acid rain research. The programs vary along similar lines throughout the other states.

What You Need to Know

Participants The average age is sixteen to eighteen, though in many states these programs use students from middle schools and junior highs. *Duration* The length of each program varies and depends on the type of testing to be done. Many programs begin in the spring, when water temperatures begin to rise, and continue through the summer, sometimes into the school year. *Pay* The positions are all volunteer. *Other* Most programs require participants to take a three- or four-day workshop.

For Further Information

For a list of forty states with monitoring programs and their addresses, write to:

Citizen Volunteer Environmental Monitoring Programs
c/o Office of Water
Environmental Protection Agency
Washington, DC 20460

Experience the Excitement of Outward Bound

It has been called "the most adventurous of all schools." One former student spoke of it as "a sort of Russian roulette on the rocks"; some well-conditioned young people who took a fourteen-day course com-

pared it to the Marine Corps—only tougher. It is known as Outward
Bound, or OB, for short.

There are about twenty-nine thousand participants every year at
the five Outward Bound schools combined. Each of the schools focuses on a different area of survival training: **Pacific Crest Outward
Bound**—sailing and mountaineering; **Colorado Outward Bound**—
mostly climbing, backpacking, and rafting; **Voyager Outward Bound**—
best known for canoeing; **Hurricane Island Outward Bound**—sailing;
and **North Carolina Outward Bound School**—rock climbing.

Most OB courses take place in the wilderness. In Colorado, for
instance, much of the outdoor action goes on at the far-flung spectacular Collegiate Range where the peaks often exceed fourteen hundred
feet, or in the rugged two-hundred-mile-long Sangre de Cristo (Blood
of Christ) mountain range. In Utah, Outward Bound operates in the
stark, painterly Canyonlands; in Arizona, in no less than the Grand
Canyon. In Maine, OB's sailors fly lively Atlantic waters in primitive sailing craft and land at nameless, rainy Maine islands.

The Outward Bound Schools are well known for their survival programs and instruction in rock climbing, backpacking, white water rafting, and even sailing. Outward Bound makes no secret of its characteristics;
its literature describes the courses as "strenuous and bold." The instructors are "adventurers in their own right." Students have to run a mountain mile at dawn. Then they plunge into an icy mountain stream. They
scale high walls and practice *bouldering* on giant rocks, followed by
inching along a two-hundred-foot-long rope strung across a river or
thirty feet above ground. Outward Bounders also do much mountain
walking, backpacking, and high-altitude camping, and they get instruction in *rappelling*. Yet with all these wilderness and fitness activities,
serious accidents are extremely rare. The rock climbing and backpacking
classes include first aid instruction, and even a session in how to treat
hypothermia.

After an initial training, groups of eight to ten go on their first
"expeditions"—i.e., they trudge off to remote locations. They learn river crossing skills, how to handle climbing ropes, and map reading. Then

each participant is led to an uninhabited, primitive area where he or she must stay for three days and three nights. This three-day solo is the most important event of each course. The equipment is minimal: a bit of line and a hook, a sleeping bag, eight matches, a nine-foot square plastic sheet, a first aid kit, two quarts of water, and a knife. The food supply depends on skill and knowledge of edible plant and animal life. Being alone for such a long period allows time for reflection and solitude; the sparse foods bring out survival skills. As a student at the Hurricane Island Outward Bound School in Maine remembers, "Three days on a fifty-by-one-hundred-yard dot of land with a few matches and a tin can for boiling water. . . . For food, I found mussels, clams, and snails."

The Hurricane Island School is located ten miles off the rugged coast of Maine at the entrance to Penobscot Bay. Other islands serve as temporary course bases from time to time. Extensive seamanship, ocean sailing expeditions, and emergency medical aid highlight the course. The first days are spent in physical conditioning and skills training. Expeditions play a major role at Hurricane Island: participants operate twelve-man, thirty-foot-long open pull boats to remote islands offshore on the Eastern Seaboard.

Students are ultimately rewarded for their hardships. They later speak of mastered challenges, their own unexpected endurance, the conquest of the self, the intensity of the experience, the powerful bond of the teams, the valuable skills learned. . . . What more could one ask from a school?

What You Need to Know

"Wearing the same clothes for twenty-three days, not being able to shower, you learn not to take the luxuries of life for granted."

Participants The program serves a diverse set of participants, mainly high school and college students, but you must be at least fourteen years old to participate. About forty percent of the students are women, and the organization actively recruits students from urban centers. No outdoor experience is necessary; just be in good physical condition and be willing to try new experiences. *Duration* Courses average about twenty-two days, but range from six to forty-two days. Semester courses last from twenty-eight to eighty-four days. More than three hundred courses are offered each summer in over twenty states. *Facilities* Except for sailing courses where you live on a boat, most courses are conducted outdoors, with tents as shelters. *Cost* Outward Bound is quite expensive, with most courses costing between $395 and $2,695. Semesters can cost up to $6,695. Scholarships are available on a first-come, first-served basis, and more than 25 percent of the students are on scholarship. Financial aid is also available; forms are in the Outward Bound catalogue of courses. *Other* OB offers college credit to students working on special education or recreation degrees. Discipline is strict: alcoholic beverages, cigarettes, drugs, and guns are prohibited in all schools.

"The last two days were the most grueling. The group backpacked back to the base camp, which means marching ten miles per day. We were exhausted. For a finale, the food ran out."

For Further Information

For more information contact the five Outward Bound Schools directly or the National Office.

Outward Bound National Office
384 Field Point Road
Greenwich, CT 06830

Hurricane Island Outward Bound School
Rockland, ME 04841

Voyageur Outward Bound School
10900 Cedar Lake Road
Minnetonka, MN 55343

Colorado Outward Bound School
945 Pennsylvania Street
Denver, CO 80203-3198

North Carolina Outward Bound School
121 Sterling Street
Morganton, NC 28655-3443

Pacific Crest Outward Bound School
0110 SW Bancroft Street
Portland, OR 97201

Move Up to NOLS

The National Outdoor Leadership School (NOLS) is considered the West Point of the outdoors by America's top mountaineers and expedition experts. NOLS trains leaders. "If Outward Bound is boot camp, then NOLS is officer's candidate school," says one former student.

The programs are not for softies. Classes include ice climbing, kayaking, expedition climbing, and rock climbing. The long sessions among the cold stone slabs in the remote Wind River Range of Wyoming teach advanced climbing maneuvers like the free rappel and other intricacies of rope climbing. Here you'll become familiar with the climber's lifesaving hardware, and you'll learn valuable leadership skills, including judgment and safety, which will prove useful to you as a mountain guide. In fact, spending a summer as a student at NOLS can mean employment as a climbing leader the next summer anywhere in the world.

The Wyoming-based NOLS offers short and long trips and expeditions to Alaska, Washington State, and Mexico. NOLS groups have climbed Mt. McKinley, also known as Denali.

What You Need to Know

Participants The NOLS programs are prestigious and attract both teenagers and older students, aged twenty-five to thirty. *Duration* Some classes are as short as two weeks, but expeditions can last up to three months. *Facilities* Housing ranges from stone buildings to campgrounds and tents. *Cost* Courses range from $1,300 to $5,000, depending on length and location. *Other* NOLS offers college credit for a full semester.

For Further Information

National Outdoor Leadership School
P.O. Box AA
Lander, WY 82520

2

Government-Sponsored Programs

Volunteer in a National Park

How would you like to spend a summer amidst America's most stunning scenery? The fifty U.S. national parks offer paid positions in dozens of areas, and volunteers are also needed at our glorious national seashores, at various national recreation areas, national monuments, battlefields, and other historic sites. The National Park Service comprises 359 different units which cover eighty million acres. With volunteers needed throughout the system, it employs a massive number of people.

Every summer, several thousand wilderness enthusiasts become seasonal "VIPS" (Volunteers in Parks) who enjoy the forested mountain splendors of California's Yosemite National Park, Alaska's Glacier National Park, Utah's Zion National Park, Olympic National Park in Washington, and Shenandoah National Park in Virginia, as well as warm-weather oases such as Florida's Everglades and Hawaii Volcanoes National Park, to name just a few.

What do these incredible landscapes have in common? Historian and novelist Wallace Stegner put it best when he wrote, "The National

Parks are unmarred by signboards, hot dog stands, super highways or high tension lines. . . ." Instead, they offer such wonders as North America's highest mountain (20,320-foot Mt. McKinley, also known as Denali), its largest known caves (Mammoth), and its gorgeous scenery (as is seen in Glacier National Park).

Tourism numbers have never been higher in these parks, and volunteers are needed more than ever to keep the parks clean, accessible, and beautiful for the thousands of visitors each year. In fact, a National Park Service accountant once figured that volunteers provide the National Park Service in the Rocky Mountain region alone with the equivalent of five million dollars worth of free labor.

The seasonal VIPs assist as fee collectors at park entrances, interpretive guides (who inform visitors about a park's history, flora, and fauna), historians, and naturalists. In addition, summer VIPs are needed to assist with unskilled work on trails, forestry programs, and various maintenance activities.

Parks also employ paid seasonal park rangers. These seasonal park rangers describe a park's natural features to tourists and try to educate them about environmental issues by explaining, for instance, that picking flowers or off-trail hiking is prohibited because of the damage it can wreak on the ecosystem. Other possible responsibilities include work as interpreters, campground supervisors, and law enforcers.

What You Need to Know

Participants You must be a U.S. citizen and at least eighteen by May 13 of the year you plan to volunteer. To be a seasonal park ranger, you must have completed your third year of college. To apply for law enforcement and public safety positions you have to be twenty-one or older. You'll also need some background in recreation management, forestry, the sciences, and conservation, and you must be in excellent physical shape. A previous stint at a park is helpful. *Duration* VIPs and seasonal park rangers usually work a three-month stint from June through August. *Facilities* In certain parks, housing is provided. *Pay* VIP positions are on an unpaid volunteer basis. Seasonal park rangers are paid employees with full health benefits. *Other* The National Park Service takes applications for most summer positions between September 1 and January 15 for the coming season. The January 15 deadline is strict and it's suggested that you get your application in early; many applicants don't realize that they have plenty of competition. Remember, the competition for summer work is very keen; the number of applicants far exceeds the jobs available. Park rangers advise that if you apply on time and are not contacted by at least June 1, you will probably not be offered a job. It's wise to aim for smaller park areas, since the better-known parks—Yellowstone, for instance—mean more applicants and thus more competition.

For Further Information

United States Department of the Interior
National Park Service
Washington, DC 20240

National Park Service
Seasonal Employment Personnel
P.O. Box 37127
Washington, DC 20013

National Park Service Regional Offices:
North Atlantic Region:
15 State Street
Boston, MA 02114

Mid-Atlantic Region:
143 South Third Street
Philadelphia, PA 19106

Southeast Region:
75 Spring Street, SW
Atlanta, GA 30303

Midwest Region:
1709 Jackson Street
Omaha, NE 68102

Rocky Mountain Region:
12795 West Alameda Parkway
Denver, CO 80225-0287

Southwest Region:
P.O. Box 728
Santa Fe, NM 87501

Western Region:
450 Golden Gate Avenue
San Francisco, CA 94102

Be a State Park Aide

State parks were created for the enjoyment of all visitors. For those staying awhile, they offer excellent camping, beautiful scenery, horseback riding, hiking, and more. For locals and day trippers, state parks also often provide areas for fishing and boating, and offer the beauty of natural settings for a picnic or brief, relaxing walk.

During the last decade there has been a marked increase in the size of state parks across the nation. Each of the fifty states has its own policies of acquiring new lands and maintaining them, and all need seasonal help in running the day-to-day activities. An internship with a state park may be perfect for you if you want to be away from the noise and soot of the city and work in a healthy environment. A state park position is also a great way for students majoring in Parks and Recreation to get their feet wet.

Job duties are varied. One day you could work the entrance station, collecting fees and giving directions. Or you could participate in patrols on land or water, where you monitor maintenance or enforcement problems. The next day you may be cleaning out fire rings and dumping trash left by a careless camper. State park aides also check visitors' camping permits, collect admission at entrance gates, help patrol campgrounds, and direct visitors. They sometimes help in the construction of new routes for off-road vehicles and bicycles.

Expect to attend regional and local staff meetings for park personnel. It helps to know who is in charge of what and what the plan of each park is. You may even get the opportunity to participate in budget planning and policies.

As a summer aide, you may get a small stipend. And after your first summer, you have a good chance at being invited back for a paid position.

What You Need to Know

Participants You must be sixteen years old to be a summer aide. It's helpful to have a science or nature background to be a summer aide. *Duration* The season is usually June through August. *Facilities* There are generally no housing facilities in the state parks. *Pay* Some positions are unpaid and some offer modest hourly wages.

For Further Information

Arizona State Parks
1688 West Adams Street, Room 106
Phoenix, AZ 85007

Alaska Division of State Parks and Outdoor Recreation
225A Codova Street
Anchorage, AK 99501

California Department of Parks and Recreation
P.O. Box 2390
Sacramento, CA 95811

Colorado Parks and Outdoor Recreation
Division of Natural Resources
1313 Sherman Street
Denver, CO 80203

Florida Department of Natural Resources Conservation
3900 Commonwealth Boulevard
Tallahassee, FL 32303

Illinois Department of Education and Information
Lincoln Tower Plaza
Springfield, IL 62706

Maine Department of Conservation
Bureau of Parks and Recreation
State House Station 22
Augusta, ME 04333

Massachusetts Department of Environmental Management
Division of Forests and Parks
100 Cambridge Street
Boston, MA 02202

Montana Department of Fish, Wildlife and Parks
1420 East Sixth Avenue
Helena, MT 59620

New York State Office of Parks,
    Recreation and Historic Preservation
Empire State Plaza
Albany, NY 12238

Ohio Department of Natural Resources
Division of Parks and Recreation
Fountain Square
Columbus, OH 43224

Oregon State Parks and Recreation Division
525 Trade Street, SE
Salem, OR 97310

South Carolina Division of State Parks
1205 Pendleton Street
Columbia, SC 29201

Texas Parks and Wildlife Department
4200 Smith School Road
Austin, TX 78744

Virginia Division of Parks and Recreation
1201 Washington Building
Capitol Square
Richmond, VA 23219

Wyoming Recreation Commission
Herschler Building
Cheyenne, WY 82002

Join the Forest Service Summer Volunteers

Mary is in her second summer as a volunteer at the Mount Holy Cross
National Forest in Colorado. She's twenty-one, can carry a fifty-five-
pound backpack without complaint, knows how to put up her one-
person tent, travels alone, and loves solitude. She returned this summer
because she loves the starlit, moon-bright nights and the smell of pine

needles. Although she's not fond of litterers or off-trail, erosion-causing hikers, she's able to talk to them quietly and they pay attention. Her title is "Wilderness Guard."

U.S. Forest Service volunteers can usually choose from among a large variety of activities. "They get a chance to do the things they do well," explains one forest ranger. And, in fact, the application form specifically asks you to list the areas you'd like to work in, as well as special skills you have that might prove important to the Forest Service. The possibilities are endless, and include wildlife preservation, geology, botany, landscaping, mountaineering, campgrounds, horses and livestock, and computers. . . . Indeed, there's work for almost anyone.

The U.S. Forest Service maintains some 114,000 miles of trails, six thousand campgrounds and picnic areas, eleven hundred boating sites, and more than three hundred swimming pools. This means constant work for scores of volunteers who can help with repairs, cleanups, and various chores.

The official list for volunteer projects is a long one: preparing fences; building and maintaining trails; picking up litter; planting trees; building and installing nesting boxes; building and installing picnic tables; reinforcing stream banks; digging latrines; raking and cleaning campgrounds; painting and building signs; answering phones and greeting visitors; sorting, labeling or contributing to photo files; washing and waxing government vehicles; building barrier-free campsites, docks, and trails; and other tasks.

What You Need to Know

Participants Seasonal workers are known as "forestry aides." There are about a thousand positions open for more than ten thousand applicants. You must be at least eighteen years old and a U.S. citizen. You must be in good health and be able to perform volunteer activities without undue hazard to anyone. A medical examination may be required at the Forest Service's expense. *Duration* The season is usually June through August. *Facilities* Most national forests offer a free campground spot for your tent or camper. *Cost* The Forest Service may reimburse expenses such as transportation (gas for your car, for instance), money for uniforms, and sometimes even lodging. Bear in mind that a volunteer isn't considered a federal employee and isn't entitled to many of the benefits they receive. *Other* The Forest Service has strict rules for volunteers and employees alike. Breaking these rules usually results in immediate dismissal.

1. Use of firearms in or near a government camp or living quarters is strictly prohibited.
2. Consumption of intoxicating beverages on government-owned property, transportation of such beverages in government-owned or -leased vehicles, or use of such beverages at anytime or place while performing work for the Forest Service is prohibited.
3. Possession or use of any and all forms of addictive or hallucinatory drugs will result in dismissal. These drugs include, but are not limited to, marijuana, barbiturates, amphetamines, and cocaine.
4. Fights or use of abusive language toward the public, other employees, or your supervisor will result in dismissal.

For Further Information

United States Forest Service
P.O. Box 96090
Washington, DC 20005-4788

Northern Region:
P.O. Box 7669
Missoula, MT 59807

Pacific Northwest Region:
P.O. Box 3623
Portland, OR 97208

Rocky Mountain Region:
11177 West Eighth Avenue
Lakewood, CO 80255

Southern Region:
1720 Peachtree Road, NW
Atlanta, GA 30367

Southwestern Region:
517 Gold Avenue, SW
Albuquerque, NM 87102

Eastern Region:
310 West Wisconsin Avenue
Milwaukee, WI 53203

Intermountain Region:
324 25th Street
Ogden, UT 84401

Alaska Region:
P.O. Box 21628
Juneau, AK 99802-1628

Pacific Southwest Region:
630 Sansome Street
San Francisco, CA 94111

3

Summer Studies

Spend the Summer as an Archaeologist

There are archaeological opportunities throughout the world, in Israel, Mexico, Britain, Asia, Canada, and elsewhere. Each offers a unique blend of atmosphere, history, education, and excavations. And each will provide you with an unforgettable experience.

Although every dig has its own schedule and routines, volunteers can always attend lectures, seminars, and workshops. No matter where you are, the physical labor is not easy: You're generally bent over the ground on your hands and knees, scraping sand cautiously and waiting for a discovery that may or may not come. The physical part is dusty, dirty, hot, and demanding. Yet day after day, you find yourself getting more and more curious and fascinated with archaeology. "You get hooked," says one volunteer. "You learn to sweep gently with a whisk broom and a trowel, digging millimeter by millimeter because you don't want to disturb anything." Among other objects, volunteers have found parts of artifacts, bits of pottery, jewelry, and ornaments.

Apart from the carefully monitored excavation techniques, volunteers learn to map, photograph, and record their finds; they watch technicians analyze every bit of the newly found items. Since many programs are run through universities, volunteers attend lectures and seminars about history and techniques, often led by world-renowned archaeologists and historians. And the summer students are continually learning about cultures and peoples that existed thousands of years ago.

A few choice places follow.

Colorado

The country in southern Colorado is rich with yellow sands, mauve stones, and giant rock faces. Mesas and canyons reach across the borders of New Mexico and Arizona. This is the area where the mysterious cliff dwellings of the Anasazi of Mesa Verde were discovered. Some ten thousand of these Native Americans farmed here until about 1300 A.D.

Then they mysteriously vanished.

But the Anasazi Indians left some extraordinary dwellings, with enough pottery, seeds, and hunting tools to give us clues about the nature of their lives. Thanks to these tribes, there is a permanent and very busy research facility in the region, the Crow Canyon Archaeological Center near Cortez, Colorado. New discoveries are constantly being made here, and will continue to be made for many years. And best of all, anyone can come for a week or longer in the summer, listen to interesting lectures, participate in educational enrichment, and then help with the excavations.

Israel

Digging in Israel is like living through history. Artifacts from ancient worlds surround you and new discoveries from many cultures are scraped from the ground every day. In a Jerusalem suburb, construction crews accidentally discovered Jason's Tomb, which dates back to the first century A.D. The famous Dead Sea scrolls were also discovered by chance. And near Jerusalem's Western Wall, a well-known local archaeologist uncovered Byzantine coins, brilliantly engineered water systems, and three-thousand-year-old vases and jars.

Away from the cities, you can visit finished archaeological sites or participate in on-going digs. In Caesaria, for instance, you see evidence of the town's status as the former Roman capital of Palestine. All around you stretches the Mediterranean landscape of eucalyptus, palms, agaves, cacti. One visitor remembers cycling to the ancient Roman aqueduct which flanks a beach, where he found the shore deserted, despite the attributes of sun and sky, of golden sands and the gentlest of waves. Pedaling across the moist ground for a few kilometers, he divested himself of sandals, shorts, and bathing suit—there was not a human being to be seen from horizon to horizon. The water was perfect; the ocean-touched temperature neither too hot nor too cold.

Although many digs throughout Israel are now complete, some others (see listings) are open to U.S. volunteers with large billfolds and strong backs. Because of the heat, the workday begins early in the morning, breaks during the afternoon, and concludes in the evening, so that you're not digging during the hours of almost intolerable summer sun. The minimum age is usually seventeen.

Mexico and South America

But you shouldn't forget archaeological opportunities nearer home. Mexico and South America offer rich opportunities to unearth a culture's past and uncover life as it was. From the Mexican capital it is easy to reach Teotihuacan, site of the ancient Indian rites of worship. You can also visit the mystic Pyramids of the Sun and Moon, glorious monuments of the Toltec civilization, which rival the Pyramids of Egypt in size and grandeur. By 500 A.D., Teotihuacan itself was larger than Imperial Rome.

The Mayan ruins on the Yucatan Peninsula are about seventy-five miles away from Merida, but easy to get to by bus. One of the most intriguing and mysterious peoples who ever walked the face of the earth, the Mayans carved their unique place in history out of a dense jungle, stone by stone, more than a thousand years ago—long before the Spanish conquistadors arrived in Latin America. The Mayans erected giant temples with the precision of master builders, invented the most complete calendar in history, and gave us astronomers and mathematicians who where centuries ahead of their time. Many travelers agree that the Mayan Cities of the Dawn with their history-laden pyramids and temples at Chichen Itza, are of extraordinary archeological interest.

Whether you dig in Colorado, Israel, Peru, Greece, Egypt, or Mexico, a week or a summer on an archaeological dig is unforgettable.

What You Need to Know

Please note that the particulars of background, cost, facilities, and applications vary from dig to dig. Check with each program for specifics.

Participants Most digs require that you be sixteen years old to volunteer. In a few archaeology projects, you need an educational background in history or archaeology. Others have no such requirements. *Duration* You can volunteer for as short as a week or as long as a complete summer. Most digs have specified time periods you must commit to. *Facilities* Living conditions vary from site to site. Most provide cabins or tents. Some may even put up volunteers in houses or hotels. Food is generally included in an archaeology vacation. *Cost* Keep in mind that volunteering on a dig is not cheap: you pay not only for the instruction, but for your flight and room and board. The costs can range from $150 a week for a site close to home to as much as $2,000 in the Middle East, for instance. *Other* Some programs supply you with tools (trowels, brooms, little buckets) but others ask that you bring your own. Many excavations are sponsored by universities and offer college credit for volunteering your time and labor.

For Further Information

Hooked by archaeology? The following listings are worldwide but not comprehensive; to learn more about other digs, trips, and seminars, check with your public library. A few interesting books, information guides, and brochures follow these addresses.

American Excavations:
Arkansas Archaeological Survey
University Museum of Arkansas
Fayetteville, AR 72701

Egyptology:
American University in Cairo
Summer Seminar in Egyptology
866 United Nations Plaza, Suite 517
New York, NY 10017

American Anasazi Excavations:
Crow Canyon Archaeological Center
23390 County Road, K
Cortez, CO 80321

Empires of Ancient Morocco:
Earthwatch
680 Mt. Auburn Street
Watertown, MA 02272

Mesa Verde:
Cortez Visitor Bureau
P.O. Drawer HH
Cortez, CO 80321

Field Trips in Britain and Europe:
Young Archaeologists Club
Clifford Chambers
4 Clifford Street
York YO1 England

Archaeological Excavations in Britain:
Copper Mines of County Kerry, Ireland
Earthwatch
680 Mt. Auburn Street
Watertown, MA 02272

Council for British Archaeology
112 Kennington Road
London SE11 6RE England

Canadian Archaeology Project:
The Forks Public Archaeology Project
130 Fort Street
Winnipeg, Manitoba, Canada R3C

Israel Archaeological Excavations:
Israel Archaeological Excavations
Project 67 Ltd.
10 Hatton Garden
London EC1N 8AH England

Department of Antiquities and Museums
P.O. Box 586
Jerusalem 91911 Israel

Summer Archaeological Seminar
United Synagogue of America
155 Fifth Avenue, #504
New York, NY 10016

Archaeology Seminars
P.O. Box 14002
Jerusalem 91140 Israel

South American Excavations:
Peruvian Tourist Office
100 Bruckell Avenue
Miami, FL 33131

Information Guides, Books, Brochures

Archaeological Excavations in Israel
Antiquities Authority
P.O. Box 586
Jerusalem 91004 Israel
This brochure is also available through any Israel tourist office.

The Archaeology Handbook, by Bill McMillon
Archaeological Institute of America
15 Park Row
New York, NY 10038

The Archaeological Fieldwork Opportunities Bulletin
675 Commonwealth Avenue
Boston, MA 02215

Learn While You Vacation

There is a vast world of summer learning experiences with great hands-on programs. How about a summer session for novice actors? Wildflower walks at a western science center? A crash course for stand-up comics? Songwriting classes? A course on moviemaking? An ecology workshop? The list of possibilities goes on.

Learning vacations are put together by universities, colleges, or educational organizations like the Wilderness Society. You can spend all summer in a program or take a week-long course, and you can choose to travel or stay in your own home town. Some adult education programs demand a lot of work, others aren't as tough. There's something for everyone.

Chautauqua, New York

What can a learning vacation be like? The little cultural community of Chautauqua, New York, typifies some summer programs that may be available in your neck of the woods.

Did you always want to take painting lessons? Or learn a handicraft? Or spend a few weeks immersed in French? How about improving your writing? The Chautauqua Institution offers a wide range of classes, from one-day sessions to nine-week educational adventures. Daytime art classes mingle here with evening lectures by famous authors, theater productions with ballet and opera. All this plus golf lessons, swimming, and tennis. Who wouldn't enjoy recreation and learning rolled into one? And it's especially nice in the compact New York State community of Chautauqua.

Chautauqua is south of Buffalo and close to Erie, New York. The educational and cultural events here are varied and stimulating. Every summer evening this cozy 358-acre compound comes alive with speakers like Henry Kissinger, James Roosevelt, Roger Rosenblatt, and others, ranging from diplomats to heart surgeons to scholars to authors. Chautauqua offers more than two hundred courses each summer, including Basic Boating Safety, Gardening, Getting Published, even How to be a Clown. Classes are available all year long, but the program goes into high gear in the summer.

Chautauqua's own seventy-four-member symphony orchestra, composed mostly of New York Philharmonic musicians, performs a variety of programs, from the songs of Marvin Hamlisch to *Carmen*. Placido Domingo and Alicia de Larrocia and conductors Phillipe Entremont and Walter Hendl are regulars.

The community itself is quaint, with several hundred Victorian gingerbread cottages under old leaf trees, and U.S. and Canadian flags flying from private homes and little inns. A library, post office, lakeside beaches, and marinas complete the picture. The enclave is small, measuring a mere one-mile-by-two-miles, and sits in a pastoral nest of meadows and vineyards embroidered by maples.

Chautauqua got its start in 1874 as a Methodist center, and you still won't find any bars or saloons on the premises. Through the years, it has attracted people as diverse as author James Michener, dancer Jerome Hines, flutist James Galway, and opera singer Jessye Norman. Thomas Edison invented at Chautauqua. Noted theologians lecture here; ministers often come for self-renewal. Sousa and Gershwin composed in Chautauqua, and by 1930, the New York Philharmonic began to give concerts at this site.

A suggestion to rock-bottom economy travelers: You can get into the village on a daily basis by asking for a "shopping ticket" at the gate. It's free if you buy lunch or dinner in Chautauqua. Once inside the inner sanctum, you can listen to the greats rehearsing in the amphitheater or join a discussion group at no charge. Maybe that's why Chautauqua has been called the "poor person's culture center." It's certainly a place for the budget vacation with a little education.

What You Need to Know

Participants Anyone can attend, regardless of age or educational background. In fact, visitors are an international and cultural cross section. What connects them is a common interest in concerts, seminars, workshops, and cultural vacations. *Duration* Summer classes can last a day, a weekend, a week, or several weeks. The busiest time here is usually from the third week of June through the end of August. *Facilities* The community has several bed & breakfasts, guest houses, and little hotels. Reservations should be made in the spring. *Cost* Some of the lectures and concerts are expensive. But if you book a package vacation, that includes lodging, parking, and some other offerings, it might be well within your budget (about $500 a week) and worth saving for. *How to Apply* Concerts and individual lectures can be attended at any time, without reservations. To attend a workshop, seminar, or class, however, you'll need to write to Chautauqua ahead of time.

For Further Information

Chautauqua Institution
Chautauqua, NY 14722

Go to Summer School

Most universities offer summer programs. Some offer a range of courses that reach beyond the walls of academia, like cooking, wine tasting, ceramics, and photography. Contact nearby universities or independent adult education centers for a summer bulletin. Two of the best are the New School for Social Research in New York and UCLA Summer Extension.

If you live in Manhattan or will be in New York for the summer and want to take some cool classes, you could spend an exciting week or longer at the "New School". The summer season is a lively one.

For seven decades the New School has succeeded on the principle that if there's a public demand for a course, seminar, class, or lecture series, it should be supplied. The faculty is highly qualified and courses include poetry writing; composing and songwriting for pop music, jazz, and rap; stand-up comedy and film workshops; film history; tasting the wines of California; evening discussions; and hundreds more. The classrooms are close to the colorful Union Square Park and Washington Square Park is just a few blocks away.

For those who will be on the West Coast, try UCLA's extension program. UCLA Extension is the nation's largest single-campus continuing higher education program, enrolling upwards of 110,000 students annually. The Summer Extension offers courses and special events designed to expand the economic, intellectual, and social abilities of its students. Sessions include career workshops, training sessions, and coursework in everything from calculus to cooking. There are courses for credit and courses to broaden your mind. Classes are held daily, in the evenings, and during the weekend.

What You Need to Know

Participants Anyone who is age eighteen or over and has a hunger for knowledge. *Duration* Classes for summer sessions begin in early June. Most full-term classes take place twice a week for six weeks. Short courses and other full-term courses meet on various other schedules. *Cost* Tuition rates vary depending on length and type of course. *Other* Classes are available for credit, non-credit, and certificates. Credit courses may have some prerequisites. Both schools advise students to sign up early.

For Further Information

New School for Social Research
66 West 12th Street
New York, NY 10011

UCLA Extension
P.O. Box 24901
Los Angeles, CA 90024-0901

Take Cooking Classes at the CIA

Have you ever fantasized about being a chef? Or do you simply want to improve your prowess in the kitchen? Whether amateur or pro, you might consider the highly praised summer sessions of the Culinary Institute of America (CIA). The Institute offers five-day courses every summer, many taught by world-famous chefs.

The hands-on courses run the gamut of cuisine from contemporary French to American, vegetarian to Spanish. Advanced courses include Patisserie, which teaches the intricacies of petit fours, fruitcakes, tortes, and specialty cakes. This is no simple course: students must take a written as well as a practical test to demonstrate proficiency in the kitchen.

The program is prestigious and the setting is elegant. The campus is on eighty acres of beautiful woods, with state-of-the-art kitchens, test restaurants, a thirty-eight-hundred-volume library, and comfortable accommodations.

What You Need to Know

Participants Applicants must be high school graduates working in the food industry or with food service experience. *Duration* Most classes range from one to twelve weeks, but some courses last as long as thirty months. *Facilities* On-campus rooms are available with study areas, televisions, telephones, and air-conditioning. Morning session students are entitled to breakfast and lunch; afternoon students, brunch and dinner. *Cost* Even only a week's stay here is pricey. Double-occupancy rooms are $175 per week; single-occupancy are $250. *Other* The Institute offers two twenty-one-month programs resulting in an Associate Degree in Occupational Studies. Continuing Education units are awarded upon satisfactory completion of a continuing education course.

For Further Information

Culinary Institute of America
433 Albany Post Road
Hyde Park, NY 12638

Attend Environmental Workshops

Audubon

Awaken to the call of a loon, hear the sea waves lapping against a rocky coast, stalk screech owls at night, and sing by a campfire far away from everyday pressures and distractions. Audubon Workshops and Audubon Adult Camps offer wonderful outdoor summer learning experiences.

For more than five decades, Audubon's reputation for outstanding nature exploration, ecology studies, and bird studies has grown. Since the first camp was established some fifty years ago in Maine, campers have spent many summers in serene natural backgrounds. There, they learn about nature firsthand by sifting a pond for whirligig beetles and damselfly nymphs, dredging the ocean floor for starfish and sea cucumbers, following paths blazed by mountain sheep, searching the desert for spadefoot toads, and listening to coyotes call under a moonlit sky.

Audubon offers a wide range of field course work, including studies in geology, marine life, birds, mammals, plants, insects, weather, astronomy, population, and renewable energy. Recreation programs allow you to explore a wild island in Maine, go rafting in Wyoming, roam the lovely, lush woods of Connecticut, or explore on your own.

At the Audubon Camp in the West, students are steeped in a week of ecology studies in Wyoming; and clear, star-filled skies, evening campfires by snow-fed Torrey Creek, and wildlife such as bighorn sheep, moose, mink, beaver, otter, and eagles are the highlights.

The setting is a glaciated valley seventy-five hundred feet high in Wyoming's Wind River Mountains, among thirteen-thousand-foot snow-capped peaks. Campers live in original homestead cabins and rustic accommodations at the Whiskey Mountain Wildlife Conservation Camp (operated by the Wyoming Game and Fish Department in cooperation with the National Audubon Society).

Geology and Native American culture are alive in the rocks and surroundings of the area. Unique birds, mammals, insects, and flowers fill the natural classroom in this rugged mountain environment. In addition to partaking in ecology studies, students can stroll along a rushing glacier-fed stream or a hike to a meadow ablaze with wildflowers. During off-hours there's square dancing, volleyball on the world's most scenic volleyball court, or exciting float trips down the spectacular Snake River in Grand Teton National Park.

In addition to regular programs, Audubon offers introductory field ecology for educators in Connecticut; field ornithology in Maine; nature photography in Wyoming; and a fascinating array of international adventures in places as diverse as Kenya and Costa Rica. You must be at least eighteen years old to go on one of these trips. Special youth programs are available for participants aged ten to fourteen.

After a summer session at an Audubon camp, you'll have a new awareness of how nature works and how you can protect it. And you'll have made lasting friendships.

Wilderness Society

Don't forget that the Wilderness Society also organizes a remarkable array of summer ecology and conservation trips, all guided by specialists. The summer outings take place in remote areas in Maine, Alaska's Wildlife centers, and on Georgia's beaches (great for snorkeling), to name a few locales.

Keystone Science School

The Keystone Science School is part of Colorado's Keystone Resort, one of the most carefully designed four-season resorts in the West, with much attention paid to the environment and architectural control (no buildings may be more than two-stories high). The Keystone Science School is located in the middle of the forest on the edge of Keystone, with a charming pond for boating, serene hiking trails, horse paths, and mountain-bike trails.

The resort began offering summer courses and activities in 1976, and the studies revolve around mountain ecology, wildlife biology, botany, forest ecology, physics, avalanche safety, geology, aquatic ecology, and the history of the area's silver and gold mining era. The "school rooms" are rustic and pleasantly quiet, and the participants' cabins stand amid healthy conifer trees in a lush forest.

The choices for summer learning programs are endless and offered coast-to-coast. Wherever you choose to go, you'll surely leave with a new understanding of the world and people around you as well as yourself. What more could one ask for from a school?

What You Need to Know

Participants You must be at least eighteen years old to attend an environmental summer camp. In most cases, however, no age is specified. *Duration* Each session ranges from six to eighteen days, depending on the courses. Audubon and the Wilderness Society also offer longer programs. The subject matter of the course determines the length. In general, you can register for as many courses as you can fit into your schedule. *Facilities* In the Wyoming Audubon camp you stay in cozy homesteaders' houses; Audubon's Connecticut programs have a lodge; in Colorado's Keystone School, you are housed in comfortable cabins. *Cost* $495 to $995 for programs in the continental U.S. Audubon manages to keep its costs low, so that almost everyone can afford a week at such a camp.

For Further Information

National Audubon Society
613 Riversville Road
Greenwich, CT 06831

Wilderness Society
Advocates for Wilderness Trips
900 17th Street, NW
Washington, DC 20006

Keystone Science School
Keystone Resort
P.O. Box 38
Keystone, CO 80435

Learn to Sail

Hoist the sails, coil the lines, cast the anchor, and take the helm! Sailing schools offer a thrilling and satisfying way to spend a summer vacation. Intensive classes and on-water courses for beginners include nautical terminology, the mechanics of wind and sail, lifesaving techniques, steering with a compass, mooring, docking, and anchoring. Advanced sailing and racing classes teach you starting and finishing tactics, teamwork and preparation, boat speed and turning, and weather and wind shifts. Bareboat cruising preparation and Live-Aboard cruising courses prepare you to charter your own boat for a future voyage, or take you to exotic places like the British Virgin Islands.

In many schools, such as The Offshore Sailing School, headquartered in Fort Myers, Florida, students learn enough to become sailing instructors themselves.

If you prefer a less intense learning environment, consider a schooner trip. Schooners are wooden sailing ships, and although you will be treated as a guest, you can also steer, raise and lower sails, and haul in the anchor.

What You Need to Know

Participants Minimum age for some ships is sixteen; for others it's eighteen. No previous sailing experience is necessary. *Duration* Trips last from two to nine days. *Facilities* Usual lodging is on the ship itself, with showers and hot water on board. All meals are provided. *Cost* Costs range from $100 to $200 per day. *Other* Contact sailing schools directly.

For Further Information

Annapolis Sailing School
P.O. Box 3334
Annapolis, MD 21403

Schooner *Heritage*
P.O. Box 482
Rockland, ME 04841

Offshore Sailing School
16731 McGregor Boulevard
Fort Myers, FL 33908

Schooner *Isaac H. Evans*
P.O. Box 482
Rockland, ME 04841

Club Nautique
1150 Ballena Boulevard
Alameda, CA 94501

Chichester Sailing Center
Chichester Marina
Sussex PO20 7EL England

J World, Performance Sailing School
P.O. Box 1500
Newport, RI 02840

Study Overseas

There is a scene in a now-classic movie where a seventeen-year-old girl, played by Mariel Hemingway, is ready to take off for a study stint in London and she has a last confrontation with her middle-aged lover. He doesn't want her to go. But she resists him. And you can see why: she's excited by the prospect of a summer in Europe. Her face is flushed, her eyes aglitter. She's no longer listening to the man. The reality of the forthcoming trip—a chance of a lifetime—tugs at her. Winningly.

This is easy to understand. Foreign places, especially old Europe, are part of the sophisticated American's education. Even a few summer months have a special patina. For others, the attraction goes far beyond Europe; they seek far-flung countries. Studying overseas is one of the most popular ways to spend a summer vacation: it allows you to travel to new places and meet an interesting, diverse group of people.

In this era of the nineties, educational travel abroad is widespread and diverse. And it is more accessible and well organized than ever thanks to travel agencies, universities, and other companies specializing in this field. Hundreds of nations throughout the world, representing thousands of areas of study, are now part of the educational picture. In fact, it would take an entire book just to describe the possibilities. I'll give you a taste of them here.

University Plans

Among the university plans, you'll find programs from large universities like Columbia University as well as smaller programs from places like Goddard College. The larger programs tend to be more costly, and accommodations are often more elaborate.

A number of Americans go to Britain to study Shakespeare. Both Oxford and Cambridge Universities feature his works in their summer lectures. Try dealing with these universities directly; otherwise, you'll be paying more for a middleman.

School for International Training

One of the largest and most reputable sources of overseas study is the School for International Training, created by the Experiment in International Living. It has a special division devoted solely to summer studies. This division sponsors an incredible array of courses, such as International Business in France (Paris), Germany's Special Role in Eastern Europe (Tübingen), Peace and Conflict Resolution in Ireland (Dublin), Educational Changes in Russia (Moscow), Solving Refugee Problems (Geneva), Ecology (Belem), and a crash course in Swahili (East Africa). The course work in some international study programs tends to be cross-culturally oriented, and many classes concern social issues and ecology throughout the world. The course can be rigorous, sometimes requiring a thirty- to forty-page independent study report.

One of the more interesting and unique features of the School for International Training's Summer Academic Studies Abroad is the *homestay*, where you stay with a local family for the entire summer. You'll learn more about the country because you'll witness firsthand how its residents live.

Overseas Adventure Travel

Overseas Adventure Travel is another large firm that specializes in travel to faraway places and focuses on the way adventure and learning often go hand-in-hand. The variety of offerings is amazing: trekking through Tibet and Nepal; visiting the land of the Maasai; learning about the Cloud Forest and other ecological regions of Costa Rica; or studying the Inca Ruins of Machu Picchu.

Overseas Adventure Travel grades each trip by degree of difficulty. For example, "Easy" trips are not physically demanding, with only a bit of rough road travel. Many involve day hikes with nights spent in hotels. "Moderate" trips can involve a seven-day hike at altitudes usually under eleven hundred feet. Bicycle trips average about twenty-five to thirty miles per day on level or rolling terrain. These trips may also include river rafting and travel by bus and four-wheel-drive vehicle over rough roads. Though physically demanding, fit people will have energy left over at the end of the day. "Demanding/Difficult" trips involve hiking at altitudes of up to nineteen hundred feet. Bicycle trips average about twenty-five to thirty-five miles per day on hilly terrain. Travel may be demanding in places and it may be difficult to get acclimatized. Participants should follow a regular exercise program before embarking on such a trip. "Strenuous" trips are for strong backpackers, climbers, and well-seasoned cyclists only. The trips involve long treks and may include altitudes over nineteen hundred feet. Climbing expeditions often involve glacier travel which requires technical climbing skills. Bicycle trips average forty to sixty-five miles per day on challenging routes over all types of terrain. A medical checkup is required for climbing trips.

Council on International Educational Exchange

Another well-known educational travel source is the Council on International Educational Exchange in New York. Its endless roster of programs include two summer months in Tokyo to study Japanese business methods at a Tokyo university, a tropical biology semester in Costa Rica, and Russian studies in Leningrad.

The International Council for Cultural Exchange works in affiliation with some European educational institutions. It coordinates classes and accommodations for travelers who want to study while vacationing. Its two- to four-week summer classes focus on art, languages, social sciences, music, and dance. High school students and others can receive college credit.

Additional well-respected firms are The Institute of International Education in New York and Educational Programmes Abroad, but their programs are sometimes more costly. See addresses below.

What You Need to Know

Nuts and bolts vary with each program, but there are general rules.

Participants The students are generally between sixteen and twenty-three years old. Student groups have from six to forty participants; the size varies in each country. Some programs are for college students, others for high school students. In general, you don't need a language background or a specific major. *Duration* Courses last from one week to an entire summer. *Facilities* Facilities in larger programs tend to be more elaborate. Room and board is generally included and can feature rooms on campus, dorms, houses with families, hotels, and pensions. *Cost* Depending on your needs, a summer semester overseas can cost you many hundreds to thousands of dollars (after all, a private room in a French chateau is more costly than a room in a youth hostel). The larger programs tend to be a bit more costly, but facilities are often more elaborate. Please note that in most cases, you must travel to the location; the farther you travel, the more it will cost. Of course, it's cheaper to stay closer to home since travel is less expensive. Grants and scholarships are scarce in educational summer travel. Write to individual organizers to get details on availability. *Other* Remember that college credit is not always offered.

For Further Information

School for International Training
Kipling Road
P.O. Box 676
Brattleboro, VT 05302

Goddard College
Travel for Academic Growth
Plainfield, VT 05667

Institute of International Education
809 United Nations Plaza
New York, NY 10017

Council on International Educational Exchange
205 East 42d Street
New York, NY 10017

Summer Academic Studies Abroad
P.O. Box 676
Brattleboro, VT 05302

Overseas Adventure Travel
349 Broadway
Cambridge, MA 02139

Semester at Sea
Institute for Shipboard Education
University of Pittsburgh
2E Forbes Quad
Pittsburgh, PA 15260

Washington and Lee University
Travel-Study Tours
Office of Summer Programs
Lexington, VA 24450

Michigan State University
Continuing Education Programs
East Lansing, MI 48824-1022

Loyola College
4501 North Charles Street
Baltimore, MD 21210

University of New Orleans
International Study Programs
Box 1315
New Orleans, LA 70148

International Council for Cultural Exchange
1559 Rockville Pike
Rockville, MD 20852

Educational Programmes Abroad
2815 Scarles Drive
Yorktown Heights, NY 10598

Oxford University
Rewley House
1 Wellington Square
Oxford OX1 2JA England

Cambridge University
Madingley Hall
Madingley, Cambridge CB3 8AQ England

Learn a Foreign Language in a Foreign Country

Institut de Français

Want to learn French? How about the twenty-five-year-old Institut de Français in Villefranche, on the painterly French Riviera? Outside your window, the pines drip dark green. The sky is ultramarine, and the ocean an even deeper blue topped with tiny whitecaps. Your class is filled with people from Europe, Asia, Africa, and Canada. The classes are kept small at the institute so that you can participate more. The instruction is serious and extensive; it goes on for several hours almost daily for four weeks. The institute's slogan in English is: "Intense but pleasurable immersion. . . . "

When I was fourteen years old, I spent a summer in Italy in a school specializing in languages. Students were housed in a magnificent villa in the Florentine hills, amid stately cypresses, vineyards, and fruit-bearing fig trees, with flowers everywhere.

We were allowed to speak only the "language of the day." On Monday it might be Italian. On Tuesday it was French. "Pass me the salt" now became "Passez moi le sel." There were other days for German, Spanish, and English. Whether at breakfast or dinner, on the soccer field or during a Ping-Pong match, we were immersed in a foreign language. I remember testing my Italian on the farmers who grew grapes and figs on the hillsides; they were invaluable to my learning. There's no better way to learn a foreign language than to live it and speak it every day on native soil.

The School for International Training

The School for International Training has arranged a German-language program with the Sprachinstitut Tübingen, in a medieval university town full of steep red roofs, narrow cobblestoned alleys, and summer fruit markets. Castles greet you from the hillsides. The classes include how to analyze press and radio reports, past and present German history, and much more.

The School for International Training has other summer immersion courses throughout the world which provide social and cultural experiences and allow you to become further involved in a foreign language. For instance, they offer a French language immersion course in the Loire chateau country, which is complemented with other classes that help you understand France and the French people.

American Language Center

How about learning Arabic in Morocco? With its *medinas* (old cities), the North African country still bears an air of mystery. The Arabic Language Institute in Fez is the only institution of its kind in Morocco, and

Fez is one of the most interesting centers for language students. Established in 1983 under the auspices of the American Language Center/Fez, the institute has cultivated an excellent reputation among insiders, adventurers, foreigners, and native Moroccans. Housed in a large villa with green stucco, a serene, tiled courtyard with fountain, and a lush garden containing everything from pomegranate trees to rosemary shrubs, the atmosphere is inspiring. ALI/Fez offers a three-week crash course in Survival Moroccan Arabic, which provides a springboard for interacting with native Moroccans.

In addition to basic courses in beginner and intermediate classic Arabic, the center offers specialized courses like Moroccan Proverbs and Stories and Introduction to the Moroccan Press. There's also a unique opportunity to learn Arabic calligraphy and even business Arabic. All instructors are native Moroccans.

ALI/Fez also conducts small, guided excursions into the *medina*, Fez's native quarter. These miniature adventures offer historical, religious, and architectural insights, often not revealed by guidebooks or guides. The institute has formed amiable ties with various local artisans and craftsmen, allowing visitors a close-up view of the local culture.

El Instituto Allende

For a less expensive journey, travel to Mexico to learn Spanish in the great summer colony of San Miguel de Allende. Despite the new super highway for the 180-mile drive from Mexico City to San Miguel, the drowsy village, now a national monument, has lost neither its charm nor its slow pace.

The San Miguel houses are strewn over the hillside like pieces of colored candy squares on street vendors' carts. Donkeys still move up and across the cobblestones like Utrillo paintings. At the outdoor market, the fruit stalls remain a painter's dream: green chiles, slices of purple cactus pears, poster-red tomatoes, papayas, bananas, limes, pineapple. The church bells ring out as they did more than four hundred years ago after Juan de San Miguel, a Catholic friar, founded the town.

Daily lectures by the institute's outstanding teachers alternate with impromptu Spanish conversation. After supper many people go to the local plaza where they practice their Spanish while strolling with the natives. All of this makes for lively and creative learning. You couldn't ask for more than that.

What You Need to Know

Participants Summer language programs are for people of all ages. It's useful to already know a smattering of French or Spanish or Arabic, but in general, classes are geared to people of various proficiencies, from beginners to fluent speakers. *Duration* Classes can last from one week to a full summer. *Facilities* Villas, shared apartments, rented rooms, and private rooms with a family are among the living options; you're usually on your own regarding accommodations and food. *Cost* Class costs vary. Write to the school to find out if you need to make a deposit. Bear in mind that you must pay for transportation to the school. Program organizers may offer you seats on cheap charter airlines, but be careful since these often go out of business before your flight, taking your money with them. It may be worth the extra money to fly with a reputable airline, such as Swissair or KLM. Royal Air Maroc and ONCF, Morocco's national rail line, also offer reasonably reliable service to Fez. *Other* Americans entering Morocco do not need a visa.

For Further Information

Institut de Français
06230 Villefranche
Mer TR3 France

School for International Training
Kipling Road
Brattleboro, VT 05302

El Instituto
San Miguel de Allende
Mexico

The Arabic Language Institute of Fez
BP 2136
Fez, Morocco

Try an Overseas Internship

Are you a journalism major? How about traveling to Egypt and working as an intern for the Middle East News Agency in Cairo? Internships in hundreds of fields are offered all over the world, so you can probably find one in a subject that interests you. With an overseas internship you'll spend a summer living and working in a foreign country, and you may even decide on a future career.

Because businesses are always looking for good people to help with their work, and college students with free summers make ideal temporary helpers, many colleges and universities have agreements with schools and businesses in foreign countries. This way, companies get hard workers and students get to learn how an enterprise works from the inside. An internship will provide you with hands-on experience, and what's more, you'll have the adventure of living and working in a foreign country.

A student can find work as an assistant banker, architect, or medical researcher. Law firms, museums, and advertising agencies also hire interns, as do theaters and political groups. The competition for these jobs is keen.

What You Need to Know

Again, specifics vary with each program, but there are general rules.

Participants Preference is given to those who are fluent in a foreign language. In some cases, you must be a junior or senior in college with a minimum 3.0 grade point average, but in other instances, anyone can apply. Qualifications can vary. You must be a hard worker and a self-starter. Punctuality, reliability, and accuracy are a must for all interns. *Duration* The length of your internships will usually be an entire summer. There are exceptions, however, as some companies may hire for only a month or even less. You will spend at least three days a week interning. The other time is available for classes, your own projects, and sightseeing. *Facilities* You are expected to pay for your own lodging, meals, and travel. Your employer, however, may help you find housing. You can choose to live with host families or on your own. Some programs may hook you up with a host family. *Pay* Most interns are not paid, although some are paid minimum wage. You may be reimbursed some expenses at the end of term. You do not have to pay tuition. *Other* Competition is fierce for these internships, so apply early and work hard on your application; only the best and most resourceful people land an internship.

For Further Information

The following is only a selection of the hundreds of summer internships. You may want to write to some of the schools, foundations, and associations also listed here to find out about other internship options.

Middle East News Agency
Chief of the Board of Consultants
Hoda Sharawy Street
Cairo, Egypt
Requires knowledge of Arabic and familiarity with newspapers and the international press.

Educational Programmes Abroad
2815 Scarles Drive
Yorktown Heights, NY 10598
Arranges internships in London, Bonn, Brussels, Paris, and Madrid.

Institute of International Education (IIE)
or
Educational Counseling Center
P.O. Box 3087
Laredo, TX 78044
Sponsors an intern program for students to gain experience in the U.S. Information Service in Mexico.

The Heritage Foundation
Academic Programs Director
214 Massachusetts Avenue, NE
Washington, DC 20002

The London Research Internship
402 Main Street
Armonk, NY 10504

London Summer Internships and Summer School
American Association of Overseas Studies
158 West 81st Street
New York, NY 10024

Stella Maris School of Nursing
Apto 28, Zacapu Michoacan
Mexico CP 58680
A proficiency in Spanish will prove handy.

And lastly, a useful book is *Internships*, by Brian Rushing.

4

The Arts

Paint the Summer Landscape

A perfect late summer day. . . . Soft blue sky. . . . Pure air. The Vermont landscape is alive with rounded wooded mountains and the first hint of gold and red. You've sketched the scene before you. Now when you dip your watercolor brush into the paint, your white paper comes to life under the onslaught of color.

The instructor stops by, looks over your shoulder, and nods with approval. This praise is all the more valuable because you're not a professional artist—or even a very experienced one. In fact, the only time you've ever really painted was in grade school art class. Yet this summer you've tapped into hidden talents due to wonderful instructors and inspiring locations through a course at the Stowe Art Guild.

Art classes are available all over the world, and are sponsored by a variety of programs, such as local art guilds, individual art teachers, art institutes, colleges, art schools, and even the Chamber of Commerce in some resort towns. Listed below is a sampling of what's available. To find other programs, look through art magazines for contacts or call your local college art department.

Stowe Art Guild

Instructors at the Stowe Art Guild are longtime professionals and members of the prestigious American Watercolor Society (AWS). The AWS is known for its outstanding watercolor instructors. But at the summer art classes they also teach oil painting, sketching, and drawing. They offer five-day classes in watercolor beginning in August and lasting through September to take advantage of the dramatic color changes of the mountain area. The five-day class will teach you to see the world with a sharper focus and an eye for color.

The Stowe Art Guild was formed to allow prominent artists conduct workshops geared to the serious amateur. Their aim is to provide a creative atmosphere where talented painters can develop new techniques and where their work will be critiqued by the instructors. Each session ends with a showing of the best work.

What You Need to Know

Participants New and advanced amateur artists are welcome. *Duration* Each course is five-days long. *Facilities* Meals and lodging are available at additional cost. *Cost* $285 for five days of watercolor instruction.

For Further Information

Stowe Art Guild
P.O. Box 1544
Stowe, VT 05672

Snake River Institute

Some summer schools focus on watercolor and oil painting, teaching a few other media, such as charcoal, pen and ink, and pastels. Other schools, such as the Snake River Institute in Jackson Hole, Wyoming, also offer classes in sculpture, art history, and photography. The setting of Snake River is magnificent, with the mighty Tetons serving as an unforgettable backdrop. Classes gather at various locations chosen for their particular atmosphere. For example, a discourse on artist Karl

Bodmer takes place on the Missouri River where he painted more than a hundred years ago; in a grove of cottonwood trees, a painter demonstrates ways to capture the play of light on flickering leaves; a class on natural history is taught in a historic pine lodge nestled amidst fourteen-thousand-foot-high mountains. Each location plays its own role in bringing the seminar to life.

What You Need to Know

Participants Courses are open to anyone who's interested. *Duration* Each course lasts from one to five days; combine several for a fuller summer of learning fun. *Facilities* Snake River has its own complex, but many of the courses are held in different locations. Lodging is included in some of the courses, but meals are not. *Cost* Costs range from $65 to $700. Financial assistance and scholarships are available; contact the institute for more information.

For Further Information

Snake River Institute
P.O. Box 7724
Jackson, WY 83001

Hewitt's Painting Workshops

Come summer and some lucky people can travel abroad to be instructed in watercolor and oil painting by well-known American artists. The fame and reputation of these instructors, combined with an exotic locale, offer an incredible experience.

For example, Hewitt's painting workshops, based in San Diego, California, sends famous watercolorist Rex Brandt seventy miles up the coast to teach in Laguna Beach; Charles Reed has chosen Sorrento, Italy, for his summer art center; and California-based painter Charles Brommer concentrates on Taxco, Mexico. The amateur painter just signs up for a particular workshop and then takes off for an exciting summer.

What You Need to Know

Participants Adults of all ages can participate. You don't need to be a professional artist. Students at all levels are welcome. *Duration* Each workshop lasts from one to three weeks. *Facilities* Various, depending on the area. *Cost* Costs range from $500 to $1,500, depending on the workshop and instructor. Price might include accommodations, again depending on the workshop. There are no scholarships available. *Other* You may make travel reservations through the workshop or through your travel agent.

For Further Information

> Hewitt's Painting Workshops
> P.O. Box 6980
> San Diego, CA 92106-0980

Cleveland Institute of Art

Likewise, the Cleveland Institute of Art regularly sends its instructors and summer students to Florence, Italy and Lacoste in the colorful Provence region of France. Lacoste is a complex of nineteen buildings where student artists come to focus on their work. A six-week summer semester and a fifteen-week fall semester are available.

What You Need to Know

Participants Undergraduate and independent students are welcome. *Duration* Semesters range from six to fifteen weeks. *Facilities* Accommodations and all meals are provided, as well as a few excursions. *Cost* Costs range from $2,550 to $5,900, depending on the session. Some scholarships are available.

For Further Information

> Foreign Studies
> Cleveland Institute of Art-PKA
> 11141 East Boulevard
> Cleveland, OH 44106

Try Pottery, Weaving, or Other Arts and Crafts

Apart from watercolor, oil painting, pastels, and other fine arts, you can also learn crafts such as pottery, weaving, and ceramics in summer sessions.

Instituto Allende

In Mexico, the Instituto Allende, (also known as El Instituto) in San Miguel de Allende, offers non-credit classes in many of the aforementioned disciplines. Some visitors come for the company of artists or for a relaxing summer. Others come to work. All students are enthusiastic about the arts.

The artists often paint outdoors, against a backdrop of the institute's cobblestone terraces, arcades, and rocky parapets, the Spanish churches, and the hillsides ascending to flower gardens. In one area potters are busy leaning over their wheels, shaping, firing, and glazing clay. In another, iron welders and plaster casters are buzzing with activity, while still others are occupied with a special bronze foundry. In studios scattered amid trees and flowers, sculptors, silverworkers, carvers, textile designers, and papier mâché hobbyists of all ages practice these crafts.

In San Miguel students are introduced to graphics, printing, monotype, woodcuts, silk-screen processes, and even lithographic stone-grinding. Photographers learn the proper use of meters, exposures, filters, flashes, strobes, and even film processing, enlarging, and retouching.

The institute's faculty is international and includes a number of Americans; all speak English and Spanish, and most have been with the institute for many years. Each year the resident faculty is enriched by outstanding guest instructors.

What You Need to Know

Participants Students of all ages and nationalities are welcome. *Duration* You can take a week-long class or take a smattering of classes for an entire summer. *Facilities* The institute can refer you to a family or help you rent an apartment (it's a good idea to come early in the summer if you're looking for an apartment). You can also stay at one of San Miguel's reasonably-priced hotels. *Cost* Costs range from $100 to $600, depending on the course and subject. *Other* College credit is available.

For Further Information

Instituto Allende
San Miguel de Allende
Mexico

Anderson Ranch Arts Center

Near Aspen, Colorado, the Anderson Ranch Arts Center features an enormous range of summer classes for beginners and experts alike. In a few weeks you can learn basic woodworking, fine bookbinding, veneer and inlay techniques, basic pottery, glazing, working with bronze, printmaking, and scores of other arts.

What You Need to Know

Participants You must be at least eighteen years old to attend. Individual classes require different levels of skill. *Duration* Classes range from four to eleven days. *Facilities* Renovated log cabins, barns, and new buildings on four acres near Aspen. Full studio facilities are available for all major art disciplines. There is a cafeteria on site. *Cost* Classes range from $225 to $600. Meals, lodging, and some lab fees are extra. A shared room including meals is $245 a week, but there are other options available. *Other* College credit, student discounts, scholarships, and summer assistant positions are available. Contact the ranch for further information.

For Further Information

Anderson Ranch Arts Center
P.O. Box 5598
Snowmass Village, CO 81615

Art Schools

Many art schools offer summer courses, mostly on a non-credit basis. If you want a wide variety of classes, your best bet is to try an art school in a big city, because they usually have more of a selection than their small-town competitors. For example, the well-respected Art Students League in Manhattan offers a wide range of summer instruction in clay sculpture, color, design, composition, etching, graphics, anatomy for artists, and much more.

For Further Information

This is only a partial listing of the many art schools around the world. Look through art magazines for more contacts.

Director, Summer Program
Institute for American Universities
27, place de l'Universite
13625 Aix-en-Provence, France
Classes in a setting that once attracted France's greatest Impressionist painters.

Taos Institute of Art
Taos Valley Resort Association
P.O. Box 85
Taos Ski Valley, NM 87525
Taos is a famous art enclave with beautiful scenery.

Anderson Ranch Arts Center
P.O. Box 5598
Snowmass Village, CO 81615

Haystack Mountain School of Crafts
Deer Isle, ME 04627
A well-known and well-respected learning center.

Art Students League of New York
215 West 57th Street
New York, NY 10019
*An art giant with a great diversity of classes and top profes-
sional instructors.*

Tuscarora Pottery School
P.O. Box 7
Tuscarora, NV 89834
Offers a congenial atmosphere.

Be an Independent Artist

Maybe you'd prefer not to attend formal art classes or school but still
want to improve your skills. You can spend an enriching summer traveling and meeting other artists from around the world.

Italy

One American sculptor spent several summers in the artistic, muse-
um-rich town of Florence, Italy. Renting an unheated sixth-floor apartment in a fifteenth-century Firenze palace put him high enough to view
the medieval red roofs of the town, the churches cutting across the
Italian sky, and the lovely checkerboard towers and walls of San Mini-
ato. He'd drive with friends to a quarry near Carrara, where they'd load
up on free marble. Hammering and chiseling the stone eventually produced sculptures which were promptly sold (although the sculptor was
often not paid) by a local gallery. He was able to make a little money
by giving English lessons.

Florence percolates with young artists; the Uffizi and the Pitti museums are right in town; and the Ponte Vecchio is a perfect lunchtime
retreat; all of which make Italy a wonderful summer artist's experience.

New Mexico

But you don't have to cross the Atlantic to work on your art. How about going to New Mexico? Many new artists and aspiring artists are drawn to the serenity of Santa Fe, with its mild climate, its bright and glowing light, its quality of life, and its many art galleries and museums, some dating back to the early part of the century.

Santa Fe offers an international, culturally sophisticated, and altogether pleasant atmosphere. At an elevation of 6,950 feet, it never gets very hot, and the area abounds with vacation retreats. The architecture is fascinating, partly because Santa Fe builders must observe strict rules: In the central areas of the city, buildings may be constructed only out of adobe bricks. Plastics, flickering or gyrating lights, and tall buildings are banned everywhere.

There's another art colony in Taos, about an hour to the north. Local art surrounds you in this small town situated below the stunning Sangre de Cristo mountain range. There are almost a hundred art galleries devoted to local work; oil paintings hang in all the hotel lobbies; bookshops are filled with art books. Compact and adobe-colored, Taos is an endearing and somewhat sensual spot with a strong Native American influence. Here you'll see remarkable turquoise and silver jewelry crafted by hand and masterpieces created by local weavers and ceramists. Spanish culture shows up in every hand-carved door, window frame, and column, and everywhere colors come alive with russet bushes, ochre and pink houses, and the earth-hued Indian Pueblo.

Contact your travel agent for information on New Mexico art centers.

Mingle with Famous Authors, Publishers, and Agents at Writer's Workshops and Conferences

Every summer, writer's workshops and conferences around the country sponsor lecture series by some of America's biggest names in the printed word, from authors and journalists to publishers and literary agents.

Some seminars are like a week-long vacation with little classroom instruction. Others are very serious, with a rapid sequence of lectures, panels, discussions, and readings scheduled from morning to night. At some conferences attendees are expected to arrive with completed stories, articles, or even books. At others, people who have never written anything in their life are welcome. Most conferences fall somewhere in between, and concentrate on stimulating the writers, and helping them overcome writing obstacles and work through literary problems. A typical writer's conference will be geared toward the perceptive reader as well as to the published and unpublished author.

The mix of students, from struggling novice to advanced writer, makes for a stimulating vacation full of good talk and new acquaintances. Even the most serious seminars leave room for parties and picnics, so that, as one participant said, "You get away from the green lights of your computers and actually sit in the sun and talk . . . and talk . . . about writing!" Eventually, even beginners talk shop here, exchanging manuscripts with newly found and already trusted friends.

Good workshops invite editors, literary agents, and book reviewers to lecture and counsel. Some of these experts also act as scouts, discovering talented new writers. Some of the more important summer writer's gatherings often result in the publication of books, articles, or poems. Lecturers come from a huge selection of famous authors: Tony Hillerman, Erskine Caldwell, Gay Talese, Norman Mailer, Irving Wallace, Kurt Vonnegut, Clive Cussler, Alice Putnam, Ray Bradbury, Joe McGinniss, James Dickey, Kay Cassill, Arthur Hailey, and Paul Erdman have all shown up at writer's conferences.

Although the writing staff can't write for you, they can certainly coax you into better craftsmanship. Participants can usually submit manuscripts for individual consultation with a staff member who might explain grammatical rules or point out flaws in your work. An experienced professional will also come up with fresh constructive ideas and might help you to view your writing from a new perspective.

Most professional writers welcome the opportunity for a working vacation. I know I did when I was asked to speak at a summer conference on Rye Beach, New Hampshire. I had some beautiful times there. I spent most mornings reading manuscripts, making marginal suggestions, and trying to help aspiring writers. Then I'd meet with a class for two hours of formal instruction in the garden. And on some afternoons we'd listen to eloquent lectures on such topics as poetry.

At the Craigville Conference on Cape Cod I taught travel writing (my own specialty). Every morning at nine o'clock sharp we'd meet at a little wooden chapel where we'd discuss travel features and travel guides and travel literature with the sea air breezing freshly through the open side doors. After a question-and-answer session, we'd meet one-on-one to discuss individual manuscripts.

Writers' workshops are often held in scenic locales, such as the Cape Cod Writer's Conference which is close to the national seashore; the Alaska Adventures in Travel Writing, where students sail Alaska's Inside Passage; and the Santa Barbara Writer's Conference situated among the flowered hillsides of Santa Barbara.

Some conferences also set up fascinating side trips, offering participants an agreeable way to travel and improve their craft at the same time. The Alaska Adventure in Travel Writing allows participants to choose from among four top-ranking tours in or around Juneau. One of the most popular excursions is a ten-hour yacht cruise to Tracy Arm Fjord and the glistening twin Sawyer Glaciers. You can see thousands of icebergs and possibly whales and bears along the way.

What You Need to Know

Participants All kinds of would-be writers, unpublished writers, and professional writers are welcome. In general, you must be at least fifteen years old to attend. Very few of the conferences demand to see writing samples, though all writer's conferences allow their instructors to read manuscripts for a fee—an arrangement that benefits both sides. *Duration* Conferences can be as short as a single day and as long as two weeks. *Facilities* College dormitory rooms, bed and breakfasts, inns, and motels are the most likely accommodations. Food is sometimes included; at least one or two lunches are provided for participants. *Cost* Lectures cost anywhere from $25 to $80 per lecture. If you attend a number of lectures or workshops, you pay for each individually. There is also a nominal registration fee which varies from place to place. *Other* Workshops include fiction, nonfiction, religious writing, outdoor and travel writing, and romance writing, among many other genres. Before choosing your workshop or conference, try to look at as many writer's magazines as you can, especially the May issues of *Writer's Digest* and *The Writer.* These magazines have detailed lists of offerings. Begin in the spring to get a head start. If you can't get hold of the magazines, try the *Literary Market Place* (*LMP*), which you can find in the reference section of the library. The *Writer's Digest* ads and listings will tell you what authors or lecturers are scheduled to speak at each conference. You might find your favorite writer is being featured or that a workshop offers specialized instruction in your area of interest. If there's something that entices you, go for it. Finally, consider where the conference is being held. You'll find that your surroundings are very important to your work.

For Further Information

Cape Cod Writer's Conference
Cape Cod Conservatory
Route 132
Barnstable, MA 02668

Writers on Writing
Barnard College
3009 Broadway
New York, NY 10027-6598

Stonecoast Writer's Conference
University of Southern Maine
Summer Session
96 Falmouth Street
Portland, ME 04103

New England Writers Workshop
Simmons College
300 The Fenway
Boston, MA 02115

Writing by the Sea
1511 New York Avenue
Cape May, NJ 08204

The Writer's Center at Chautauqua
Box 408
Chautauqua, NY 14722

ASJA Writer's Conference
American Society of Journalists and Authors
1501 Broadway, #1907
New York, NY 10036

Blue Ridge Writer's Conference
2824 Northview Drive
Roanoke, VA 24015

Ozark Creative Writers, Inc.
6817 Gingerbread Lane
Little Rock, AR 72204

Southeastern Writers Workshop
Box 102
Cuthbert, GA 31740

Annual Mark Twain Writer's Conference
Hannibal-LaGrange College
921 Center Street
Hannibal, MS 63401

Alaska Adventures in Travel Writing
P.O. Box 21494
Juneau, AK 99802

Palm Springs Writer's Guild
P.O. Box 2385
Palm Springs, CA 92263

Santa Barbara Writer's Conference
P.O. Box 304
Carpinteria, CA 93104

California Writer's Conference
2214 Derby Street
Berkeley, CA 94705

Writer's Conference at Santa Fe
Santa Fe Community College
P.O. Box 4187
Santa Fe, NM 87502-4187

Taos Writing Workshop
P.O. Box 1389
Taos, NM 87571

Yellow Bay Writers Workshop
Continuing Education & Summer Programs
University of Montana
Missoula, MO 59812

Writers at Work
P.O. Box 3182
Park City, UT 84060-3182

The Naropa Institute
2130 Arapahoe Avenue
Boulder, CO 80302

Aspen Writers' Conference
P.O. Box 5840
Snowmass Village, CO 81615

Antioch Writers' Workshop
135 N. Walnut
Yellow Springs, OH 45387

Writer's Conference
Illinois Wesleyan University
P.O. Box 2900
Bloomington, IL 61702

Western Reserve Writers and Freelance Conference
34200 Ridge Road, #110
Willoughby, OH 44094

Midwest Writers Workshop
Ball State University
Muncie, IN 47306

Attend a Photo Workshop

Do you own a camera? Have you ever toyed with the idea of making a
career in photography? Or at least improving your photo skills? If so, a

summer workshop might be just the ticket. Whether photography has been a longtime hobby of yours or you got your first camera on your last birthday, you can't go wrong by attending a seminar or workshop this summer.

Programs differ, with some zeroing in on technique and camera details and others concentrating on marketing finished work. A long-time photo teacher says that if you think that photography is more than just a sharp, clear picture, you should consider attending a photo workshop. A workshop is for you if you think you have a special way of seeing the world and want to find ways to get that vision onto film and into prints. Photo workshops are for people who want to learn as much as possible in a short time.

Fortunately, you will now find dozens of workshops in the U.S. Name a specialty, and there is probably a week-long rendezvous on it somewhere in the country. You can attend outdoor photo sessions like the Wilderness Photography Workshops in the West, where you'll photograph local wildlife including bighorn sheep, mountain lions, moose, elk, deer, coyotes, and eagles—sometimes from the porch of the lodge.

Many universities also run summer field trips and lab sessions through their extension departments. And photographic centers in major cities, especially in New York and Los Angeles, feature well-known speakers. A few of these offerings are summer commitments; most are only a few days to a week or two.

Summer programs can be eye-opening, stimulating, and inspiring. Students agree that the photo workshop is much more helpful than home-study courses (which are often overpriced). A book might be able to give you technical data, but a summer workshop propels you into close quarters with a professional photographer who watches you work and offers constructive criticism based on your individual needs. You might compare the learning experience with the summer writer's seminars described in this chapter. Naturally, the approaches and hours vary from one workshop to another. Each day usually consists of informal lectures, discussions, and critiques of the students' output, all run by professional, and often well-known, photographers.

Some of these programs are thorough affairs, with plenty of lab instruction. Students might be up at dawn and work with their instructors for ten to fourteen hours each day. Others are more relaxed, like a vacation or wilderness photo session. It's a good idea to ask for a brochure for information about specific workshops.

Remember that photo workshops do not perform miracles. Don't expect to become a photography genius in one week. Although great changes might not occur right away, with the daily cycles of processing-critique-response assignments, everybody's work improves somewhat. You'll test new approaches, explore new techniques, and tap hidden talents. Also, remember that, although a one-week workshop isn't a quick pathway to riches and success (be wary of instructors that promise a workshop can lead to selling fine-art photographs), you'll certainly learn a lot. On top of that, you'll have a great vacation and make interesting friends.

What You Need to Know

As one photography instructor explains, "The 'teacher-at-the-elbows' situation is great when a student wants to learn what it's really like to be a photographer, in all possible senses. A week-long workshop is intense, because it must provide answers to basic questions and actions, teach attitudes, demonstrate change, provide criticism, and promote accessibility in a very short period."

Participants You don't need to bring a portfolio, but if you have one you might want to take it along to review with an instructor. In fact, you don't require any kind of photo background to attend; just an enthusiasm for photography. *Duration* Some workshops run only a day or a weekend; more serious courses might be one to two weeks. *Facilities* Facilities range from spartan campsites in the wilderness to dormitories on college campuses or accommodations in condos. Bring your best camera equipment, but don't worry if you only have the basics. *Cost* Workshops cost $50 and up, depending on the workshop length and the reputation of the instructor. Most workshops are non-credit, though a few do offer credits. Check individual programs for details.

For Further Information

Here's a sampling of workshops and conferences offered in the U.S. Call or write for brochures.

New England Photo Workshop
P.O. Box 1509
New Milford, CT 06776

Mark Warner Photo Workshops
P.O. Box 142
Ledyand, CT 06339

The Maine Photographic Workshops
2 Central Street
Rockport, ME 04856

Immersion Photographic Workshops
311 Good Avenue
Des Plaines, IL 60016

Pine Lake Farm Photography Workshop
Station 5
Osceola, WI 54020

Santa Fe Photographic Workshops
P.O. Box 9916
Santa Fe, NM 97504

Sierra Photographic Workshops
875 A Island Drive, #222
Alameda, CA 94501

The Snake River Institute
P.O. Box 7724
Jackson, WY 83001

Ron Sanford Photography Workshop
P.O. Box 248
Fridley, CA 95948

California Wildlife Photographic Safaris
P.O. Box 30694
Santa Barbara, CA 93130

Travel & Outdoor Photography Seminars
P.O. Box 1511
Arlington, TX 76004

SouthWest Photographic Workshop
P.O. Box 19272
Houston, TX 77224

Touch of Success Photo Seminars
P.O. Box 194
Lowell, FL 32663

Visit a Music Festival

The power of the trumpet, the brilliance of the pianist, the sweet strains of violins. Music is emotion and can move your heart. And music can be an adventure.

There are all kinds of musical goodies offered throughout the U.S. all summer long.

Spoleto

My favorite festival is the Spoleto Festival U.S.A. in Charleston, South Carolina, held yearly. Opening toward the end of May and lasting for seventeen days, it's known as America's foremost festival of the arts.

Spoleto has always attracted big international names like composer Gian Carlo Menotti, playwright Arthur Miller, dancer Alexander Godunov, soprano Renata Scotto, cellist Yo-Yo Ma, pianist Misha Dichter, and conductor Zubin Mehta. Menotti serves as artistic director, stage manager, librettist, spark plug; you may also discover his distinguished face among the audience or in a walk-on part in one of his famous operas.

Spoleto was created in Spoleto, Italy, with such luminaries as the late actress Colleen Dewhurst, the late playwright Tennessee Williams, and violinist Pinchas Zuckermann, among others in attendance.

Spoleto U.S.A. takes place in Charleston's municipal auditorium, and in various local theaters, cathedrals, and churches in Charleston.

Year after year Spoleto attracts important orchestras, ballet companies, chamber music ensembles, jazz players, choirs, and theater groups, all of whom perform around the clock. When Menotti started the festival, the composer let it be known that he "sought the most gifted artists; if there is no audience, at least *we* will enjoy the performances."

All these doings take place against an Old South background. Charleston was founded in 1670 as "Charles Towne" and today overflows with two thousand beautifully restored buildings. You'll glimpse charming flower gardens, ornamental gates, and handsomely crafted columns as you amble across cobblestones. Roof terraces, walled courtyards, antique shops, and blooming magnolia trees will greet you on your rounds, while horse-drawn carriages clatter through the streets.

For Further Information

Spoleto Festival U.S.A.
P.O. Box 704
Charleston, SC 29402

Tanglewood

In the East, in that lovely hilly country known as the Berkshires, there's the yearly Tanglewood Berkshire Music Festival in Lenox, Massachusetts. Because this is the summer home of the Boston Symphony Orchestra, Tanglewood always attracts some of the world's best musicians. On sunny days you can picnic on Tanglewood's beautiful lawns while you enjoy the day's concerts. The festival takes place from the end of June through mid-August, with the Boston Symphony Orchestra playing Thursdays through Sundays. Tanglewood also offers chamber music, recitals, and a minifestival of contemporary music. Midweek there are occasional chamber and small orchestral concerts given by the students at the Berkshire Music Center, located on the fringes of the Tanglewood estate.

For Further Information

Tanglewood Music Festival
Lenox, MA 01240

Marlboro Music Festival

Farther north, in Marlboro, Vermont, is the site of the yearly Marlboro Music Festival, a highly respected Vermont tradition. For two months, musicians of all ages and backgrounds come together to study chamber music. There is no formal instruction at Marlboro; rather, students learn from each other as they rehearse eighty to one hundred pieces of music. Much of the quality here comes from the prestigious Marlboro Music School.

For Further Information

Marlboro Music Festival
Marlboro, VT 05344

Chautauqua Institution

Meanwhile, in New York State, the Chautauqua Institution has its own seventy-four-member symphony orchestra, composed mostly of New York Philharmonic musicians, and a few from Boston, Massachusetts, and nearby Erie, Pennsylvania. All tastes are catered to here, from classical to opera to show tunes. A wide variety of musical stars, from Placido Domingo to Alicia de Larrocha, from Phillipe Entremont to Walter Hendl, are regulars. For instance, in a typical week you can listen to Marvin

Hamlisch in the amphitheater and the next day hear Marvellee Caria-ga perform an aria from a little-known Blitzstein opera titled *Regina*.

For Further Information
Chautauqua Institution
Chautauqua, NY 14722

Wolf Trap

Wolf Trap, in Vienna, Virginia, offers more than classical concerts. This famous summer festival also features all kinds of jazz, country, and other music. Depending on the season, performers range from Martha Graham to the Preservation Hall Jazz Band to the Metropolitan Opera.

For Further Information
Wolf Trap
1624 Trap Road
Vienna, VA 22180

Ravinia Festival

In the Midwest, the well-known Ravinia Festival is held all summer long in Highland Park, Illinois. Symphonic and chamber music are the main fares here, but there's also dance, folk music, and jazz.

For Further Information
Ravinia Festival
Highland Park, IL 60035

The Aspen Music Festival

Situated in the West, the Aspen Music Festival is probably the most famous and most exciting of all the U.S. festivals. The great symphonic events, chamber orchestras, ballets, and lectures are enhanced by the scenery and various cultural doings of Aspen. The soloists appear formally in the Aspen Music Tent, but you can hear them rehearsing outdoors for free (there are also several free concerts each week). There's a lot going on at the Aspen Music Festival from the end of June through the end of August.

For Further Information

Aspen Music Festival
425 Rio Grande Place
Aspen, CO 81611

Central City Festival

Closer to Denver, the old mining town of Central City is the site of the yearly Central City Festival. Whether or not you like classical opera, you'll be impressed by the choices here. For one thing, all operas are sung in English. Central City itself has a lot of Victorian character, and is the perfect locale for the *Ballad of Baby Doe,* a western opera based on the famous Tabor story and first sung here by Beverly Sills. Central City also produces a memorable *Carmen* and *La Boheme.* Every spring, the opera house here attracts apprentice singers, some of whom graduate to the chorus or get minor singing parts in the opera productions.

For Further Information

Central City Opera
621 17th Street, Suite 1601
Denver, CO 80293

Santa Fe Opera

With the spectacular Southwestern sunset as a backdrop, buses gather small groups of people from hotels and head up five miles through mountains adorned with sagebrush, piñon, and russet sands to the famous Santa Fe Opera House. Each summer, this magnificent outdoor theater shines with the moon and stars overhead and the lights of Santa Fe blinking behind the audience.

After a steady international search for the most talented cast (some eight hundred singers audition for a few dozen roles), the chosen performers prepare for six months, so the resulting shows are spectacular. The Santa Fe Opera has produced a wide array of great productions, including a much-acclaimed *Magic Flute* and a memorable *La Traviata*. Some seventy-thousand listeners come to enjoy the half-dozen or so operas each season.

From the traveler's viewpoint, the Santa Fe Opera complex has more atmosphere and more charisma than the indoor setups found in many larger cities of the world. The outdoor amphitheater allows you to breathe mountain air full of wild herbal and conifer scents. As you listen to the rousing tones of Verdi, Puccini, and other composers, you begin to feel in tune with the wide Southwestern landscape.

For Further Information

Santa Fe Opera
P.O. Box 2408
Santa Fe, NM 87504

Be a Street Musician and Travel Around the World

Are you a young musician in search of adventure? Are you a vagabond at heart? Then street performing may be the perfect summer job for you.

Across the nation, downtown communities are trying to provide a "carnival" atmosphere to bring shoppers back from the suburban malls. They begin by closing entire city districts to cars and opening up "pedestrian zones" for shoppers, street musicians, and performers.

During the summer months (May to September) in the university town of Boulder, Colorado, you can encounter a barrage of freewheeling entertainers. At the steps of an historic building a young man plays acoustic guitar; a few people gather around him, singing along; others pass by, tossing handfuls of odd change into his guitar case. Around the corner a pair of juggling, fire-tossing performers on unicycles amuse shoppers who stop to see their fifteen-minute set of tricks.

Street performing is more than a job; it's a lifestyle. It's one of the few professions that can be done all over the world. As a street performer, you determine your own schedule. There's little stress. Young people adapt to the occasional rules and regulations regarding where they can perform. One performer comments, "It sure beats playing in a smoke-filled bar for a bunch of drunks."

Street performing has a long history. During the Renaissance in the fifteenth century, people congregated in the cities to trade their wares at the markets. Traveling minstrels and bands of troubadours entertained throughout Europe. In Spain these musicians were usually Gypsies, Jews, and Moroccans who lived harmoniously, traveling from city to city; their unique blend of flute, guitar, and violin is known today as *flamenco*. Today, street performing serves as an ideal training ground for future professional musicians. Rod Stewart, for instance, polished his act on the street, and Tracy Chapman got her start playing in the streets of Harvard Square in Boston.

Some students find street performing a nice way to travel. You learn about local culture, meet interesting people, and may earn enough money for room and board. In European cities like Munich, Salzburg, Florence, Barcelona, Prague, and Athens there is real camaraderie among the street musicians. They often meet in the local cafés to discuss the day's earnings and work out who will play at the choice locations during the afternoon and evening.

GETTING STARTED

Since playing outdoors means braving a variety of weather conditions, you should not consider this work unless you're in good health. You also have to be comfortable camping or staying at cheap pensions, because you won't be able to afford much more (but remember that youth hostels are often a better option and are usually close to the action).

You'll need to develop a dynamic repertoire lasting at least forty-five minutes and pick a suitable place for the performance. The best spots are sheltered (for good acoustics), such as an arcade far away from cars and other sources of noise, and have plenty of passing pedestrians and enough room for people to stop and listen. Be sure not to block an entrance to a store.

Because ordinances vary from city to city, it is difficult to generalize about the need for permits. But they're usually fairly inexpensive, costing five dollars and up for three months to two dollars and up a day. Rules, too, vary from city to city, but local ordinances typically limit the maximum number of performances you can give. For

Best Cities in the U.S.:

Boston, Massachusetts

Try Quincy Market, in the downtown harbor district. This pedestrian market is located in a historic area, easily reached by taking the subway to the government center. In Boston, musicians must audition before one or two members of the local retail association, which screens applicants and schedules performance times. Musicians need not be members of the association. The schedule for performances is booked two weeks in advance. Jugglers, large acts, and unusual instruments do especially well at Boston's Quincy Market.

Boston's North End (also known as the Italian Section) is accessible from Haymarket Station. This is a quaint spot in front of Bank of Boston on Hanover; best for violinists, classical guitar, and mandolin. The shop owners in the area prefer classical music. You'll find less competition there than at other local hot spots. Best, and only time, 6:00 P.M. to 9:00 P.M.

Harvard Square, in the student city of Cambridge, has wide sidewalks and arcades at Brattle Street that offer as many as ten acts on any summer evening. You'll need an amplifier unless you can play at the Harvard Coop entrance ("Be sure to get there early," warns one musician). All kinds of acts are performed here, but businesses prefer it if rock bands limit their play from 5:00 P.M. to 11:00 P.M. You'll need a permit to play at Harvard Square. Performance locations are available on a first-come, first-served basis.

Boulder, Colorado

Pearl Street Mall, in downtown Boulder at Broadway and Pearl Street, is a four-block-long pedestrian street with many spots to play. Folk music and classical do well, and acoustic music is preferred. You'll also see other successful acts here, even a tightrope walker and fire swallower. You'll need to get a permit from the Downtown Management Association on the mall; permits are available on a walk-in basis. You can then play any time from 11:00 A.M. to 11:00 P.M.

There is no dress code on the Pearl Street Mall, but most performers dress to fit their role. For example, a classical musician might wear coat and tails while a renaissance juggler may appear in brightly colored tights and a harlequin patterned vest.

instance, in Munich, Germany, you may only perform two days in any three-week period. Rules also limit the hours during which you may perform (usually between 11:00 A.M. and 11:00 P.M.). They specify where you may use an amplifier and where you can only perform acoustically. Also, most municipalities require that you play for free or for donations only: you may not charge for a performance and you must not harass an audience to tip you. If you want to sell tapes of your performances, check whether that might classify you as a vendor and require a tax license.

How much can you really make as a street performer? It's hard to know exactly, but you can earn anywhere from ten to fifty dollars an hour. This usually covers your living expenses. Musicians—especially singers—usually work for about three to four hours a day (it's difficult for them to last longer), but other acts might be able to exceed four hours. If there's more than one performer, tips are usually split evenly.

Seattle, Washington

Pike Place Public Market is an outdoor market located on the waterfront at Pike and First Avenue. It's a four-block district with some covered areas. The best spots are near the fish shops under the clock tower, but stairwells in the retail mall are suitable for acoustic or solo guitar. You might have to wait to get a good spot, so arrive early. You must obtain a permit from the Market Management in the market building, but they're pretty inexpensive. Special current acts include mimes, dancers, and Tico the balloon man who makes exquisite balloon unicorns. Rules include no amplifiers, no drums, and no horns.

The University District at Broadway and the Seattle Center (the World's Fair site) is also a great place to perform, especially during civic festivals.

Best Cities in Europe

If you're going to Europe, buy your return ticket before you leave the U.S. so you'll be able to get back home if you run low on cash. Bring enough money for train fare within cities, and remember that European transportation is often more expensive than the stay itself.

Munich, Germany

The City Hall building is located on the Marien Platz, which has a *Fussgaenger strasse* (pedestrian street). It is a big venue with good earnings. You must get a permit from the city to perform here and the number of performances allowed every day is limited, so plan to move on after a few days.

Salzburg, Austria

Salzburg is the birthplace of Mozart and is a real music city; if you're a talented classical musician, you'll be in high demand here. American tour groups often pay big bucks to hear Austrians play. *Mozart Platz* is the most prominent square in front of the Cathedral. Amplifiers are prohibited here.

Florence, Italy

The best places to perform are around the center of the city near the Duomo, the Uffizi Arcades (especially for portraitists) and the Ponte Vecchio bridge at the fountain (probably the best spot on earth). Sunset violin or classical music is a sure sell. Permits are required in some locations; check with the local *carabinierie* (police).

Athens, Greece

The *Plaka*, the old historic Roman city under the Acropolis, is the best place for street performers (and the food is cheap). Here the shop owners actually encourage you to play in front of their shops since it attracts more business. They've even been known to donate! Acoustic British or American music does as well as anything romantic or gypsy. "Regulations are taken casually in Athens," says one musician. "If you attract too large a crowd, however, the local gendarmes may appear."

One final piece of advice. Your best bet is always to talk to other, more experienced musicians about the laws and ordinances. Thanks to a camaraderie among performers, you'll get straight answers. If there are no other musicians around, try the nearest tourist office, convention bureau, retailer's association, or mayor's office. Or stop off at the nearest musical instrument store, where they can tell you when and where to play.

5

Building Houses and Hearts

Habitat for Humanity

Meet Tina, a volunteer for Habitat for Humanity in Tijuana. She spends a week of long, hot days each summer helping to put up house walls, mix and pour concrete, and install windows. At night, Tina sleeps in a tent. There's no electricity in this part of Tijuana, no running water. What's Tina doing in Tijuana, Mexico? She's helping to build a home for a poor local family.

Habitat for Humanity is an organization that helps in the building and renovating of some seventeen thousand homes for homeless or less fortunate individuals and families as well as for victims of disaster. Founded in 1976, it is a Christian organization run by volunteers, and is active in some eight hundred projects located around the world, and in fifteen regional offices in the U.S.

Habitat for Humanity has earned a remarkable reputation in the U.S. When Hurricane Andrew destroyed hundreds of homes and businesses in 1992, Habitat was on the Florida and Louisiana scenes to rebuild, putting up new roofs and clearing debris. After Hurricane Ini-

ki blew into Kauai, Hawaii, with 227 mph winds Habitat's people immediately sprung into action. Its volunteers have helped renovate inner
city areas, made repairs in thousands of homes of the disadvantaged,
and restored hundreds of dilapidated buildings. The Christian faith of
Habitat's founder, and of many volunteer workers, attracted ex-Presi-
dent Jimmy Carter and his wife to the programs; the Carters regularly
spend a week carpentering for one of the myriad projects.

Habitat for Humanity solicits funds from various corporations and
individuals to help finance land and materials. The bulk of the hard
work is done by a volunteer army of construction workers—carpenters, bricklayers, electricians, roofers, and plumbers—who donate their
time and skills to this worthy cause. The Habitat for Humanity has
dozens of affiliates in U.S. cities that are constantly searching for people who want to share their skills for a week or longer. There is also a
perpetual need for unskilled workers, especially young people who
want to do some good during their summer and aren't afraid of hard
labor. The homeowners help in the effort to build, too. In fact, that's
one of Habitat for Humanity's few rules, known as "Sweat Equity." These
homeowners must also make a small down payment for their future
home and then pay reasonable rent.

The quality of the homes is astonishing when you consider how
little they cost. Some years ago, for example, Habitat built a low-income
housing development in Florida. Though these same homes would
eventually be in the path of Hurricane Andrew, they were some of the
few that were barely damaged by the storm.

What You Need to Know

Participants Habitat is highly selective in accepting volunteers, because
their workers are sent into a variety of cultures where it can be difficult
to adapt to different attitudes and customs. You must be sixteen years
old to volunteer, though you can be as old as eighty-six. You don't need
any particular skills to work with Habitat for Humanity, but skilled volunteers usually get preference. Your willingness to do physical work is
most important. You should also have a Christian outlook. *Duration*

Habitat requests that you volunteer for three months. Shorter stays can be arranged, though they're not favored. *Facilities* Most volunteers who commit to a three-month stint get help in arranging for housing. *Pay* U.S. projects pay a small stipend toward food and housing, which varies from project to project. Overseas projects provide an allowance for personal living, housing, and project-related travel expenses for those who have committed for three years. *Other* You can volunteer in any state you choose. To volunteer overseas, ask for the International Partners project applications when you contact Habitat.

For Further Information

Contact the headquarters for application information. The application form is long and tedious; Habitat requires that you provide an exorbitant number of references, and they will be asked very personal questions about you and will be grilled ruthlessly about your background (for example: "How do you assess the applicant's family and/or marital relationships?"; "What weaknesses might reduce this person's effectiveness?").

> Habitat for Humanity
> 121 Habitat Street
> Americus, GA 31709-3498
> *Check your local telephone directory for additional addresses,*
> *since Habitat has many branches around the U.S.*

Earthwatch

In Big Bend National Park in Texas, a team of volunteers and several scientists hike through the spectacular high desert to collect rock samples, map the landscape, and perform magnetic surveys. In central Ontario, Canada, a group of American and Canadian volunteers under the direction of an ecology professor portage and paddle canoes into the remote Temagami wilderness. They measure the age and size of the trees and research past forest fires. At night, the teams sleep in tents. In western and southern New Hampshire, crews examine and identify soil types and rocks under the direction of an experienced geologist. At night, they stay in a log cabin. In Honolulu, Hawaii, a group of volunteers studies dolphin intelligence. They spend a month in and out of the sea and at a Marine Mammal Lab.

These are just a few examples of the 140 exciting projects sponsored throughout the year by a remarkable organization named Earthwatch. Earthwatch operates in some fifty countries around the world, and its volunteers have put in almost 500,000 hours in various science projects, such as monitoring plant health in Scotland, studying coyotes at Yellowstone National Park, and excavating an ancient tomb in North Africa.

Earthwatch's mission is "To improve human understanding of the planet, the diversity of its inhabitants, and the processes that affect the quality of life on Earth. We are non-commercial, incorporated as a charitable institution under the host country's laws; we provide services and projects that educate, inform, and inspire citizens to see problems and solve them. We depend on our members—individual, corporate, and foundation—for the funds that enable us to do this work."

What You Need to Know

Participants Earthwatch recruits actively in the U.S. for volunteers. You must be at least sixteen years old to volunteer (and volunteers range in age from sixteen to ninety). The only other requirements are curiosity and good health. *Duration* Program lengths vary from six days to three weeks, with two weeks being average. You must stay for the duration of the program. *Facilities* Accommodations range from tents to field stations to rented houses. Meals are usually included. *Cost* "Contributions" range from $495 to $2,200, depending on the program. You pay your own travel expenses to the expedition sites—so costs also vary depending on where you volunteer. *Other* School credits may be available; check with Earthwatch. Each year, about thirty-four hundred people apply to Earthwatch and this giant organization accepts most

**FUTURE EARTHWATCH
PROGRAMS INCLUDE
RESEARCH ON:**

- human adaptation to changing environments
- the relationship between resource availability and distribution
- alternative energy sources and agricultural systems
- new or traditional uses of resources in threatened ecosystems
- restoration of degraded ecosystems
- protection of threatened species
- botanical surveys and inventories
- global food security
- women's health and education in developing countries
- conservation of cultural diversity, including language, art, architecture, ethnomusicology, folklore, and textiles.

of them. If you have a preference, you can request a program or location from among Earthwatch's many offerings.

For Further Information

Earthwatch
680 Mount Auburn Street
Watertown, MA 02272

International Voluntary Service (IVS)

International Voluntary Service, or IVS as it's known, does good deeds all over the world. Unlike the Peace Corps, IVS isn't associated with the U.S. government, but is a private, international development agency. The organization was founded in 1922 by a pacifist with humanitarian concerns. IVS volunteers swoop into dozens of countries to assist in a variety of ways. IVS is committed to the idea that Americans can make a valid contribution to other countries through face-to-face contacts with their people, and by performing activities that the host country chooses.

The IVS work force helps out all over the world, including Europe and North America; camps exist in Turkey, Greece, Finland, and former Iron Curtain countries, among others. And volunteers are always needed. Each work camp is sponsored by a local group, such as an environmental organization, a village council, or a special community. Among the many projects the IVS maintains are:

- Running a day-care project in Northern Ireland
- Renovating a woman's shelter in Germany
- Preparing the grounds for a Native American Festival in California
- Educating people about pollution in the countries of the former Soviet Union
- Building a shelter for the homeless in Washington, D.C.

At the moment, IVS teams are also planting seeds and tree nurseries, building irrigation ditches, and constructing community housing.

IVS operates primarily in summer because that's when most of its volunteers—young people who are flexible, strong, and healthy—are available. The IVS volunteer must adapt his or her efforts to meet the needs, interests, and abilities of the people in the host country.

A letter from a volunteer in Russia says, "We have cleared most of the remaining land, using hand tools, most in poor condition. We have made some beautiful vegetable gardens along the fence line and are about to plant crops in the space just cleared. Small as this space is, it will be the largest plot under irrigation in the area. Everyday the people watch us. Seeing Americans sweating and dirty has gained us respect."

Becoming an IVS volunteer is a great way to meet people from all over the world and gain insight into a host country. A former IVS volunteer in Italy recalls: "It really was an incredible, enlightening, educational, fun experience. We were able to do so much and I was exposed to aspects of Italy which would otherwise have been unattainable to me as an independent tourist."

What You Need to Know

Participants You must be at least eighteen years old to volunteer. *Duration* You'll commit to work on an ongoing project from two to four summer weeks. You can specify which weeks are best for you and IVS will try its best to match them. *Facilities* The local community takes care of food and accommodations. Housing can range from tents to mud huts to farmhouses and bunkhouses. *Cost* Volunteers pay for their transportation to the work camp site from their home. A fee of $35 is charged for U.S. locations; $75 to $100 for foreign locations. The fee includes accident and illness insurance. *How to Apply* Registration forms are available from IVS. Choose your location on a first come, first served basis.

For Further Information

Service Civil International/International
Voluntary Service (SCI/IVS)
Innisfree Village
Route 2, P.O. Box 506
Croset, VA 22932

The American Friends Service Committee (AFSC)

The seventy-five-year-old American Friends Service Committee (AFSC) is a Quaker organization, so in all of its projects pacifism and peace are emphasized above all else. Through organized projects, AFSC workers use their social and technical skills to help people in the U.S. and developing countries discover and utilize their own power and resources.

In the past seven decades, AFSC volunteers have helped families in the slums of Peru become self-supporting; shared experiences with young Southeast Asians in a seminar in Japan; helped refugees in Hong Kong start new lives; established community services in African villages; and created a preschool center on the Gaza Strip, among many, many other projects. The campaigns are held in places as diverse as Lebanon, Nicaragua, Mexico, Chile, Colombia, Zambia, California, Mali, Indochina, Laos, Thailand, the Gaza Strip, and Florida. AFSC's volunteers are particularly welcome in Mexico's programs, repairing schools and clinics, digging irrigation ditches, and planting gardens.

The AFSC operates on a very small scale in its overseas programs. These programs usually have only one or two expatriate staff members working with local people on projects of importance to the community. Volunteers work in groups of fifteen supervised by two leaders.

In the U.S., volunteers have built shelters for the homeless in Oakland, California; erected housing in Florida; counseled homeless families in New York; trained inmates for their release from jail in New Jersey; and run a Native American youth camp in Montana, to name a few of their projects. If you're motivated to do good in the world, your AFSC summer will be a memorable one.

What You Need to Know

Participants Volunteers are from eighteen to twenty-six years old. Volunteers not only share the work on a project, but participate in the daily activities of the area they are in. Overseas volunteers must be physically and emotionally qualified for service under conditions that at times may demand long hours and adjustment to primitive living conditions. Health exams are required. You must be able to speak Spanish to work on projects in Mexico. *Duration* Most projects run for six weeks, from June to mid-August. *Facilities* Meals and lodging are provided at the project site and may be primitive or spartan. *Cost* AFSC operates on a shoestring budget, and requires a $700 contribution. This money covers orientation, food and primitive lodging, plus health and accident insurance. Volunteers are responsible for transportation costs to project destinations. *Other* College credits may be available; ask AFSC for details.

For Further Information

American Friends Service Committee (AFSC) Offices:
National Office:
1501 Cherry Street
Philadelphia, PA 19102

Regional Offices:
Southeastern:
92 Piedmont Avenue, NE
Atlanta, GA 30303

Middle Atlantic:
4806 York Road
Baltimore, MD 21212

WHAT IT'S LIKE TO
VOLUNTEER OVERSEAS

It can sometimes be difficult to spend a summer on foreign soil; you're not familiar with the food, customs, or people. Many organizations recommend that you already know something about the place you'll be traveling to, so that you can adapt once you arrive. Often they'll help you get ready, sometimes through a special department in the organization specifically designed to prepare you for the great adventure. There are also some independent firms that specialize in relocation training. They'll provide you with background knowledge of the area, including a study of regional history, religion, and geography. Among other subjects, they also cover social customs and ways of conducting business, such as:

• What will offend the people of the host country?

• What will please them?

• What might you find strange in local customs, behaviors and values, and how should you learn to cope with that?

Although many volunteers suffer no anxiety in their adjustment to local conditions, a few organizations require you to meet with psychologists or recruiting experts just to be sure. This is done not only for your benefit but to reassure the organization and host country of your abilities and social skills. It is not uncommon for participants to suf-

New England:
2161 Massachusetts Avenue
Cambridge, MA 02140

Great Lakes:
59 East Van Buren
Chicago, IL 60605

North Central:
4211 Grand Avenue
Des Moines, IA 50312

New York Metropolitan:
15 Rutherford Place
New York, NY 10003

Pacific Southwest:
980 North Fair Oaks Avenue
Pasadena, CA 91103

Pacific Mountain:
2160 Lake Street
San Francisco, CA 94121

Pacific Northwest:
814 NE 40th Street
Seattle, WA 98105

Council on International Education Exchange (CIEE)

The Council on International Education Exchange (CIEE) acts as a placement agency for hundreds of young people who want to spend their summer in a foreign country. The volunteers do construction and renovation and perform environmental tasks. An even larger organization than IVS, CIEE has contacts in such exotic areas as Morocco, Algeria, Bulgaria, and Hungary.

CIEE is a reliable, well-known organization. The organizers emphasize that volunteers must be adaptable, outgoing, and ready for a challenge. You're guaranteed a unique and exciting summer as a CIEE volunteer. You could be involved in forest conservation in Czechoslovakia, care of the elderly in West Germany, construction of a water trench in Turkey, renovation of historic sites in France, or archaeological digs in Spain.

What You Need to Know

Participants You must be at least eighteen years old to volunteer. *Duration* Projects usually last from late June to early September. *Facilities* Food and housing are provided. *Cost* CIEE charges a steep $125 application fee and you pay for your own travel to a work camp destination. Strictly volunteer work; no salary.

For Further Information

Council on International Education Exchange (CIEE)
International Voluntary Service
205 East 42d Street
New York, NY 10017

Global Volunteers

The Kingdom of Tonga in the South Pacific is the "land where time began," and the site of the mutiny of Captain Bligh's ship, the *Bounty*. It is also one of the eight locations around the world where Global Volunteers, a sort of miniature Peace Corps, offers exciting travel opportunities.

Global Volunteers works with local people on community projects.

fer culture shock, the disorientation most people experience when they move for an extended period of time into a different culture from their own. They may feel irritable, resentful, homesick, depressed, withdrawn, bored, or even hostile toward the host nation. Many individuals get over these symptoms quickly, but sometimes they linger, and some people might have to be sent home.

A few pointers on behavior might be useful too, to give you an extra edge in an interview and to help you once you're on location.

For starters, it's best to be open to new ideas and ways of doing things. While an attitude that everything American is superior has no place in these programs, to the other extreme, you shouldn't put down American ways of doing things either.

Many European cities are more formal than American cities. Men often dress in a shirt, tie, and jacket. Be friendly but not familiar; use first names only when invited to do so. In some countries, an early use of first names is not understood in the friendly sense we intend; it is often considered a condescending familiarity.

Do not ignore age, rank, degrees, or titles. Doctors of philosophy and jurisprudence are referred to as "Doctor." When dealing with a group, treat all members with equal respect until the leader is identified.

Above all, accept the basic rules of a host nation.

As a GV, you can spend two fascinating summer weeks building a playground in a remote Jamaican village; restoring a much-needed community building in Jonestown, Mississippi; teaching English to the Rural Solidarity Farmers Union in Zbuczyn, Poland; or developing a clean water supply for a school in Pommern, Tanzania.

The local village or host organization identifies the specific needs and projects for Global Volunteers to focus on. As invited guests, the volunteers are not there to set the agenda, but to implement what the village wishes done, as long as the work benefits the entire community. Some recent projects included building tables, chairs, and desks for a school; digging latrines; tutoring children; drilling water wells; counseling small businesses; and identifying crop diseases.

A summer with Global Volunteers is time to learn about another culture and its philosophy . . . and to learn a bit about yourself.

What You Need to Know

Participants You must be at least eighteen years old to volunteer. *Duration* Most projects last about two weeks. *Facilities* Accommodations with the local people are usually available. Dormitory accommodations may also be expected. *Cost* Costs range from $600 for a U.S. location to $1,825 for a project in Poland, for instance. Volunteers must pay for their own airfare.

For Further Information

Global Volunteers
375 East Little Canada Road
St. Paul, MN 55117

Amigos de las Americas

How would you like to spend a summer immersed in the culture and customs of Mexico and Central America, learn more about public health care systems, and brush up on your Spanish? If you would, Amigos de las Americas could be the right summer group for you.

Amigos de las Americas sends students to Brazil, Costa Rica, the Dominican Republic, Ecuador, Mexico, and Paraguay to work as interns in public health. Program activities include digging water wells, administering immunizations, teaching dental hygiene, and improving community sanitation methods. An intensive training program is given prior to leaving the U.S., and the overall experience is an unforgettable one.

What You Need to Know

Participants Applicants must be sixteen years old and should have studied Spanish for a year or more before volunteering. *Duration* Internships last from four to eight weeks, depending on location and project. Most run from mid-June to mid-August. *Facilities* Host families or community centers provide housing and food. *Cost* Volunteers must cover all other expenses, including airfare to Houston and insurance. Total monetary outlays range from about $2,300 to $3,000, and include transportation to the host country, training, and field supplies. The training kit includes a fund-raising packet that will help you raise money through donations from family, businesses, and anyone else who will contribute. Limited scholarships are also available. *How to Apply* The deadline for applications is March 1 for the following summer. *Other* It's not especially hard to get onboard: of seven hundred or so summer applicants, at least six hundred are accepted overseas as volunteers.

For Further information

Amigos de las Americas
Recruitment
5618 Star Lane
Houston, TX 77057

Institute of Cultural Affairs (ICA)

The Institute of Cultural Affairs has been in the forefront of international group efforts in developing nations for more than twenty-five years.

ICA volunteers are invited by more than thirty nations to train self-supporting villagers in new facilitation skills and development. The organization is known for its involvement in local culture and resource management; they conduct on-site programs with schools, businesses, and social services. ICA plans and orchestrates community development in such areas as medicine, sanitation, and literacy. It then gradually shifts all the responsibilities back to the local population.

The volunteer takes a sixteen-day course called Leadership Options, which teaches volunteers how best to work with local community agencies and nonprofit organizations to assist needy people.

As an ICA volunteer, your work will be varied, and may include livestock upgrading, organic farming, building a children's playground, taking local senior citizens on excursions, or performing blood pressure tests.

One former volunteer remembers, "I worked with the ICA in Cairo, Egypt, for two weeks, while I was visiting an older brother. As a twenty-year-old, third-year architecture student, I designed my first building there: it was limestone and was built with funding from the Ford Foundation. It was a school and training center which housed twenty-six cultural development students and was designed to provide training to health care and sanitation technicians. I felt extremely useful because I was able to discuss the workers' needs and provide a simple design to fit the area."

What You Need to Know

Participants You must be between the ages of twenty and twenty-four, with two or more years of college behind you. *Duration* Programs vary from two weeks in a South American village to a three- to nine-month stint as an intern in a residential setting. *Facilities* ICA volunteers live in staff housing, training centers, or with families on a prearranged basis, depending on the location. Accommodations can be arranged by ICA. *Cost* You cover all costs while on assignment as well as the costs of training, orientation, travel, room, and board. ICA handles expenses of project-related work only. Costs vary, so check with ICA for specifics.

For Further Information

Institute of Cultural Affairs (ICA)
4750 North Sheridan Road
Chicago, IL 60640

La Sabranenque in Provence

The southern part of France, known as the Provence, is famous for its blue sky. The sun seems to always shine on the rich flora and fauna of the region—cypresses, fig trees, olive trees, and vineyards. The celebrated French Impressionist painters loved the Provence. And you can easily see why—the pastoral beauty of the landscape is hard to ignore.

Not far from Avignon, the little village of La Roque-sur-Ceze and the red Mediterranean roofs of Saint Victor-la Coste climb up the hillsides. From below, one can hear the hammers of stonemasons, the clanging of picks and shovels, the saws of amateur carpenters, the shouts of tile layers. Here are the international volunteers of La Sabranenque: about 150 Americans and Europeans who come every summer to enjoy the bright daylight and to brush up on their restoration skills . . . and their French.

Sabranenque also has a few projects in Italy. Here, volunteers restore and renovate old villages and their medieval buildings and monuments. The work is sweaty, but the volunteers are in love with the surroundings and the renovation projects. "With La Sabranenque, you enter another 'world zone,'" says one American.

What You Need to Know

Participants You must be at least eighteen years old. You'll be trained at the site; no prior skills or training are required. *Duration* Each project is two or three weeks long and you have the choice of several two-week periods. *Facilities* Most volunteers stay in a village room at their own cost; the Sabranenque office can provide leads. Volunteers pay for their meals, which they eat together, usually outside, or *al fresco. Cost* A two-week session costs about $490 and three weeks will run between $860 and $915. You must pay for your own flight to Paris, which can be expensive.

For Further Information

La Sabranenque maintains both a U.S. and a French office.

La Sabranenque
c/o Jacqueline C. Simon
217 High Park Boulevard
Buffalo, NY 14226

La Sabranenque
rue de la Tour de l'Oume
30290 Saint Victor la Coste
France

Part II

Earning Adventures

6

Fruits of the Vine and of the Soil

Pick Peaches

As you approach Grand Junction, Colorado, Interstate 70 allows you to exit to Palisade, the state's major peach country. The Chamber of Commerce claims "354 sunny days a year." The valley is ringed by brown and mauve mountains that surround the Grand Mesa, the largest flat-topped mountain in the world. You can see the dryness of the climate in the color of the terrain.

Here's where some of the West's best peaches grow. The pickers tan and sweat, sweat and tan; yet many of them feel an exhilaration as they gather their bushels of fruit. These are real action jobs—you're up and down the ladder, reaching and picking.

Harvesting fruit can give you a high, can make the endorphins dance. Some people go from orchard to orchard and from state to state, arriving in time to pick at each place. In the words of one longtime picker and writer, "The fruit fields get into our blood. Our fingers are itching to pick fruit. . . ."

Palisade (population 1,600) has 310 growers and about 300,000 peach trees. Unless there has been a winter freeze or another horti-

I spent one summer picking peaches, and won't ever forget the experience. Every day I worked side by side with many Mexicans; the work is hard, but the exercise felt good all over. I earned all of ten dollars in a day. If you want to make real money in the orchards, you work long back-breaking hours. (I worked only from 8:00 A.M. to 12:00 noon.) Some orchards don't have bathrooms, just latrines, and the migrant Mexicans wash their laundry on old-fashioned washboards. While most of the labor force stays in tents, barracks, or rickety trailers, I slept at the Grand Junction Holiday Inn. "Lucky you," someone observed. "You can take showers." Showers are a writer's privilege.

cultural disaster, the area needs some 4,000 harvesters to pick the golden ripe Elbertas. The yearly crop is 18 million pounds. Thus, there are lots of opportunities for workers.

The people are interesting: An abundance of students; bearded vagrants and their ragged girlfriends; local Colorado folks; some "fruit tramps" (pickers who travel from state to state and who know the ropes). A number of them own RVs. Many of the pickers obviously didn't intend to make a career of it; they were just between jobs or on school vacation. Then there are the authentic, experienced, needy, exploited Hispanic migrant workers . . . Indeed, most of the workers are Latinos. Some are undocumented "aliens" or in the U.S. on false papers, which the orchard owners keep mum about.

Peach picking isn't for you unless you're in excellent shape. It's hard to scale ladders all day, to stretch your limbs until they ache; the string of your filled harvest sack bites without mercy into your shoulders or neck. You must continually lug forty-eight-pound bushels. A week of peach picking guarantees to make almost anyone lose weight. And there is always the chance of your ladder (or you) slipping, of branches breaking and hitting you, of hernias and other health problems.

Some orchards—especially on those sun-baked, wrinkled Colorado plateaus and in California—get extremely hot. There's almost no shade. The canopy of trees is pierced by the sun's rays. In Colorado, that means from eighty-five to a hundred degrees. You're cool only at 7:00 A.M. when you start, and in some parts of the country at 6:00 P.M. when you finish.

Some newcomers also forget about the peach fuzz. You won't feel it for a few hours, but after a day or two, it stings. Be careful, since some people are allergic to the fuzz and break out in hives. Talcum can help the average harvester. But the fuzz remains a problem.

Harvest workers can generally gather fruit from the ground for their own use. Some people thus manage to sweeten away a year's supply. Actually, many workers who eat too many of the juicy fruit wind up with diarrhea during their first few days.

In addition to picking jobs, there are positions available to help with cultivation, spraying, thinning, and irrigating throughout the summer. The fruit must also be sorted and crated after it is picked. All this creates many temporary jobs, including some in the packing shed. Fortunately, mechanization still has a way to go when it comes to harvesting most types of peaches.

From the job seeker's viewpoint, the advantage of the peach industry is that it's spread throughout North America. You may not have to go far; wherever you live—in the East, the South, the northern half of the Midwest, or the West—there are probably peach orchards. (See detailed list with addresses at the end of this section.) The time span for harvesting is great, too, which allows you to choose a period that is suitable to you.

The harvest seasons for peaches vary with the geographical location from south to north. The earliest fruit is usually picked in Florida around mid-May, the last peaches in Pennsylvania, Michigan, and Colorado during late August or early September. Some areas have long harvest seasons because growers planted varieties that ripened in succession. In other regions most of the fruit is harvested and shipped between a period of two weeks to a month.

According to U.S. Department of Agriculture figures, California leads other states with about 1,800,000 pounds taken each year. In fact, California produces most of the nation's dried fruits and nearly all of our canned cling peaches, in addition to canning virtually all of the fruit cocktail.

Georgia, South Carolina, New Jersey, and Michigan all figure prominently for their peach crops. Nevertheless, there are almost no jobs—except for a few rare regulars—until harvest time.

Naturally, the actual job openings depend on the area. In some places down south there is an abundance of local labor most of the time. Many orchardists hire through crew leaders, some of whom return to the same spots year after year. A few orchards even import people from Puerto Rico. On the whole, however, the situation is promising enough for anyone willing to work cheaply. A spokesperson for the National Peach Council puts it this way: "Willing harvest workers who can and will stay on the job would be welcomed by many orchardists."

What You Need to Know

Participants People of any age can harvest; in some orchards you see kids as young as fourteen, and students working alongside adults. Being in good shape is paramount here, meaning you need a tough physique and plenty of stamina. The huskier the harvester, the better. *Duration* The harvest lasts from two weeks to a month per state. Some pickers follow the ripening peaches all over the U.S. *Facilities* In a few places, you may be able to get free accommodations. But they're primitive, and you may have to sleep in bunks. Facilities in these shacks are used by many pickers. *Pay* You do okay when the trees are full and you can fill your sacks at high speed. The individual bushel rate varies from year to year and from region to region. In some parts of the U.S. pickers are paid by the hour. This method is used when orchard owners believe in high quality and they want you to pick ripe fruit only. Remember that there are no unions to bolster your income. Most growers pay you less money than they should. Some orchardists hand out paychecks only when the entire peach harvest is in. If you worked by the bushel or by the bin (twenty-seven bushels) you might get a bonus when the harvest is in. The pay-later system makes sense for the orchardists; they hope you stay for the length of the harvest. Usual payment is by the bin and can range from $10 to $15 per bin, with a worker averaging from two to six bins per day.

For Further Information

It would take a long book to list all the orchards in the U.S. But an adequate assortment follows. Forget about writing letters. Fruit farmers don't have the time to answer. Instead, try the state capital's state labor offices, often known as Job Service, Employment Developments Department, or Employment Security. Go a few months ahead of the harvest. Find out about the labor practices in the state's peach orchards.

If they don't use migrants or regular crews exclusively, get in touch with the nearest agricultural extension service (or USDA office) and ask about the season's harvest dates. (In California, they're mid-July to September.) A few days before D-day thumb a ride or drive to the area and hightail it to the local state job service. Or report directly to some of the big growers on the list. Bigger orchards cannot guarantee you a job; but sometimes the small peach grower has more openings and can help you get started.

California State Agencies:
Employment Development Department
1204 E Street
Marysville, CA 95901

Employment Development Department
P.O. Box 216
Geres, CA 95307

Employment Development
2600 Fresno Street
Fresno, CA 93721

Some leading California orchards:
Praudt Farms
Reedly, CA 93654

Sun Valley Farms
Del Ray, CA 93616

P-R Farms, Inc.
2929 E. Copper Avenue
Clovis, CA 93612

Colorado:
James A. Clark Orchards
Palisade, CO 81526

Sisson Peach Orchard
R.R. 1
Palisade, CO 81526

Dale Ferguson Orchards
Palisade, CO 81526

W. Wohland Orchards
Palisade, CO 81526

Peter Forte Orchards
Palisade, CO 81526

Idaho:
Symms Fruit Ranch
Route 6
Caldwell, ID 83605

Washington State:
Thompson Farm
Old Natches Highway
Natches, WA 98937

Y & Y Farms
54th Avenue
Fife, WA 98443

Georgia:
Department of Industry and Trade
230 Peachtree Street
Atlanta, GA 30301

Agri Personnel
5120 Cook Road
Atlanta, GA 30349

Byron Plantation
103 William Street
Reidsville, GA 30453

Michigan:
Michigan Information Bureau
333 South Capitol Avenue
Lansing, MI 48933

Michigan Department of Commerce
P.O. Box 30226
Lansing, MI 48909

Rocky Top Farms
Route 1, Essex
Elsworth, MI 49729

New Jersey:
New Jersey Department of Commerce
20 West State Street
Trenton, NJ 08625

Tak Moriuchi, Inc.
Fellowship Road
Moorestown, NJ 08057

South Carolina:
Labor Finders
1366 Rosewood Drive
Columbia, SC 29201

SC Peach Growers Association
RFD 1
Moore, SC 29369

For more information on all states, contact the Extension Office of the Department of Agriculture.

Join the Cherry Harvest

Cherry harvests start as early as May in California's San Joaquin Valley, Sacramento Valley, and in the foothills of the Sierra Mountains. In June, you can find work in Washington State's lower and upper Yakima Valleys, in Oregon's fertile Willamette Valley and the Dalles, or in Utah. In northern Colorado, both sweet and tart cherries are plucked from trees during early July; this is also the time for Michigan's big crop, and for the Hudson Valley's in New York State. The harvest is generally short, lasting only a few days. When it comes to quantities, the cherry harvest doesn't compare with that of apples. Yet in Washington State, for example, some thirty-thousand pickers are kept busy. Three-fourths of the nation's sweet cherries come from the Pacific Northwest; in poundage, the entire U.S. harvest only amounts to 127,000 tons a season.

In some states, the harvest is in the hands of contractors who contact the Texas-based harvest crew chiefs. The contractor deals with the cherry grower who indicates the number of needed workers. The crew chiefs find the harvesters and drive them north in trucks. The crews are often made up of Mexican families. What if you don't have a crew chief? Then you are single or a "loner" and find your own work as you go. The pay is mediocre but the Bings and Royal Anns taste great.

In fact, the work can be rather pleasant.

Your services will be especially welcomed in some parts of the U.S. A labor expert from the Dalles, Oregon region, for instance, paints this favorable picture: "Hot weather, forcing a rapid harvest, could produce a shortage of pickers in any given year. Mechanization still has no significant impact on the local cherry industry."

Bear in mind that bad weather can also wreak havoc with the delicate ripening process of the small, juicy fruit. During many years, the entire crop of tart cherries is ravaged by freezes. In short, ask the near-

Author Toby Sonnenman admits to being a "fruit tramp"; even after decades of picking, she hasn't lost her enthusiasm, especially when it comes to cherries. Toby explains in her book Fruit Fields in My Blood:

"In spite of all the frustrations, delays and disappointments, there is nothing so satisfying to a picker as a good day of fruit picking. It's a rare day when the weather is perfect, not too cool or too hot, and a promising row of loaded trees stretches out ahead. The camaraderie of the crew is pleasant and the boxes of cherries seem to fill almost effortlessly with plump fruit. These days are rare even in the best harvest, but they are always what a picker hopes for at the beginning of the fruit run and remembers long after the last fruit of the season is picked."

est agricultural agent about the season's prospects before hitching a ride to the orchards. Some orchards encourage families to pick their own instead of hiring you and then marketing the output. One of the great U-pick areas—where anyone can come to pick their own fruit— is the San Gorgonio Valley region of California. One man who came with his wife tells about his experience: "You are furnished a ladder and buckets and assigned a certain tree. You bring your own boxes for carrying the cherries home. U-Pick prices are based on the Los Angeles wholesale market."

What You Need to Know

Participants When the cherries are ripe around the U.S., all hands are welcome, regardless of age or education. Good health is all that counts if you want to join the army of pickers. *Duration* The harvest lasts two weeks to a month at the most, unless you travel from state to state.

For Further Information

National Cherry Growers Institute
1105 NW 31st
Corvallis, OR 97330

U.S. Job Service Centers has employment offices in:
The Dalles, OR
Hood River, OR
Milton, OR
Freewater, OR

California Cherry Growers and Industries Foundation
48 East Oak
Lodi, CA 95240

The Job Service Center
Loveland, CO 80537

Traverse City Area Chamber of Commerce
P.O. Box 387
Traverse City, MI 49684

Gather Apples

Though most of the opportunities mentioned here arise during summer months, if your school year starts late or if you have some spare weeks in early fall, you might want to try apple picking.

Poets praise the fruited grove; painters set the boughs and top-heavy limbs of apple trees to canvas. When you reach up for those gleaming balls, the sweet smell will waft into your nostrils. And if one apple a day "keeps the doctor away," one thousand or more a day should keep you in fine shape—and give you a little pocket money besides.

In most parts of the U.S. the apple harvest follows on the heels of the peach harvest, and some of the same crews move on to the new bonanza. The Pacific Northwest is especially blessed with apple orchards; so are California and New England. You'll also find some action in between the two coasts. The harvest figures seem as dazzling as the red, gold, and green fruit: California's San Joaquin and Sacramento valleys plus the northern and central areas yield a yearly 472 million pounds of Rome Beauties, Golden Delicious, and other varieties; Washington's Yakima Valley produces almost three times as many pounds, providing seasonal employment for some forty-thousand pickers. Even Virginia's one thousand commercial growers, backed by some fifteen thousand seasonal workers, bring in ten million boxes of fruit each autumn. Oregon, Michigan, and New York are all prospects for harvest jobs.

New England

The states of Maine, New Hampshire, and Vermont comprise more than one million apple trees in almost seven hundred orchards. New England's harvest season and picking methods are fairly characteristic for the nation.

Apple picking season here usually lasts for six weeks, from about the first week in September until around the third week in October, and sometimes into early November, depending on the year's weather. The Northeast has a temperate climate, averaging seventy to eighty-five degrees during the summer and cooling rapidly before autumn. As a picker you are often subject to warm seventy-degree days under clear blue skies, with fifty-degree nights. By the end of the harvest, you may well experience freezing temperatures, or at least days in the forties and nights in the thirties. But New England's changing leaf colors in October are the picker's bonus and consolation for the hard work.

New England grows mostly dessert apples. They're meant to be eaten as individual fruit instead of being canned or made into apple butter. The growers want quality fruit without bruises. This means you may neither toss apples nor pick unripe ones.

Apple picking takes a day of training. You'll have to learn how to carry and place the fifteen- to twenty-four-foot ladders, which can weigh up to thirty pounds. Your picking bucket shouldn't bump against the rungs. Of course, new hands must learn how to detect ripeness, and must learn how to "gentle" the fruit into the picking buckets. The buckets hold about twenty-five to thirty pounds; they go into bushel boxes or bushel bins and later into boxes in the sorting sheds. Growers often insist on a ten-hour workday, six days a week.

There's a great turnover in workers, in part due to some of the hazards involved. For instance, some harvesters suffer heat exhaustion; others poison ivy; and there's a risk of sprained ankles in the grove. It also rains frequently, and some workers leave because of the freshly applied pesticides and insecticides. What with modest pay, some feel it's not worth it.

What You Need to Know

Participants Almost anyone who can work full time for a few weeks—and who will stick on—is eagerly welcomed by any orchard. You should also be in good physical shape, dependable, and motivated. Although ages generally range from early twenties to thirties, you'll see a few teenagers and some older folks as well. A few of your co-workers may want to be growers themselves someday. Others just enjoy being outdoors. Pickers come mostly from local communities, but there are also Canadians, Hispanics, and Jamaicans. *Duration* The season usually lasts about six weeks. *Facilities* In some parts of the country, growers furnish free housing, a communal kitchen, and some bedding; on occasion, especially in the Pacific Northwest, there are recreational facilities such as volleyball courts or a soccer field. As a picker, you can eat all the apples you want, but you provide your own meals. You also must bring your own sturdy work clothes, boots, and overshoes for wet grass. *Pay* Your pay is usually based on a piece-rate basis which varies from coast to coast. It's lowest in the South (including Virginia) and highest in the Pacific Northwest, the Midwest, and New England. Still, each bin (almost twenty-seven bushels) brings you no more than the average price of a dinner at a decent restaurant. But some pickers have learned to harvest so fast and efficiently that they take as much as $1,500 home after the season. By working long hours, some pickers make around $200 a week. In Washington State you're paid from $6 to $8 an hour if you're not on the piece rate. On occasion, particularly when the growers face severe labor shortages, you can earn even better money.

For Further Information

Just before the harvest, you might want to contact the State Labor offices, State Employment Services, the Apple Commissioner, Job Service offices, or farm bureaus in the counties with large numbers of apple orchards. Don't write or send a résumé; inquire by phone or in person. Here are the most lively areas (check with your local library for addresses and phone numbers):

Washington:
Chelan, Okanogan, Yakima counties

Colorado:
Hood River Valley, Delta County

New York:

Hudson Valley, Wayne, Orleans, Niagara, Monroe, Onondaga Counties, Ulster, Columbia, Dutchess, Orange, Saratoga, Clinton, Essex

Michigan:

Kent, Oceana, Ottawa, Ionia, Macomb, Berrien, Van Buren, Allegan, Genesee, Oakland, Lapeer, St. Claire, Manistee, Benzie, Leelanau, Grand Traverse

New Jersey:

Gloucester, Camden, Cumberland, Monmouth, Burlington, Middlesex, Warren, Sussex, Hunterdon counties

California:

Sacramento Valley, San Joaquin Valley, Santa Cruz, Sonoma, Monterey, Mendocino, El Dorado, Ventura, Tulare, Kern, and San Bernardino counties

Apple Associations and Guilds:
International Apple Institute
P.O. Box 4556
McClean, VA 22101-4556

Washington State Apple Commission
P.O. Box 18
Wanatchee, WA 02193

Washington Association of Apple Growers
801 Summitville
Yakima, WA 98902

New England Apple Council
Weston, MA 02193

Apple Processors Association
1629 K Street
Washington, DC 20006

United Fruit Growers Association
144 Kluge Avenue
Palisade, CO 81526

Apple Orchards in the U.S. (east to west):
Mack's Apples
Londonderry, NH 03053

Rickler Hill Orchards
Turner, ME 04282

Baxter's Echo Hill Orchards
Wilbraham
Monson, MA 01057

Rice Fruit Farm
757 Main North
Wilbraham, MA 01095

Hepburn Orchards, Inc.
P.O. Box 212
Hancock, MD 21750

Stanford Orchards
2391 South 25th Road
Cedaredge, CO 81413

Rogers Mesa Fruit Company
Highway 92 & Lerous Gulch Road
Hotchkiss, CO 81419

Skyland Apple Orchards
Delta, CO 81416

Stahl Orchard
4006 P Road
Paonia, CO 81428

Ace Apple
2771 East French Camp Road
Manteca, CA 95336

Appleseed Ranch
1834 High School Road
Sebastopol, CA 95472

Hurst-Darrel Twin Hill Apple Ranch
1689 Pleasant Hill Road
Sebastopol, CA 95472

Martwelli Apple Ranch
3360 River Road
Windsor, CA 95492

Follow the Citrus Crops

Citrus fruit grows only in warm climates, so if you're looking to pick citrus, you'll find yourself out there in good sun, under a good blue sky. The citrus harvest work on the high stepladders is no harder than other fruit picking. Since citrus crops don't lend themselves to mechanical harvesting, growers must rely on seasonal workers. Keep in mind that your employers need more than just pickers; somebody—in fact, many bodies!—must also wash, sort, grade, and pack the vitamin C-rich fruit. Each type of citrus fruit is unique. Orange trees, for instance, never shed their leaves; so you work under a fairly shady canopy. Russ

Leadabrand, a well-known California harvest watcher, tells us: "The lemon harvest goes on the year round. In fact, there is no time of the year when lemon trees are not simultaneously bearing buds, blossoms, and ripening fruit.

"A lemon takes about six months to ripen. Picking crews work over each tree every six weeks. They pick, not by color, but by size—taking only the lemons that do not slide through a wire measuring ring. In the course of a year a single good tree may bear three thousand lemons."

In most citrus-growing regions, ripe grapefruit is picked each month, December through April, so there aren't many summer jobs available in the grapefruit harvest.

To be sure, working conditions vary and are not always ideal. In one West Coast orchard, long owned by an insurance company, harvesters complain fiercely about defective ladders and the lack of first aid equipment. In some other parts of the country, rattlesnakes are not uncommon.

What's more, the pay is modest. Experienced migrant workers slaving in the citrus orchards from sunup to sundown manage to earn from twenty to thirty dollars per day. The average summertime picker rarely matches this, being hard put to work as fast. Moreover, in some labor camps, the worker is charged large sums for food and drink, even for a bed. This results in even more modest earnings.

Essentially, there are three basic citrus-growing areas in the U.S. Despite hurricanes and other disasters, Florida leads the other citrus states with its quantities of oranges, grapefruits, and lemons. California comes next, producing about forty million boxes of oranges, along with other fruit. (A box usually weighs seventy pounds.) Texas follows, with a goodly crop of grapefruit, especially in the lower Rio Grande Valley, which has about five thousand grapefruit groves. You'll find many trees near the following Texas communities: Weslaco, Edinburg, McAllen, and San Benito. And there is also some activity in Arizona. Laborers are employed mostly in the winter, though.

Easterners and midwesterners might as well head for central Florida. Find Ocala on any map; the jobs are south of that city, all through the central belt of the state. According to the Florida Department of Agriculture, "Harvesting work can be obtained through registration at a Farm Labor Office of the Division of Employment Security, Florida Department of Commerce. However, many workers simply make themselves available at well-known pickup points during the harvest season and wait for an employer to come along."

Or how about California?

Statisticians estimate that the count of orange trees in the state is presently around nine million. These include Valencias and Navels. Valencias are picked from spring (about May) through early winter (November); Navels during the winter through May. You're quickly aware of the season when you see the first roadside stands hawking their pretty wares. For oranges, your best bet is to drive into the amazingly fertile Joaquin Valley or into the Sacramento Valley. You also see plenty of orange groves in the lower Sierra around San Diego.

Your best California counties for lemons are: Ventura, Riverside, Santa Barbara, San Bernardino, San Diego, Tulare, Kern, and Fresno. The Oxnard Plain is also an ideal country for lemons. That's the area between the Pacific and State Highway 126. Other sites with lemon groves are in Goleta, around Carpinteria, between U.S. Highway 101 and the beach. Some of the business is also in the hands of Sunkist, who you should contact to learn the names of its many growers. (See addresses.)

What You Need to Know

Participants Growers will accept willing hands of all ages, as long as you're physically fit. Sorters as well as pickers are needed. Remember that migrant crews fill many of the jobs. *Duration* Harvests last all hot summer long and the whole year round. *Facilities* Mostly shacks and barracks, some tents (if you bring your own), plus some small trailers. When the accommodation is provided by the orchard owner, it's often free, or at least inexpensive. *Pay* Earnings vary from coast-to-coast and often from orchard to orchard, but generally range from as little as $20 a day to $60 a day if you can work fast.

For Further Information

Sunkist Growers, Inc.
P.O. Box 7888
Valley Annex
Van Nuys, CA 91409

Orange County Farm Labor
South Rosalina Avenue
Orlando, FL 32801

Citrus World Growers
Lake Wales, FL 33853

Citrus Products Co-op
Winter Garden, FL 32787

Dole Citrus
2151 E Street
Ontario, CA 91764

Sunkist Growers, Inc.
Sherman Oaks, CA 91423

Indio Grapefruit Company
Indio, CA 92201

Castaic Junction
Orange Co-op
Castaic, CA 91310

Sam Perricone Citrus Company, Inc.
1601 East Olympic Boulevard
Los Angeles, CA 90021

PPI Del Monte Tropical Fruit Company
21136 South Wilmington Avenue
Long Beach, CA 90810

Aderhold Groves
Sharp Road
Edinburg, TX 78539

Oxford Groves, Inc.
3 ½ Mayberry Road
Mission, TX 78572

Texas Citrus Exchange
U.S. Expressway 83
Mission, TX 78572

Pick Grapes in a Vineyard

California's wine country, especially up north, is a handsome sight. Many of the mountainous areas look as they did centuries ago when the padres planted the first vines. In the faint light, even when the fog and smog rolls across these hills, the landscape affords a pleasing symmetry. Somehow, the tradition-bound grape farmers have managed to keep out greedy land and housing developers and their bulldozers.

The U.S. has about 900,000 acres of vineyards. California alone sells some 415 million gallons of wine per year, which means employment for at least thirty thousand people, especially in Napa and Sonoma counties. There are also vineyards in New York State and elsewhere on this continent (see page 122).

Each year the harvest means employment for an army of pickers who work the vines by hand. Mechanization has not yet taken place on a large scale and probably won't for some years. One reason may be the sheer cost of a mechanical harvester: few small vintners can afford the

$150,000 per machine. In addition, the machines cannot handle the steep grades of some vineyards.

The industry must therefore rely on people for the next decade. Vine owners often call on friends, relatives, family members, and neighbors to help cut ripe grapes. In some areas, migrants do most of the work, returning home after the harvest. Everywhere, the industry employs not only pickers but cellar workers and bottling staff as well.

First, someone has to pick the grapes. Someone else has to get the wine grapes to the winery, eating grapes to the packing shed, and raisin grapes to the drying trays in the fields. So there's always room for an extra pair of able, hardworking hands.

Get Ready for the California Wine Country

Some of California's famous grapes are ripe by early August or September. The best time to explore for a job is in June, before the actual harvest. You can drive or take a bus into the wine country. An official wine tour can be a bit touristy, but at least it will get you acquainted with the larger vintners. Almost all California wineries set up free tastings and lectures on growing and harvesting grapes and making wine. For the best research, go on a weekday, since vintners tend to get bombarded by tourists on weekends. This will allow you to develop some leads. Talk to the cellar masters and professional technicians who test grapes for maturity and sugar contents. At the very least, sample some of the wines: If you're of age and experienced enough, you may even get lucky and land a job as a wine-tasting server.

Bear in mind that not every winery grows its own grapes; some well-known vintners buy the fruit from outside vineyards. But at least you'll get a foot in the door and gain some insight on the season's possibilities.

Begin in the San Francisco area, where you'll see vineyards and wineries in every direction. Some of these properties date back to the Spanish missions. Plan a day trip to tour these beautiful areas. Many of the best wineries in the U.S. lie north of the city in Napa and Sonoma counties. Vines and wineries dot the area all the way to Calistoga, and the hill-strewn acres of vineyards make for beautiful scenery.

Or try the fertile Santa Clara Valley, easily accessible to the south from San Francisco via U.S. Highway 101; head east into the rocky Livermore Valley and neighboring Solano County via Interstate 580; explore the wine tours in the Sacramento area; or drive south on State Highway 99 through the San Joaquin Valley to Lodi, whose wine-makers are known for their brandies as well.

More vineyards cluster around Los Angeles and San Diego in the Cucamonga District. While these specialize in table grapes and dried fruit, the vineyards on California's north and central coasts produce much of the supply of wine grapes.

A ripe cluster of grapes is a beautiful sight; the golden or blue circles shine in the sun and stand out against the sky. If you're a picker, though, you can easily lose sight of the beauty, especially in some of California's areas (like the central valleys), where the heat is fierce. Most harvesters start working in the first daylight to avoid the oppressive sun: They prefer the cool dawn to the scorching afternoon.

All grapes, whether table grapes or wine grapes, must be separated from their vine stems. You'll generally use a small curved knife or small shears for the task, and you may cut yourself on occasion. And, since you work faster without gloves, you'll probably get stung by insects. Remember, too, that when you pick grapes, you'll also be filling up pans, lugging boxes, baskets, or crates, and emptying them into gondolas holding anywhere from two to five tons of fruit.

At some vineyards, a picker is expected to cut as many as one thousand to five thousand pounds per day, not including leaves. You'll need a strong back and strong abdominal muscles. Supermarket-grape picking is no easier, since the fruit usually goes into fifty-pound boxes or crates in the fields, and someone must haul them in. The work with the raisin trays is a little easier, since the filled drying trays are not as heavy.

The U.S. is now the sixth largest wine producer in the world, and when you start clipping grape bunches, you'll become part of this fascinating world. Elegant-sounding varieties like California Chardonnay, Chablis, Chenin Blanc, or Riesling (all of them white wines) will become part of your daily vocabulary. Or you might help produce the local Burgundies, Zinfandel, Cabernet Sauvignon and Pinot Noir. You'll hear wonderful tales about vintages and learn about the ancient traditions of the vintners.

What You Need to Know

Participants You must be at least eighteen years old to pick grapes. A strong back and good health are useful. *Duration* Keep in mind that the work lasts for only about two weeks of fast-paced, intense action. The California harvest begins in some areas as early as August 20, and may end as late as November 1. (Contact state of California Farm Labor Offices—addresses below—for exact dates). *Facilities* Some employers provide basic accommodations and food. Other grape farmers require that you make your own arrangements. *Pay* Wages vary from one vineyard to the other. Some harvesters get paid by the hour, from minimum wage to about $8, with occasional bonuses. (In the case of migrant labor, the hourly pay doesn't always conform with the minimum set by the U.S. Department of Labor.) Unionized pickers can earn a lot more money, and as a summer picker, you may be eligible to join the union. Contact the local chapter, if there is one, of the United Farm Workers. Most vineyards also have a small, year-round staff (who receive medical benefits as well) to help out with pruning, fertilizing, and so on during the off-season.

For Further Information

A personal visit to the vineyards and wineries listed below should yield information about local customs and clue you in on where the jobs are. Make your calls at least one month before the grape harvest. This may be an outstanding year!

Beaulieu Vineyards
Rutherford, CA 94574

Calistoga Chamber of Commerce
P.O. Box 321
Calistoga, CA 94515

Domaine Chandon (Champagne)
California Drive
Yountville, CA 94599

Gallo Winery
Modesto, CA 95353

Louis Martini Vineyards
St. Helena, CA 94574

Beringer Vineyards
St. Helena, CA 94574

Martini and Prati Winery
2191 Laguna Road
Santa Rosa, CA 95401

Inglenook
1991 St. Helena Highway
Rutherford, CA 94573

Napa Chamber of Commerce
1900 Jefferson Street
Napa, CA 94559

Mumm Napa Valley (Champagne)
8445 Silverado Trail
Rutherford, CA 94573

Sebastiani Vineyards
P.O. Box AA
Sonoma, CA 95476

Paul Masson Vineyards
13150 Saratoga Avenue
Saratoga, CA 95070

Sterling Vineyards
1111 Dunaweal Road
Calistoga, CA 94515

Simi Winery
16275 Healdsburg Avenue
Healdsburg, CA 95448

Wine Institute
425 Market Street, Suite 1000
San Francisco, CA 94105

Other Areas

Outside of California, the most important wine-growing districts are
the Finger Lakes district of New York State, noted for its Champagne
and table and dessert wines, and the Sandusky-Lake Erie Islands region
of Northern Ohio, also a Champagne and table wine producing area.
Other districts are the Yakima and Columbia Valleys in Washington; the
Willamette Valley of Oregon; all of southwestern Michigan; the Hudson River Valley of New York; the area centering around Charlottesville
in Virginia; the eastern coastal plains of North Carolina; and areas in
the Ozark Mountains in Arkansas.

If you want to choose an area near your home, your local State
Labor office, Farm Bureau, or Job Service office should know about
some openings for seasonal workers. A few of these major wine producers are worth a visit, too.

Adair Vineyards
75 Allhusen Road
New Paltz, NY 12561

Baldwin Vineyards
1786 Hardenburgh Estate
Pine Bush, NY 12566

Benmarl Vineyards
Highland Avenue
Marlboro, NY 12542

Brimstone Hill Vineyard
49 Brimstone Hill Road
Pine Bush, NY 12566

Rivendell Winery
14 Albany Post Road
New Paltz, NY 12561

Taylor-Great Western-Gold Seal Wine
County Road 88
Hammondsport, NY 14840

Walker Valley Vineyards
Walker Valley, NY 12588

Widmer's Wine Cellars
1 Lake Niagara Lane
Naples, NY 14512

Colorado Cellars
3553 E Road
Grand Junction, CO 81501

Carlson Vineyards
461 35th Street
Palisade, CO 81526

Plum Creek Cellars
3708 G Road
Grand Junction, CO 81501

Work on a Farm

Have you ever plunged your hands into soft soil just to feel the warm earth between your fingers? Picked plump green beans in a garden? Watched tomatoes grow under your window, then redden and ripen in the bright sun? If these thoughts warm your heart, then you might enjoy a summer on a farm, getting to know the land.

The midwestern corn and wheat fields stretch to the horizon, richly-colored and tall, ready for the harvest. The Kansas hay shimmers under the noon light, waiting to be transformed into compact bundles. In Oregon, asparagus fields await the arrival of the cutting crews; and California's avocados and artichokes are green and ripe for picking. Wisconsin's large dairy farms require plenty of manual labor, as do Hawaii's pineapple fields and Florida's varied vegetable crops. In the Pacific Northwest, strawberries, lettuce, and celery are still picked by hand.

According to the U.S. Department of Agriculture, the number of farm workers stands at almost three million per year. During a typical summer month, some 1,800,000 seasonal workers are employed on two million U.S. farms. Moreover, in recent years farm labor has become younger, with farms employing more people under the age of twenty-four than ever before. So there are plenty of opportunities waiting for you if you're healthy and strong.

Even so, getting summer work on a farm isn't necessarily a piece of cake. For one thing, sophisticated new machines are taking the place of more and more people every day; already, a percentage of the tomato, pea, raspberry, potato, and other crops can be handled by mechanical harvesters. For another, certain U.S. jobs require experience; a few employers want dependable, year-round people instead of seasonal workers. And many harvests are brought in year after year by a migrant labor pool that moves from state to state, following the harvests. The majority of this pool consists of Spanish-speaking Americans as well as Mexicans who know little English. In some sections of the U.S., Anglos join the migrants.

Farm work is easy to find around harvest time if you know how and where to look. Begin in spring with a visit to the nearest library to look through the year's U.S. Department of Agriculture Handbook on "Usual Planning and Harvesting Dates." Check with the Job Service or State Employment Office in your chosen area. The counselors can give you most of the information you need over the telephone.

Shortly before the start of the harvest season, call up the State Farm Labor Bureau (in some areas this office has a different, though similar, name). This office can be found either in the state listings of your telephone directory, usually under the state employment department, or in the county listings under the extension service or agricultural agent.

A yearly agricultural survey indicates that Montana, New Mexico, California, and Ohio will offer the best chances for seasonal farm work during the next few years. Some Oregon harvest jobs, such as raspberry picking, have been known to open up so suddenly that the Job Service can't find enough labor to pluck the ripe fruit. In Michigan, large farms are often desperate for experienced, dependable dairy workers. Florida uses more hired farm labor than any state except California and Texas.

What are the negative aspects? Field work can be dangerous because growers often use noxious defoliants and other chemicals. It can also be monotonous; some farming country may be dull or too hot, and it's often less stimulating and physically harder than city life. And so far, unions have only made a dent in California, so workers elsewhere often get low wages and minimal benefits.

If you want to do farm work throughout the summer, you may have to follow the harvests the way migrant farm workers do. There are several major travel patterns. The annual migrant movement generally originates during the early spring, with the two peak harvest periods occurring in May-June and October-November.

"The Central Stream," the most heavily populated route, covers the midwestern states. The first crop may be spring lettuce, but most of the harvest is beans and tomatoes. Other field workers head into the Mississippi Valley through Arkansas and southeastern Missouri, onto Illinois, Iowa, and Wisconsin, and across Indiana en route to Michigan. Arkansas's major crop is broom corn; Wisconsin has a tomato harvest; Michigan grows corn and broccoli; and Colorado farmers grow large quantities of sugar beets. Most of the early spring work consists of thinning and hoeing these crops. Other agricultural workers make their way through Oklahoma, Kansas, Nebraska, North and South Dakota, western Iowa, and Minnesota. This group starts in May or early summer, eventually helping bring in wheat and small grain harvests.

The "Atlantic Coast Stream," as the name suggests, flows along the eastern seaboard. Starting in late March, farm laborers move north from Florida and Georgia, into the Carolinas, Virginia, Maryland, Delaware, Pennsylvania, New Jersey, and New York. In mid-May, South Carolina's tomatoes must be picked, followed in June by Maryland's. By midseason, July, most of the states are harvesting tomatoes. By late summer, New Jersey farms gather onions, green beans, asparagus, and blueberries.

Despite the large migrant labor force from Mexico, many opportunities exist for young people to help bring in the harvests. If the migrant force moves on to another harvest or doesn't show, the farmers may suddenly need extra labor. Because they're strong and healthy, young people are especially welcome to help.

Field work, though often tiring, is renewing and cleansing. The smell of the freshly tilled land, the scent of fragrant plants, and the pure air of a farm can be invigorating. Even if you do field work for just a few weeks—on a long vacation or in between studies—you'll get all kinds of physical and emotional benefits.

While it's true that you won't get rich laboring on a farm, you will
be a kind of apprentice to the land. Consider it a possible step toward
a future in farming; you may gain valuable experience in the fields
toward a time in which living off the land plays at least a part in your
life.

What You Need to Know

Participants Any adult can volunteer for farm work. *Duration* Temporary work can last from a day or a weekend to a full week or several weeks. Regular labor pools, as well as migrants, work for several
months by traveling from crop to crop. *Facilities* Primitive housing in
barracks and other basic shelters; some farmers expect you to find your
own accommodations. *Pay* Pay ranges from minimum wage to $15 an
hour, varying with your skills (such as being able to operate machin-
ery) and the state (the southern states generally pay the least). *Other*
Whether you're a man or a woman, in your twenties or older, you'll
need a certain amount of idealism to work on a farm. Call it love of the
land. . . .

7

Harvests Abroad

Join a Vineyard Harvest

Almost all of the opportunities in *Summer Adventures* occur during the summer months. Here comes an exception, though. Let's say you're an American language student who spent a happy July and August in Europe and now wants to round out the experience with a week of social activities, physical action, and a few francs. Or maybe your school year starts late. All over France's vineyards, young people are helping to harvest grapes. Specifics follow.

France

The area around the town of Beaune in northeastern France is famous for its wines—Pommards, Meursaults, and Montrachets, to name a few. The vineyards occupy the hillsides in orderly fashion, with the vines in perfect symmetry. Pruning, harvesting, pressing, and wine-making are a great tradition in the area. It is said around here that even the Romans drank Beaune wines. There is a wine museum in Beaune and many of the multicolored buildings contain huge wine cellars. The commerce of *le vin* is significant in this region; it's even more important than the tourist industry.

Once a year, from about mid-September to late October, paid workers descend upon the vineyards to pick the grapes. The French call it *le vendange*, which means gathering grapes. How does an American get a job in these vineyards? Simply by showing up in any of the many French wine regions. The work is hard, but meals, complete with Beaune's vintages, are free, and you'll also get a little pocket money.

France's main regions are, from south to north, Roussillon, on the Mediterranean adjacent to the Spanish border; Languedoc, between Toulouse and Montpellier; Côtes de Provence, which has vineyards from Marseille to Monaco; the Côtes du Rhone, which stretches for 120 miles from Avignon and Lyon; Bourgogne or "Burgundy," from Lyon to Dijon; Bordeaux, the largest wine producing area in France, which begins at the edge of Bordeaux itself and moves east; Cognac, centered around a town by the same name; Val de Loire, stretching nearly from the mouth of the Loire River on the Atlantic deep inland to Nevers; Alsace, along the German border and Rhine River; and the famous Champagne region, which reaches north to Reims and almost to Paris. (See listings at end of this section.)

These major regions are listed south to north because that is also the harvesting sequence. The season may vary each year, though the work usually begins around the second week of September in the southern regions. The Côtes du Rhone area bustles around the third week in September, or even at the end of August. The beginning of October should signal the start of picking in Bourgogne. And by the middle of October, Bordeaux and Cognac get busy. An average grape-picking stint lasts two to three weeks, depending on the size of the estate. You're expected to stay a minimum of ten days. And, since there's heavy competition for jobs, especially from Spain, Britain, and naturally, France, you should begin scouting for work early in September. You won't need an official work permit because you'll only be staying a short time.

If you can speak French, you can call on the farmers yourself by

The experience is one you won't soon forget. Here's how one volunteer described a typical day: "It's nearly 7:00 A.M. when we join the other grape pickers on the edge of Tavel, the village north of Avignon. The early morning here is breathtaking: the tiled village roofs stand out in soft apricot hues against a rose sky; the hillsides roll toward the horizon. The vines' autumnal leaf colors remind me of a French Impressionist painting.

"The vineyard owner's wife rolls up in an old truck, greeting us with Latin warmth, so typical for the South of France, and we are introduced to our co-workers. Among them is the grower's aging mother, a couple of cousins, a nephew, a niece, and three middle-aged village women. Plus two Spaniards, an Egyptian who speaks little French beyond 'Merci' or 'Bon Jour,' and two of us Americans.

"Monsieur Planterin, the burly, friendly owner drives his tractor to our morning's work site. Planterin and his immediate family know these hillsides; they spend much time here during the year, planting, replanting, pruning, plowing. But now comes the most intensive work period for these people. And that's what we're here for. There are about ten pickers in the field, each working one row, nine coupeurs (cutters), and one porteur (porter) who ferries the full three-gallon buckets to the wagon. We normally cut two or three clumps before tossing them into the bucket. Our hands get black and sticky from the juice and grit.

going door-to-door and asking for work. You will probably find that a phrase book is very useful for this approach. Never write for a job; most vintners have little time to correspond. Instead, call in person. There are also several French offices that match pickers and growers (see list below). Many European-based organizations can provide you with information on the vintner. But beware of U.S. organizations that charge a fee.

When you ask for work, a French grape pickers' vocabulary comes in handy. Remember these words: *vendanger*: to gather grapes, vintage; *le lodgement*: lodging; *la nourriture*: food (board); *mal aux reins*: backache; *le seau*: bucket; *la tondeuse* or *sicateur*: clippers; *vignoble*: vineyard; *les raisins*: grapes; *mur*: ripe.

Before starting, you should also be aware of the various jobs in the vineyards. The *coupeurs* (cutters) work the rows of vines, picking grapes along the way. The work of a *coupeur* is very tiring and hard on the back. The *porteurs* (porters) collect the grapes and dump them into the wagon. There is normally one *porteur* for a dozen or so *coupeurs*. A *porteur* must have strong legs and shoulders, since the work is strenuous. It is also difficult to work as a tractor driver or help in the presses, and in every job, your employers expect you to work hard.

The financial arrangement varies from vineyard to vineyard, but in any case, don't expect to receive more than minimum wages. If your employer provides room and/or board, your salary will probably be less. Bring a tent just in case a vintner doesn't have housing. In any case, you'll always receive some basic foodstuffs plus wine, and, since you won't have much opportunity to spend any money during the two or three weeks you'll be working, you will come out slightly ahead financially. Whatever you do, always discuss your working conditions with your employer before you start.

For Further Information

In the United States:
French Government Tourist Office
610 5th Avenue
New York, NY 10020

French Government Tourist Office
645 North Michigan Avenue
Chicago, IL 60611

French Government Tourist Office
9454 Wilshire Boulevard
Beverly Hills, CA 90212

In France:
The following French offices can put you in touch with labor-needy vineyards.

Agence Nationale pour l'Emploi
20 Rue Berthe Nolly
68021, Colmar (Alsace)

Agence Nationale pour l'Emploi
40 rue du General Sarrail BP 502
51331, Epernay (Champagne)

Centre de Documentation Rurale
92 rue du Dessous des Berges
75013, Paris

Centre d'Information et de Documentation Jeunesse
101 Quai Branly
75740, Paris

Centre National des Jeunes Agriculteurs
14 rue de la Boiti
75008, Paris

Centre Départmental des Jeunes Agriculteurs
19 Avenue de Prades
66000, Perpignan (Roussillon region)

"At 9:00 A.M. we pause for a few minutes and share the owner's breakfast. Excellent smoked ham, bread and, naturally, Tavel Rosé wine. As the sun climbs the morning sky we set to work again. The song of the French women keeps us in good humor. (Fluent French is by no means necessary here, but a little knowledge makes your experience more meaningful and proves useful on occasion.)

"We finish one long swath of vines and move to the next. The proprietor lets me maneuver the little Renault tractor. At 11:00 A.M. the truck takes us back to the wine grower's estate. Monsieur Planterin furnishes potatoes, onions, tomatoes, and all the wine we want. I eat extremely well.

"After a nap of half an hour or so, we take the truck in the opposite direction, past the old fountain and the rustic church. Since they've been growing grapes here for over two thousand years, the vineyards are scattered piecemeal all round the village. The Tavel Rosé and the Chateauneuf de Pape, also grown nearby, are justly famous.

"The afternoons are warm. The harvest goes on. The gathering of grapes continues until 5:00 P.M. After a light supper we stroll into the village. We are delighted by the ancient dwellings and the narrow cobbled streets. The scent of the new wine is everywhere. It drips from wagons and overflows from casks. Wine odors even waft from the courtyards arcaded by grape arbors. Wine growers and pickers coalesce in warm taverns. Before turning back, we join them for an evening talk."

Centre Départmental des Jeunes Agriculteurs
Maison du Payson
13 rue Foy
33000, Bordeaux

Comité Interprofessionel des Vins
17 rue des Etats
44000 Nantes (Val de Loire)

Groupment de Development Agricole
Hotel de Ville
83470, Saint Maxim
(Côtes de Provence)

Centre Départmental des Jeunes Agriculteurs
rue Barbaroux
83170, Brignoles (Côtes de Provence)

Maison du Tourisme et du Vin de Medoc
La Verrerie
33250 Pauillac

Vineyards:
M. de Thelin Vineyards
11700 Capendu, France

Canard-Duchene
1 rue Edmond Canard
51500, Ludes

Chateauneuf de Pape
84370, Bettarides

George Goulet
¼ avenue du General Giraud
51100 Reims

Grasse & Files (Sons)
32800 Eauze

Charles Heidsieck & Henriot
51100 Reims

Piper Heidsieck
51 boulevard Henri-Vasnier
51100 Reims

La Vielle Ferme
Route Jonquiéres (Vse)

Joseph Perrier
51000 Chalons-sur-Marne

Louis Roederer
21 boulevard Lundy
51100 Reims

Taittinger
9 place St-Nicaise
51100 Reims

Germany

The German wine industry isn't as large as France's. At last count, Germany had some thirty thousand vineyards, with a total cultivated area of 210,000 acres. Even compared to California's abundant acreage, that's small. But working in a smaller vineyard for a short time can be a rewarding experience because you're closer to the people. And the history of the village surrounds you; you remember that a medieval farmer once stood where you are more than five hundred years ago, harvesting the very same field.

A few notable areas to try for work follow.

The Mosel includes such famous vineyard towns as Bernkastle, Piesport, Zelfingan, Trittenheim, and Trier. All yield well-known wines. The Mosel region comprises approximately twenty-seven thousand acres of river valleys in western Germany.

The Pfalz (Palatinate) includes the well-known eighty-kilometer-long Weinstrasse ("Wine Road"), with such well-respected wine centers as Bad Duerkheim. The road begins in the northern village of Kleinbockenheim, adjacent to Bockenheim, near the Hessian border. The vineyards stretch for some distance to the north.

The Rheingan is the poetic region along the Rhine River consisting of Assmanhausen, Lorch, Ruedesheim, and Bingen. The upper Rhine also produces good wines. Try to get to Koblenz or Boppard.

Likewise, the Neckar, Main, and Danube Rivers are all flanked by many vineyards.

Along the way, you'll see some glorious scenery and magnificent ancient cities. Gleaming space-age buses shuttle between all the historic old points from Cologne south, along the steep, castled valley of the Rhine; west from Mannheim to the wine country and to ancient Trier; and east to staunch old Heidelberg and the slow-flowing, green-banked Neckar River. The dewy, stately Black Forest region, the German Alps, the cold beaches northwest of Bremen, and the well-preserved historic cities of Nüernberg and Wüerzburg are all worth visiting before or after the harvest, along with famous German spas like Baden Baden.

If you intend to work in romantic Rhineland, it would be wise to stay in Assmanhausen because it isn't touristy or expensive, and it's more intimate; the Assmanhausen vistas are just as dramatic as in Bingen-am-Rhein. Try the little wine communities along the Rhine, which can be reached by the local river ferry or by bus.

Traditionally, U.S. students augment the German labor force, especially in late summer. Germany has a fair tourist industry then. With farmers busy in their fields, vineyards, and orchards, students can be employed for at least two months in agriculture. Though you must travel to Europe at your own expense, you'll receive the same pay as the Germans once you're there. Many Americans come to improve their German, and some to become acquainted with the land, the people, and their way of life.

Apply by February since there's a lot of competition.

For Further Information

The following organizations are useful in arranging student work programs:

Zentralstelle für Arbeitsvermittlung
Feuerbachstrasse
42 6000 Frankfurt 1

Bundesanstalt für Arbeitsvermittlung
Zeil
57 6000 Frankfurt a.M.

If you speak a little German, call on the grape grower associations, agricultural employment offices, or the major German vineyards directly.

Vineyard Associations:
6900 Heidelberg
Kaiserstrasse 69-71

8700 Würzburg, Ludwigkai 2-3
8000 München 15
Thalkirchner Strabe 54

A week before the grape harvest in the Rhineland, I was wending my way up the unpaved road that winds through the terraced vineyards above Assmanhausen. The Rhine River wove a silver band far below, with many barges moving ponderously through the waters. To the north was the Loreley Rock; to the south were old castles on both sides. The trains whirred along the riverbanks three thousand feet below, moving toward Switzerland.

I stopped to sample the dewy grapes that hung against a morning sky, alone among the ancient vineyards. All around, the light breeze fluttered the colored ribbons meant to keep birds away from the ripening fruit.

It was late September, six days or so before the <u>Weinernte</u> (harvest). When the harvest moves along the Rhine, the Mosel, the Saar, and the Weinstrasse, many local villagers lock up their businesses and join other workers to collect the valuable fruit. Local chefs, eager tourists, and students of all nationalities are welcome to snip the "Trauben" clusters off the vines. Each basket of fruit weighs about fifty to a hundred pounds.

Bundesverband der deutschen Weinkommissionaire
Mainz, Postbox 1571

Verband Deutscher Weinexporteure
Bonn
Dorotheenstrasse 241

Vineyards:
Zeltinger Schlossberg
Zelfingen, Mosel

Bernkastle Doktor Vineyards
Bernkastle, Mosel

Sonnenuhr Vineyard
Wehlen, Mosel

Johannisberg Vineyards
Johannisberg, Rheingau

Ritter Vineyards
Rüdesheim, Rhein
Mosel

Mosel Valley
Verkehrsamt, Endertplatz
D 5590 Cochem
Winzerverrein
Bad Dürkhein
Weinstrasse

Weingut Oster & Franzen
5599 Bremm/Mosel
Weingut J.H. Selbach
D5553 Zelfingan

Südliche Weinstrasse
Büro für Tourismus
Postfach 2124
D-6740 Landau

Other Contacts:
German National Tourist Office
122 East 42d Street
New York, NY 10168

German National Tourist Office
11766 Wilshire Boulevard, #750
Los Angeles, CA 90025

Kreisfremdenverkehrsamt
Philipp-Fauth-Strabe 11
D-6702 Bad Dürkheim

Try Other Vineyards in Europe

The little Duchy of Luxembourg shares borders with both Germany
and France. Luxembourg also grows a lot of grapes, especially along
the lovely banks of the Mosel River. You can help pick grapes for a few
days in the bilingual (German and French) communities of Wasserbil-
lig, Grevenmacher, Remich, Schwengen, and others.

As with other countries, it's not very helpful to send a letter from
the U.S. requesting employment. Instead, just drop in.

The Luxembourg Youth Hostels are always a good place to obtain
leads. Also try the Office of Tourism.

Although Italy, Spain, and Portugal are all big wine countries, the
local people always handle the harvests, and opportunities for Americans to pitch in for a week or two are rare.

There's a bit of work to be had in Great Britain. Suffolk Vineyards
in East Anglia grows more than thirty acres of vines in a rolling countryside. The Beaulieu Abbey Estate in Hampshire, where the old monks

used to grow their grapes, is the site of another vineyard. There are others on the Isle of Wight. At Horma, Sussex, south of London, the Merrydown Wine Company first planted vines twenty years ago. There are twenty more growers nearby.

You may also try Pilton Manor near the Mendip Hills in Somerset. In England's northeast there are more than three hundred vines prospering on the Cathedral grounds in Lincoln.

What You Need to Know to Work on a Vineyard

Participants People of any age can work on a vineyard, as long as they have strong backs to bend and cut grapes. College students are a common sight in France, Germany, and Great Britain. *Duration* The harvests take place in September and October. The length of each harvest varies depending on the region, so ask the locals. *Facilities* You can eat as many grapes as you want, and you'll be given vegetables and bread by the farmers. As for accommodations, look for the nearest youth hostel or *pension*. *Pay* Pay ranges from nothing (*rien*, in French) to minimum wage, and varies from vineyard to vineyard. But applicants are plentiful, so you're in no position to argue. Most vineyards also provide you with plenty of food and wine (though be careful, since too much wine in the sun can be hazardous). *How to Apply* Just knock on doors and smile.

For Further Information

In addition to the French and German addresses provided earlier, try the following:

Luxembourg Office National du Tourisme
Luxembourg
place de la Gare
Syndicat D' Initiative
Remich a l'Hotel de Ville

The official Luxembourg Employment office is:
Administration De l'Emploi
38 Rue Phillipe II L-2340

British Tourist Authority
625 North Michigan Avenue, Suite 1510
Chicago, IL 60611-1977

British Tourist Authority
40 West 57th Street, Suite 320
New York, NY 10019-4001

English Vineyards Association
Cricks Green
Felsted, Essex
England

Work on a Foreign Farm

You might want to consider some seasonal farm employment beyond North America's borders. A work camp in Israel, three summer weeks on a Swiss dairy farm, berry picking in England, and other European adventures can be yours with ease.

Switzerland

In the words of an old Appenzell folk song, "Life is glorious up in the high pastures; Up in the high pastures, I'd like to be. ..." The meadows here climb and climb toward the Saentis peaks. As you look up from the valley, you see a sunny tableau of knee-high grasses, herbs, sedges, wild-flowers, and buttercups. The brown cows find nourishment in these pastures; you can hear their bells pealing from every alp.

The world in the Appenzell elevations hasn't changed for centuries. Life is peaceful in these mountains. This is dairy and cheese-making

TRANSPORTATION: GETTING AROUND IN EUROPE

It's very expensive to rent a car in Europe and, unfortunately, airline travel on the Continent has become extremely costly. So, unless you come with unlimited funds, you're best off traveling by <u>Zug</u> (train). It's actually very enjoyable to see Europe by train. Take in a relaxing view of Vienna's wine region and the vineyards of the Mosel valley; Switzerland's grape-growing hillsides seem even lovelier; and French vineyards roll past from one end to the other.

If you plan to work at vineyards or wineries in more than one country, you might consider the popular Eurailpass or the Eurail Youthpass, which allows Americans and Canadians to enjoy unlimited first-class train travel through seventeen countries. Just ask your travel agent. With the Eurailpass, you decide how long you want to travel, from a few days to weeks or even one month. You can stop off to visit vintners in the Beaune region one day, at Lake Geneva the next, and in Siena or southern Germany a few days later.

country with nearly a thousand-year tradition. Swiss history books describe how farmers delivered Appenzell cheese in 1282 to the nearby Monastery of St. Gallen. Although the recipe for the cheese has remained a secret for generations, tourists can now visit part of a commercial dairy in the little hamlet of Stein. There you'll see a publicity movie and then watch the cauldrons where the creamy milk is boiled. You'll also get to taste Appenzell's delicious specialty.

Any healthy hiker can reach the high summer pastures where it feels as if you just stepped back in time. Several thousand feet above the villages, the *Senner* (herdsmen) still churn their own butter and make their own Appenzeller *Kaese*, which has holes like Swiss Emmenthal, but is softer. The herders live and work in primitive, one-room stone shelters. A hiker or backpacker can help with the cattle or the cheese making or the hay pitching, in return for sleeping quarters in a hayloft.

Whether you do farm work or help the high-altitude *Senner*, you'll have an unforgettable experience. If stay through fall, you can watch the descent of the dairy herds to the valley. The lead cow will be adorned with its bell and flowers and large wheels of golden cheese. The local villages celebrate with costumed musicians, plenty of dancing, and music from the three-meter-long Alphorn. The occasion? The autumnal descent of the cows.

A good place to look for work is in the Swiss lands above Appenzell, Trogen, Rehtobel, Speicher, and other local villages, where you may be hired by a herdsman in midsummer (although you won't get paid much). In recent years the Swiss have restricted the number of full-time foreign workers by withholding working permits, refusing to renew permits, and not replacing workers, but they haven't restricted temporary labor. If you're prepared to put in eight to twelve hard hours a day at low wages, you'll likely find work.

Officially, any American can visit for three months. If you want to extend your trip, you must report to the Immigration Office, which is also called the *Police des Etrangers* (police for foreigners). Normally, your employer must obtain permission for you to work before you leave the U.S., but for seasonal farm work, the Swiss farmer can usually arrange a work permit.

You probably won't get an answer if you write to a farm. Your best bet for finding a job might be to just canvass some larger Swiss farms in early summer. If you can learn a little Swiss German before you begin, it will be much easier, since almost no farmers speak English. You'll find the phrase, *"Haben Sie Arbeit?"* ("Do you have work?") quite useful. Most seasonal farm workers are between the ages of eighteen and thirty.

What You Need to Know

Participants People of any age can work on a farm, as long as they're strong and willing to work long and hard hours. *Duration* The work period ranges from one week to three months, and each day lasts from dawn to dusk. *Facilities* Swiss and German farmers may offer their hayloft or a room on the farm. Some temporary workers set up tents. Most farms provide generous breakfasts or lunches and evening meals. *Pay* You'll earn pocket money: $10 to $25 a day (in marks or francs in Switzerland and Germany, respectively). Food is free. *How to Apply* Ask at local labor offices and farmers' associations, and visit individual farms. *Other* Except for those in England, most farmers won't speak English. It will pay to learn a few phrases, like *"Haben Sie Arbeit?"* ("Do you have work?").

For Further Information

Swiss Farmer's Union (Bauernverband)
Laurstr. 10
5200 Brugg

Landdienst-Zentralstelle
Postfach 6331
8023 Zurich

Swiss Wine Growers Association
P.O. Box 1346
CH-001 Lausanne

One American worker hiked from farm to farm in the St. Gallen region asking for work and he found paid temporary employment with a Matzingen dairy farmer. He described a typical day: "I get up at 5:00 A.M. and shovel grass into the troughs for the cows. They're milked and then attached to a mechanical sucking device. At dawn, I join Herr Keller in the fields, where we heave heavy bales, hoe sugar beets, load hay into silos, plant seedlings, and clean the cattle stalls. The grandfather is eighty-four years old but still rises at 5:00 A.M. to help clean out forty stalls and spread fresh straw. I've even seen him in the fields pulling a huge rake behind him. The work is demanding, but the food is fantastic! A huge breakfast at 7:00 A.M., followed by a prodigious <u>Mittagessen</u> (brunch) at noon, and at 4:30 P.M. a hearty <u>Abendbrot</u> (dinner). The whole family eats together. Work continues until 7:00 P.M., since the cows must be milked again and other work finished. I'm in bed by 10:00 P.M. I earn only about twenty dollars per day in Swiss francs, plus room and board. But I'm learning a lot and meeting wonderful people."

Schweizerischer Bauernverband
Stellenvermittlung
Laurstr. 10
5200 Brugg

Wochenende für Volontäre
Speerstrasse 7
8305 Dietlikon

Weekend farm work.
In the U.S.:
Swiss National Tourist Office
608 Fifth Avenue
New York, NY 10020

Swiss National Tourist Office
150 North Michigan Avenue
Chicago, IL 60601

Swiss National Tourist Office
222 North Sepulveda Boulevard, Suite 1570
El Segundo, CA 90245
contact: Eric Buhlmann

Swiss National Tourist Office
260 Stockton Street
San Francisco, CA 94108

Switzerland Cheese Association
P.O. Box 5013
New York, NY 10022

Scotland and England

If you can manage to get seasonal work in the British Isles—and there's a good chance you can—you'll be very happy you did. You'll find that Scottish and English people are polite and hospitable, and you don't have to worry about struggling with the language.

England remains a small, comfortable island whose hamlets aren't marred by shopping centers or eight-lane highways. The countryside is lovely, with flower boxes outside many houses, and the climate is fair, although it does rain a bit.

Seasonal farm work is generally available for Americans, although the pay is very low. You don't need a work permit or visa, just your passport. Demand for workers grows each year. Volunteers are needed in British-based international farm camps, where young farm labor is used to the best advantage. A typical workday is at least six hours long, and the season can last anywhere from two to six weeks.

There are many different ways to find work in England. For example, you can do weekend work on an organic farm where you swap your work for food and sleeping quarters. One organization, Working Weekends on Organic Farms (see address below), joins (mostly) vegetarians who want to learn about farming without chemicals, and who are willing to work very hard. Participants are usually between seventeen and twenty-two years old, but must be at least seventeen, and should be physically fit.

To get a summer job, you should apply at least six months in advance. Season after season, the same camps put ads on the various European bulletin boards at schools, universities, YMCAs and youth hostels. Write to the farm camp and enclose an international reply coupon for their answer. (You can buy the coupon at any U.S. Post Office.)

For Further Information

If you happen to live in Europe, or find yourself in London, you could also apply to the following offices in person:

"We picked strawberries on a Scottish fruit farm," reports a girl from Ohio. "Other Americans were working on English strawberry and raspberry farms." If you talk to people who return after a summer in the British Isles, you invariably get an enthusiastic response. Most of the berry pickers are under twenty, and many try to spend a week or two after the harvest exploring the high country. "The British Isles are crowned by 4,406-foot Ben Nevis, in Scotland. What splendid rock climbing in the Highlands! And there's ample terrain for hikers, or 'hill walkers,' as the British call them. The English Midlands and Wales thrive with opportunities for short or long 'rambles' across the hillsides. The Pennine Way goes on for some 250 miles, connecting Derbyshire with the distant Scots Cheviot Hills. In between, there are curvy paths across two-thousand-foot elevations and down into flowered valleys where villages have poetic names like Windy Gyle."

National University
Student Employment Office
3 Endleigh Street
London W.C. 1

British Tourist Authority
Thames Tower
Black's Road
Hammersmith, London W6 9EL

World University Service 5
United Kingdom Council
260 High Road
London, N 15

Quaker Work Camps
Friends House
Euston Road
London, NW1, 2BJ

4 International Voluntary Service
91 High Street
Harlesden, London NW 10

Camps and Farms
Contact these prominent camps and farms by mail.
Apple Pie Farm
Cranbrook Road
Cranbrook, Kent TN17 4EU England

Ashton Fruit Farm
Castle Grounds
Ashton, Leominster, Herefordshire
England

Barnyards Farm
Beauly, Inverness-Shire
IV4 7AQ Scotland

Cartford Limited
Brompton Farm
Brompton Farm Road
Strood, Rochester, Kent ME2 3QZ England

Fiveways Fruit Farm
Fiveways
Stanway, Colchester
Essex CO3 5LR England

International Farm Camp
Tiptree, Essex, CO5 OQ5 England

Working Weekend on Organic Farms
19 Bradford Road
Lewes, Sussex BN7 1RB England

Canada

Agriculture has always been one of Canada's largest industries. And although much of it is now mechanized to cope with the vastness of the country, temporary farm labor is still often needed. While the pay doesn't generally compare to that in the U.S., you'll find promising situations in the provinces of Manitoba, Saskatoon, and Ontario. Organic farms all over Canada need willing volunteers. Year-round work is available, but opportunities are especially plentiful during June, July, and August. Sites include small homesteads and large farms. Duties range from marketing, garden work, milking goats, and working with horses, to all other general farm work. You'll receive no pay, but room and board are provided free of charge. Each September, however, volunteers are paid to harvest the fields of ripe blueberries in Nova Scotia's Cumberland County. Again, rather than writing to these farms, it is best to just turn up in the towns of Amherst, Springhill, Pugwash, Parrsboro, or Minudie, and you'll probably land some work.

For Further Information

Tourism Yukon
P.O. Box 2703
Whitehorse, YT Y1A 2C6

Willing Workers on Organic Farms
RR2 Carlson Road
Nelson, British Columbia, V1L 5P5

Experience Life on an Israeli Kibbutz

Israel is a fascinating place; it has more museums and sightseeing than most countries its size (it's only 240 miles long and 10 miles wide). Israel's Mediterranean beaches are beautiful, its hilly terrain breathtaking. Few other nations in the Middle East can boast religious shrines of Moslems, Jews, and Christians, all within walking distance of one another.

Israel is colorful, vivacious, and youth-oriented. The variety of farms here is tremendous, especially among *kibbutzim* (plural for kibbutz, or communal farm). The kibbutz is unique to Israel, where it has existed for more than seven decades. There are 280 of these Israeli farm settlements, and they account for about fifty per cent of Israel's agricultural production.

The farms vary greatly: some are sophisticated and urbane and even operate assembly plants; others are primitive and sit in the hot, barren desert. For instance, the Ketura Kibbutz, near Elat, grows dates and onions and breeds turkeys. Kibbutz Kfar Blum does scientific farming and tourism (offering hotel space to visitors). A kibbutz may have anywhere from 50 to 2,000 people; most have about 250 to 500. Some communes are filled with Russian immigrants.

For the seasonal American farm worker the kibbutz is ideal. You can visit a kibbutz in the hot summer (although they're a lot more crowded then) or in the winter, whether for a few weeks or a few months. To enter Israel, you'll need a passport but no visa. Some people stay in Israel a full year and work on a communal farm while they study at a university part-time. Most temporary kibbutz dwellers are in their early twenties, but many kibbutzim offer special youth programs in summer for people ages fifteen and up. For example, the kibbutz movement allows young Americans of any religion to participate in a month (or longer) "work camp vacation." Workers live with a kibbutz family and labor in the fields for six hours a day, six days a week. The fee is sixty-five dollars plus airfare, and all meals are provided. This and other more extensive (and expensive) programs are sponsored and operated by Kibbutz Aliya Desk.

While on a kibbutz, you're expected to work tremendously hard. You'll be out in the fields, the orchards, and the chicken coops. You may be draining swamps, picking oranges, apples, nuts, potatoes, or carrots, or grading fruits and vegetables for export shipments. *Kibbutzniks*, people who live on kibbutzim, plow fields, drive tractors, milk cows, spade gardens, work in construction, dig irrigation ditches, wash dishes, and peel potatoes. Inside it will be steamy; outside excruciatingly hot. Israel's summer inland climate may be compared to Arizona's; it seldom rains. Agricultural mechanization means that you may get greasy, and the fields get you dusty. The work can be tedious, unpleasant, dirty, and sometimes boring, but it's important to be a good worker.

The food won't always be great and the accommodations will be mostly dorm rooms. And you won't receive any wages for your work.

But the benefits are outstanding. An American kibbutznik describes the area to a friend: "We're not far from the ocean, and we bike there after work. The landscape is full of laurel, sycamore, palms, and pines. Roman ruins are less than a kilometer away from the beach...."

Israel isn't for everyone, though. This has nothing to do with whether you're Jewish or not; it concerns your personal philosophy and sensitivity. Remember that parts of Israel are like a potential war zone.

Security is written here with a capital "S". You're searched several times before your flight out of Israel; then you're taken to the airfield where you must identify your baggage (an unidentified suitcase could contain a bomb). Sky marshals often sit with you all the way over to Ben Gurion Airport. You'll run into soldiers at every turn: at the airport, on the back roads, exercising, on buses, even in stores. Even the collective farms are not immune from the weaponry. One American remembers his first impressions:

"On the road we pass several jeeps loaded with men and machine guns. These 'soldiers' are the men of the kibbutz. You might have asked one to pass the butter, or seen another spraying dates just the day before. Now they are armed fighters; they are the security force of the community."

Everyone seems involved in the present-day military situation, either as soldiers or as soldiers' relatives.

Remember that thousands of temporary people like yourself have been employed on kibbutzim. For you it may be a great adventure; for the kibbutznik, it's not. So don't be surprised if your enthusiasm is not returned at every corner. Kibbutzniks know that most volunteers are temporary and some don't seek close friendships with them. But in general, you'll find the community warm and inviting and you'll leave with wonderful memories.

What You Need to Know

Participants You don't have to be Jewish, but you'll need a certain amount of spirituality to fit in on a kibbutz. Minimum age varies from place to place so ask for specifics. Good health and stamina are important qualities in a kibbutznik. *Duration* You may stay any amount of time from several weeks to several months to a year. *Facilities* Dorms, youth hostel-type accommodations, or a room (sometimes shared) are always offered, and plenty of food is provided. *Cost* Kibbutz programs may or may not include the flight, but in general you'll have to pay for your airline ticket. And bear in mind that kibbutz stays require a fee on your part. It can be as low as $70 a week, but some arrangements cost as much as $2,000 a month (plus an expensive airline ticket). *How to Apply* The screening process at a kibbutz is strict; not everyone is accepted, and complications can arise. Many ask you to fill in a long form; some send an even more complicated form to your doctor. Still others require a character reference from your rabbi if you are Jewish. *Other* Kibbutzim do not tolerate drugs of any kind.

For Further Information

American Zionist Youth Foundation
110 East 59th Street, 3d Floor
New York, NY 10022

Israel Ministry of Tourism
350 Fifth Avenue
New York, NY 10018

The Jerusalem Post
211 East 43d Street, Suite 601
New York, NY 10017

Kibbutz Aliya Desk
27 West 20th Street, 9th Floor
New York, NY 10011

Masada
4 East 34th Street
New York, NY 10016

Volunteers for Israel
330 West 42d Street, Suite 1318
New York, NY 10036-6092

8

The Sea Life

Work on a Commercial Fishing Boat

The heavens are burgundy and gray; a bruise-blue sea churns beneath the boat. The ocean swells lift and tilt you in several directions. You've been on deck since dawn, breathing deeply the cool, salted air.

As a salmon fisherman in Alaska you'll marvel at the grace of the killer whale as it slashes the surface with a hiss; you'll follow the flight of an eagle careening downward, talons outstretched toward a herring; you'll learn not to be astounded by deer and bear roaming certain beaches. At night you'll stand watch on the return to home port, passing ferries with their myriad of lights, your nets yielding a writhing mass of opulent salmon.

Alaskan salmon runs have been at record levels for the past decade. Fishing means freedom from time-clocks, traffic lights, and dress suits. It's also a lucrative endeavor. But the good money in most fisheries is no gift: The hours are long and because fishing jobs are seasonal, the pay often ends up being equivalent to that of other jobs.

You should also know about the unpleasant sides of fishing. The claustrophobic bunk located down below, adjacent to the engine room is stuffy and reeks of diesel. There are often stinging jellyfish among the thrashing salmon layering the deck. Rough weather and high waves will smash you back and forth. You must concentrate on the work at hand to keep your mind and your stomach off the restless horizon. A twenty-four-hour day is taken in stride.

Certain personal traits should be considered mandatory for a crew member on a fishing boat. You need physical stamina and coordination, some mechanical aptitude, and the ability to get along with people in tight, cramped situations that allow for little privacy. If you think you have these attributes then read on.

If you've never worked on a fishing boat before (which means you're a "greenhorn") then you'll have a harder time getting a job, whether you try to get aboard a Gulf shrimper, a California tuna boat, or a king crabber in the Bering Sea.

The Alaska Department of Labor warns, "Most jobs for fishing crew members require at least basic experience and skills. Finding a job as crew man can be difficult without having some previous connection with fishermen. Generally crews are hired back year after year when they have proved to work well together and can bring in a good catch."

But even if you've never been on a boat in your life, you still have a chance of finding work. Perhaps more than with other pursuits, becoming a fisherman is a matter of being at the right place at the right time.

Writing a letter won't get you very far here; you must apply in person. Many young people can spend weeks pacing the docks of Kodiak, Alaska, without result, while others may be approached by a captain on their first morning in town. Although fate certainly plays a large role, the well-informed greenhorn will be more likely to get hired than one who saunters onto the dock for a lark.

Before you head for the nearest harbor, learn where the centers of the fishing industry lie; what sort of fishing boats are more likely to ask you aboard; and the best times to hit the various ports. Decide where and when to go based on climate considerations, seasonal variations, and the type of fishery involved. Then, scout the waterfront early, one or two weeks before the season begins.

Once you arrive, make a survey of the fishing fleet in the harbor.

In the U.S., Alaska and California rank first and second, respectively, in value of their commercial catch. Many thousands of fishermen are employed annually from the Pacific to the Bering Sea. Important fishing centers in this vast area include Astoria and Newport, Oregon; Kodiak, Ketchikan, and Petersburg, Alaska; Seattle, Washington; and San Diego, California. Alaskan salmon fishing pays the most; depending on job specifics, you can earn from three thousand to fifty thousand dollars per season.

Alaska may be the easiest place for a novice to get into the business. Because of its relative isolation from large population centers, Alaska is a state that continues to offer temporary job opportunities. The seasons for shrimp, salmon, crab, and halibut overlap, and docks like Kodiak in the Gulf of Alaska hum almost all year long. More than half of the fishermen employed in the Pacific work in Alaskan waters. It rains a great deal in the southeastern part of the state and winters are quite severe. The rest of Alaska can have mild weather in summer.

It's fairly inexpensive to fly from Seattle to Anchorage; in the summer months the Alaska Marine Highway System runs ferries from Seattle up the Inside Passage to Haines at reasonable rates. (Remember, though, that these ferries are not at all like cruise ships.)

Texas and Louisiana are first and second in the value of their commercial catch on the Gulf of Mexico. Many fishermen find employment in the Gulf area. In the Chesapeake Bay area alone, a very large number of commercial anglers work on boats.

When you're through reading this chapter, you'll be able to recognize what kind of fishing is done on different boats. Don't judge a ship by its paint job; some good skippers still fish with old ragged-looking boats.

Try to make the rounds of all the vessels two or even three times a day. In a smaller town especially, let as many people as possible know you are looking for work on a fishing boat. A hotel clerk, a waitress, a supermarket cashier, may all prove to be valuable contacts. Ask everybody you see if they have heard about any shorthanded boats. Keep your ears perked. Most fishing ports have a harbormaster who maintains the docks and keeps track of the comings and goings of the fleet. Get acquainted with him or her and check in often; the harbormaster probably knows more about the boats and fishermen than anyone in town. Some harbormaster offices have bulletin boards where you can put up an ad offering your services. A desperate skipper with a sick crew member could get in touch with you at the last moment. Have your belongings in a semipacked state so that you will be ready to leave at any time.

Be aware of local conditions by talking with fishermen you meet. How was last year's season? Is this season supposed to be good? How much are local canneries paying for their product? Ask questions that show you're genuinely interested.

Observe how the fishermen are dressed and be aware of where you can purchase such work garments if you get hired. In most fisheries you will need rubber boots and full rain gear.

A final hint: learn the opening and closing dates of fishing seasons by checking at the local outlet for State Fish and Game releases. You will then know when fishermen will most likely be looking for crew members. In some states, you'll have to purchase a commercial fisherman's license to work on a boat. You can find out where by checking at the State Fish and Game Departments. A few states also have a Commercial Fishing Commission or Department.

Ask whoever you see if they know of any boats (be specific about what kind, since this shows some knowledge on your part) that are shorthanded. Or ask if there is a vessel that needs another deckhand for the season. You'll have lots of competition, so don't be timid. While it would not be proper to go inside the cabin uninvited, it is normally acceptable to go up the gangplank and knock on the cabin door, but only if there is no one to be seen on deck.

In short, persevere. Pester local fishermen until they agree to take you out on "just one trip." One fisherman advised me, "You gotta bug the heck out of 'em."

If the captain is in the market for help, he'll start by asking if you've ever fished before. It's important that he know the truth since this is dangerous work, especially for the novice, and teaching you takes up valuable time. Do not lie; imagine the captain's disgust if he were to discover you cannot coil a line properly (fishing gear is very expensive and improper handling can cause damage). But have faith; many skippers agree that everyone begins as a greenhorn, and they'll take the time to train you.

As a newcomer, play up your other credentials. If you're a good cook or if you have some background in electronics or diesel mechanics, tell the captain. If the captain seems shorthanded but is stalling, suggest that you'd be willing to "fish for groceries" on your first trip. Though you won't get any pay, you'll have a chance to gain some experience. On a second trip, you may wish to accept a smaller cut of the catch than the other crew members—but never fish for free on the second trip.

Before you accept any job on a fishing boat make sure you and your employer are in agreement over the financial conditions of the first and following trips. Crew members on most fishing vessels are paid on a share basis. At the end of the season the cannery tallies the value of the total catch and divides the amount into shares. Food and fuel costs of the season are deducted from each crew member's final check in equal amounts. Each crew member usually gets one share. Some members' pay depends on their level of experience and responsibility. A greenhorn may receive only a half or quarter percentage for his first trip until he has proven himself a capable worker.

In most cases, the cannery or plant pays you, but in some fisheries the skipper is an independent agent and pays the crew members himself. During the season you can ask for draws against your final settlement for pocket money.

Be prepared for backbreaking work. You'll wake up early and be expected to learn quickly. Never forget that the captain is boss. The skipper will expect you to get along with the rest of the crew and to remember your place as a greenhorn. Be observant and fulfill your duties; react quickly and listen.

For Further Information

The following addresses will help you begin your search for work on a commercial fishing boat:

Alaska Department of Fish & Game
P.O. Box 3-2000
Juneau, AK 99802

Fisheries Project Coordinator
P.O. Box 11080
Juneau, AK 99811

Alaska State Employment Service
Sea Level Drive
Ketchikan, AK 99901

Juneau Job Service
Glacier Highway
Juneau, AK 99801

Anchorage Job Service
P.O. Box 107024
Anchorage, AK 99510

Kodiak Employment Center
309 Center Avenue
Kodiak, AK 99615

Atlantic Salmon Federation
P.O. Box 807
Calais, ME 04619

National Maritime Fisheries Service
709 West 9th Street
Juneau, AK 99801

Fairbanks Employment Center
P.O. Box 71010
Fairbanks, AK 99707

Sitka Job Service
Cathedral Apartment Building
Sitka, AK 99855

Follow the Salmon Runs in the Pacific Northwest

Salmon hatch from eggs in freshwater streams and lakes and then migrate downstream to spend their adult life in the open sea. After between four and seven years, the fish return to the stream or lake they came from to spawn. Then they die.

In Alaska, Washington, and Oregon, salmon are the principal fish sought commercially. Their heaviest concentrations are near shore between May and October, with the bulk of the catch landed in July and August. Because the future of salmon stocks depends on the numbers of fish able to migrate upstream and spawn, the salmon catch is one of the most regulated of all. The opening and closing of seasons in various districts is determined by the different state Fish and Game Departments. Salmon are caught commercially by three different methods, and you should know how they work before you approach a ship.

Purse seining

A *purse seine* is a long rectangle of net with corks attached to the topside for flotation and a bottom line strung with lead weights to keep the net vertical in the water. The seine is stored on the stern of the mother ship. A secondary vessel, called the *power skiff*, takes control of one end of the net. With both boats plying in opposite directions, the seine is set out in the water. If the salmon are running in schools, the skiff-man will bring his end back around to the main boat quickly, thus encircling the fish. But usually the skipper will just instruct the skiff-man by radio to maneuver the seine into a "C" formation to face the oncoming tide.

After twenty minutes or so the skiff-man brings his end back around. Once the skiff reaches the mother ship it relinquishes control of its part of the net. Along the lower edge, or the *lead line*, of the seine, there are a series of bridles bearing hand-sized brass rings. These are spaced along the entire length of the lead line. A purse line is laced through the rings while the net is still on deck, so that now, with the seine in a circular form in the water, this line is drawn in like a purse string to close up the bottom of the net.

A hydraulically-powered pulley, known as a *power block*, begins bringing in one end of the seine. The power block is mounted on the boom above. As the seine winds down through the pulley, it is laid out on the stern by three men. One crew member "stacks cork," another "pulls web," and the third "pulls lead" and deals with the rings attached to it. All three components must be arranged so that they will flow out smoothly at the next go-around. The very last portion of the net, called the *money bag*, is where the fish bunch up.

The entire procedure of getting the seine into the water, encircling the fish, and hauling the net with its bounty back aboard is called a *set*. A fast crew under the right conditions might make fifteen or more sets per day. After the money bag is emptied on deck and the gear is ready for the next set, the fish are pitched into the hatch. Besides salmon, the seine captures extraneous matter such as jellyfish and a mess of seaweed.

At the end of each fishing day most of the crew goes down into the hold to pitch fish into a *brailer* basket that is hoisted and swung over to a *tender* ship, which is contracted (or owned) by a particular cannery to ferry the salmon from the sea to the plant. On the tender the salmon are weighed and then dumped into its cavernous belly. Crew members must keep five varieties of salmon separate since each is worth a different amount to the fisherman.

Salmon seiners can be easily recognized by the power skiff that rides piggyback on the stern when not in use. The large round power block that hangs from the boom is also quite prominent. The ships range from forty to sixty feet in length and have a low house forward and work space aft. You should be able to see the seine with its stacked corks on the stern.

There are purse seine fleets in Chignik, Kodiak, Kenai, Homer, Valdez, Cordova, Hoonah, Sitka, Kake, Petersburg, Wrangell, Ketchikan, and Klawock, Alaska. The purse seine fishery is not active along the coasts of Washington southward.

Salmon seining is not a particularly dangerous fishery as Pacific fisheries go. But there are definite hazards, including the burn of jelly-fish (which you'll experience throughout every day, especially in south-eastern Alaska). But seining does offer beautiful views and fascinating wildlife.

If you don't manage to get on a boat by the time the season starts, you may want to try getting a job on a cannery tender. You'll be earning a good daily salary and you'll be in close contact with numerous skippers should an opening occur. You'll also gain some experience in operating hydraulic equipment and some other useful skills.

What You Need to Know

Participants Crew size on a salmon seiner varies with the skipper's preference and the labor supply. The bare minimum is five people, including the skipper. The average number of crew is about seven, though some boats have up to ten. Because of the large crew size and the variety of duties, a beginner has the best chances of getting aboard a seiner. *Duration* For seiners the season usually opens in early July. Get to the docks by the third week of June to begin looking for a boat. In the Copper River area (Cordova) there is an earlier season that begins in late May or early June. Salmon seining slows down in September and is normally over by October. *Pay* See general fishery description above.

Gill netting

The gill net is a long, straight net with floats on the top edge and weights on the bottom so it hangs in the water like a wall. The mesh of the gill net is a fine nylon web, translucent green in color, and is designed to allow a specific size of salmon to pass part way through but no further. When the salmon struggles to free itself the mesh slips behind the gill cover and prevents it from backing out.

The drift net is free-floating and is set to drift with the current. Other nets are either set from shore or anchored in open water; these are called *sets*. When the net is fixed from shore the fishermen catch the fish at low tide. Otherwise, fishermen tend them from a skiff.

Gill netting is usually done from smaller vessels in the twenty- to fifty-foot-range. Gill netters are recognizable by the *drum*, which is mounted on the stern. This giant spool sets and retrieves the net.

The most productive salmon district in all of Alaska is Bristol Bay, part of the Bering Sea, on the north side of the Alaskan Peninsula. This region used to be dominated by gill netters. Dillingham, Togiak, and Naknek are important fishing communities in this area. Elsewhere in Alaska one can find gill net fleets in Kodiak, Kenai, Anchorage, Homer, Seldovia, Valdez, Cordova, Yakutat, Douglas, Hoonah, Kake, Sitka, Juneau, Petersburg, Wrangell, Ketchikan, and Hydaburg. There is a significant gill net industry in the Puget Sound region, which includes Port Townsend, Bellingham, and Seattle, Washington. The Columbia River is the scene of a large gill net fishery centered in Astoria, Oregon.

What You Need to Know

Participants Most of this type of fishing requires only two people, although some boats may have three crew members. A gill netter is often managed by a couple or a father and son. For these reasons greenhorns won't find it an easy fishery to crack without contacts. *Duration* As with the purse seine fishery, the season is heavily regulated. The bulk of the catch is made in July and August. In the Puget Sound area, the season lasts well into September. In the Columbia River the season is very long, lasting from May to October. *Pay* Because of the small crew, a fisherman on a gill netter can earn a good living. In Bristol Bay, individual crew members can make $8,000 in three months. The owner of the boat earns even more. But because of their more limited range, a gill netter may do very poorly if a certain area sees few fish or if the decrees of the Fish and Game Department are to their disadvantage.

Salmon trolling

In troll fishing, four or more long lines with lures or baited hooks are towed behind a slowly moving boat. To achieve spatial distribution of the lines, *outriggers* or *spreader poles* slant from the side of the vessel. The fishing lines are attached to tag lines which are fastened to the trolling poles. When salmon strike the lure, a bell at the end of the pole rings and alerts the fisherman.

A crew member called the *puller* will have to perform a wide range of tasks, including working the lines; re-baiting or resetting them; navigating at intervals; cooking, cleaning, and icing the fish; cutting bait; and keeping the boat tidy. If there is only one crew member, he or she assumes the roles of the puller, skipper, navigator, engineer, and all-around deckhand. A crew member must know the different types of baits and lures and which ones to use in which depths. He or she must also know the areas to fish, the speed of trolling, and so forth. Since there are so many variables involved, trolling is considered by most fishermen to be an art in itself.

In many fishing communities trollers make up the majority of the boats. Trolling boats are small, about twenty to forty-five feet long. Trollers are most easily singled out by their paired outriggers: long poles that tower over the rest of the boat when not in use.

There are sizeable trolling fleets in Ketchikan, Petersburg, Sitka, and Wrangell, Alaska. In the Puget Sound area of Washington there are numerous trolling centers, including Port Townsend, Bellingham, and Seattle. In small ports along the entire West Coast there are little groups of trollers. Newport, Astoria, and Coos Bay, Oregon and Eureka, California are host to trolling fleets.

What You Need to Know

Participants Many trollers are operated by only a single fisherman, with help from a friend or family member. Rarely does a greenhorn find work on a troller. Also, because of the intimate conditions on such a small boat, most skippers of trollers would never consider taking anyone aboard they didn't know well or who wasn't recommended to them by a reliable source. *Duration* In Alaska the salmon troll fishery begins in June and continues through September. In Washington and Oregon it begins in April and often continues through October.

Trawl for Shrimp

The Alaskan shrimp fishery is relatively new. Only since the late fifties has the shrimp fishery developed in serious proportions. In one year Alaskan fishermen landed more shrimp than Texas or Louisiana Gulf shrimpers. Today, the per-boat yield is substantially higher for Alaskan boats than for Gulf of Mexico boats.

Shrimp are bottom-dwelling species, traveling in large schools. They are harvested with trawl gear, with the most widely used trawl being the *otter trawl.* It is constructed of heavy nylon webbing and shaped so that when pulled behind the boat it takes on the shape of a broad-mouthed funnel.

When the skipper feels he has trawled long enough, the towing cables are brought in and the trawl is hoisted aboard. The sock-like end, called the *cod end,* is then opened and the shrimp and other sea creatures spill out on deck. The fish and algae are sorted out from the shrimp and thrown overboard. The shrimp is then shoveled into the flush hatches on deck and layered with ice by a crew member.

Shrimp trawlers are usually gone from port for three or four days, depending on the distance to the fishing grounds; they may have trips as brief as two days before they bring their catch to the cannery to be processed. As with almost every other fishery, the crew will be busy in port buying food, fuel, and other supplies before returning to the fishing grounds.

You can spot a shrimp boat by either the double towing booms or the huge steel outriggers that are secured to the main mast. During the season their sterns are covered with net gear. Sometimes the trawl is wound on a big spool mounted on the stern. This is most often the case on smaller vessels.

Kodiak is the focus of the Alaskan shrimp fishery. Elsewhere in Alaska try Chignik and Petersburg. There are also minor shrimp fisheries based in Newport and Coos Bay, Oregon. But don't limit your search to the docks of the main boat harbor; many shrimpers are tied up at cannery wharves.

The doors of a shrimp trawl weigh up to fifteen hundred pounds. In rough weather these doors may sway back and forth while they are being lifted out of the water. If a crew member is not extremely careful he could be struck and seriously injured. There is great tension on the towing lines and always the possibility of malfunction. Also, during the later months of the season the weather can become very nasty.

What You Need to Know

Participants In the Alaskan fishery, most shrimp boats carry a crew of three or four people; there are smaller shrimp trawlers that get by with two, and others that have up to five crew members. *Duration* The Kodiak shrimp fishery begins in April, and after a slack period in May, continues through the year until December. The most productive time, when most boats are engaged in the fishery, is July and August. *Pay* Crew members on average boats do well, especially because of the relatively long season. Each person earns several thousand dollars per month. The more experienced the skipper, and the more he is familiar with the shrimping grounds, the more the shrimp boat will haul in and the greater the money each individual crew member will earn.

Southern Shrimp Fishery

As in Alaska, most of the catch is harvested by otter trawls. The mechanics are basically the same, though crews may be somewhat smaller. In the Gulf region two-man crews are quite common, although three-man crews are more normal in operations further away from shore. Many of the larger boats fish far from home ports and land their catches in South American ports.

The Southern shrimp fishery extends from Beaufort, North Carolina to Brownsville, Texas. The most productive states are Texas, Louisiana, and Florida, in that order. Some centers of this fishery include Port Lavaca, Brownsville, Port Isabel, Corpus Cristi, Freeport, Galveston, Aransas Pass-Rockport, and Port Arthur, Texas; Morgan City, Empire, Dulac-Chauvin, New Orleans; Houma, Louisiana; Biloxi, and Pascagoula-Moss Point, Mississippi; Tampa, Ft. Myers, Key West, St. Petersburg, and Panama City, Florida; Mobile, Alabama; and Brunswick, Georgia.

Southern shrimp are fished all year long. The largest catches come in June and July and catches remain sizeable until November when they slack off.

One tried-and-true strategy for getting on a shrimp boat is to work at a cannery that processes shrimp (see the section on canneries). The secret is to get on the unloading crew, where you will have the most frequent contact with skippers and crew members of the ships. Every time a boat comes in, talk to the captain and let him know you want to work for him. Put in exceptional efforts on the unloading crew and the word will eventually reach the skipper. Be informed about when the vessel will be heading out to the grounds again and appear just before they leave to see if they are shorthanded. Greet the skipper wherever you see him and tell him frequently that you want to go shrimping. Assure him you'll fish for free on the first trip.

The best time to start working at a shrimp cannery is at the beginning of the season. At this time some boats are still assembling or testing their crews. You'll have far less competition at that point than in summer when the docks of Kodiak are crawling with greenhorns.

Join the Great Crab Hunt

There are three species of crab caught in this general fishery: king crab, tanner or snow crab, and dungeness crab. All three varieties are harvested in a circular or rectangular trap called a crab pot. This mesh-covered pot has a funnel opening the size of which depends on the type of crab desired. The crab can enter the baited pot but cannot escape. Crab pots are set on the sea bottom and are marked by a buoy secured to the trap by a sturdy line also used to bring the pot to the surface.

The pots are tended regularly. After the fisherman hauls up a pot with a specially designed winch, he empties it and sorts the crabs. The pot is then re-baited with chopped clams or fish heads placed in a plastic container with holes in it.

As with most fisheries, the hours are long and strenuous. A fisherman on a crabbing vessel will often put in sixteen- to twenty-hour days. There are usually four crew members including the skipper, although some of the smaller boats will have only three. A trip lasts anywhere from five to seven days. Because crabs spoil rapidly, they are kept alive in seawater circulating holds. The crabs must reach the cannery alive or else they are worthless.

Crab boats are easily distinguished by the usual neat stacks of crab pots on deck and the brightly colored and marked buoys placed inside the vacant pots or strung about the cabin. Boats in the king crab fishery are usually quite large, ranging from 60 to 150 feet, since they must weather seas masthead-high or higher.

Dungeness crab is the only one fished from California to Alaska. It is the smallest of the three species with a maximum leg-spread of about two feet. No predominant center exists for the Dungeness fishery, though boats operate in Kodiak and Homer, Alaska; the Puget Sound area of Washington; and in Astoria and Newport, Oregon in summer months. In extreme northern California, Oregon, and Washington, Dungeness are fished in the winter months.

Tanner or snow crab are fished in primarily Alaskan waters. From Ketchikan on the southernmost tip of Alaska to the distant islands of the Aleutian, cabin pots for tanner crab are set. Primary ports are Kodiak, Homer, and Dutch Harbor. Tanner crab is landed in the greatest quantities between March and June.

King crab are the largest of the three varieties. They can weigh up to twenty-four pounds and span five, even six, feet from tip to tip of outstretched legs. King crab pots are massive, rectangular steel frames covered with wire mesh. The pots alone weigh up to four hundred pounds! Few greenhorns get on king crabbers because the skipper must be sure of his crew. The focus of the king crab fishery is Kodiak and Dutch Harbor (on Unalaska Island of the Aleutians). There are minor fleets of king crabbers in Cordova, Kenai, and Homer, Alaska. The king crab season gets under way in September or late August and thrives until January.

The winter months happen to be the peak months of this fishery, so both boats and fishermen face incredible hazards. Winds, especially in the Bering Sea, often top a hundred knots. Waves can be mountainous. Temperatures of twenty-five degrees below zero, with a wind factor bringing them lower, cause dangerous icing of decks. All of these factors combine to make crabbing one of the more dangerous occupations in the world. Imagine the exquisite skill and timing required to take a four-hundred-pound pot with perhaps a thousand pounds of crab in it aboard a pitching, rolling boat. Injuries and damage to equipment are far more frequent on these vessels.

But it is a rich fishery. And there is fierce competition to get a job on a crab boat, despite the dangers. If you're in the right place at the right time, or if you know the right people, you may get on.

Learn the Difficult Halibut Trade

Halibut are a bottom fish. They can weigh up to five hundred pounds and grow to seven feet in length. The basic unit of halibut fishing gear is a *skate* which has a ground line three hundred or more fathoms long. Hooks are attached at intervals of ten to fifteen feet via five-foot gangens. Each skate contains 100 to 120 hooks and is coiled and baited prior to fishing.

The first step in setting the gear is to throw over a buoy with a flag marker and an anchor to which the topmost end of the coiled skate is attached. After the long line has been fished or "soaked" for a sufficient period (usually six to eight hours), one end of the skate is retrieved and the skates are brought in. A fisherman at the rail of the ship controls the power gurdy which hauls in the line. As the fish are brought to the surface, the skates are recoiled, baited, and made ready for resetting. The catch is thoroughly cleaned and iced down in the hold. The handling and care of the halibut during this operation determines the quality of the fish and its subsequent value.

Most of the vessels in the Pacific halibut fishery are fifty- to eighty-feet long and hold up to fifty tons of iced halibut. Halibut boats are recognizable by the chute on the stern and the neat bundles of skates stored in a sheltered alcove on the aft deck. Many halibut vessels have what looks like a miniature sail stretched between the mast and lowered boom. This is used to help stabilize the boat in rough weather. Another way to distinguish a halibut boat from others is to look for bunches of bright pink buoys and flag markers. The markers are bamboo poles topped with red banners.

Seattle is home port to many halibut schooners during the off-season and perhaps a good place to scout around a month or so before the fishing begins. This is the period when most of the boats head up to more northerly waters. Kodiak, Seward, Homer, Cordova, Ketchikan, Sitka, and Petersburg are among the more significant ports in this fishery. The fishing grounds may be as far away as six days and a trip may last well over two weeks.

Halibut fishing is an exceptionally hard fishery. It demands extremely precise teamwork from its crews. Their skills and timing are not something that can be picked up in a week or even a season: Old-line halibut fishermen claim that it takes three seasons to turn a greenhorn into a fairly competent worker. Given the speed with which they are handled and their sheer numbers, hooks pose an ever-present danger. A minor scratch can, in a matter of hours, develop into a severe infection. And the waters frequented by halibut fishermen are known to be tumultuous much of the year.

What You Need to Know

Participants Crew size varies from five to nine fishermen. Because of the large crews, many beginners have found jobs as halibut fishermen. *Duration* The season starts in April or May and continues through October each year, depending on the regulations of the International Halibut Commission. *Pay* As with the king crab fishery, halibuting can be financially rewarding since the price per pound for halibut is rising steadily.

Join the Crew of a Seiner

Most of the tuna canned in the U.S. is landed in purse seines. The seines used in tuna fishing are much larger than those for catching salmon. Tuna seines can be as long as six hundred fathoms and as deep as forty-five fathoms. Tuna are normally fished a hundred miles or more off shore. They travel in schools that stalk "feed fish" such as herring and anchovy. Because tuna are a diving fish, the skiff brings around its end of the seine rapidly and the net is pursed as quickly as possible.

In bad weather there is tremendous pressure on the steel cables used as purse line. They sometimes snap and can easily result in fatal injury.

The seiners are usually large fishing boats with capacity for 350 tons of tuna, and are similar to salmon seiners in appearance. Most tuna seiners have enclosed "crow's nests" from which a spotter watches for schools of tuna.

Primary centers for tuna seining fleets are San Pedro, San Diego, Terminal Island, Monterey, and San Francisco, California. Some tuna boats are based in Newport and Astoria, Oregon.

It is very difficult to get hired if you're inexperienced and without contacts. And because California is a heavily populated state, the docks are worn thin by greenhorns trying one boat and the next. But be persistent.

What You Need to Know

Participants The crew consists of from twelve to twenty people, each hired to perform a specific task. There is a cook aboard, a full-time engineer, and a navigator. *Duration* A trip normally lasts two months. While tuna are fished all year long, the most productive period is from July to August. *Facilities* Quarters and provisions are rather lavish compared to fishing vessels in most other fisheries. *Pay* A beginner usually starts out with one-fourth share for his first trip. On each successive trip he earns one-fourth share more until he is making a full share. A full-fledged crew member might earn as much as four to five thousand dollars per trip in summer on a good boat (minus food and fuel, of course).

Try Sport Fishing

Scattered all along the East and West coasts, from San Diego to Seattle to Alaska's Inside Passage, and from Key West to Portland, Maine, are charter boat outfits that rent to sport fishermen. In the trade these deep-sea fishing boats are known as *pukers*. The vessels are usually manned by the skipper and one other person who handles the bait. The duties of this "bait boy" include preparing the rods and fishing gear for inexperienced tourists, keeping hot coffee and seasickness medicine ready, washing down the boat, cleaning fish, and so forth. During the best summer months these sport fishing boats make several trips per day. A wide range of fish are landed, from albacore to salmon, sea bass to shark.

The best time to look for work as a bait boy is in May before the tourist rush; by the time the tourists get there most of the vessels already have their steady bait boys (usually high school kids from the neighborhood). Working for a month or so will teach the raw landlubber some basic seamanship skills, such as tying up a boat and coiling lines. Though you probably won't earn more than between thirty and sixty dollars per day, you will be able to assess the fisherman's life without breaking your back. Scenic spots such as Depoe Bay, Oregon, will appeal to the greenhorn's romanticized visions of being a fisherman.

For Further Information

Alaska's Glacier Bay Tours & Cruises
520 Pike Tower
Seattle, WA 98101

Sea Ruby
P.O. Box 1369
Valdez, AK 99686

Seward Fishing Adventures
P.O. Box 2746
Seward, AK 99664

Captain James M. Heston
Seaview
P.O. Box 331
Valdez, AK 99686

Something Fishy
375 Miller Hill Road
Foks, AK 99709

Captain Howard Short
Rosie Ann
P.O. Box 3284
Valdez, AK 99686

Stan Stephens Charters & Cruises
P.O. Box 1297-FVG92
Valdez, AK 99686

Captain James C. Long
P.O. Box 601
Clear, AK 99704

Hook, Line & Sinker
Corner of Kobuk & Chitna
Valdez, AK 99686

Nicholson Yacht Charters
432 Columbia Street
Cambridge, MA 02141

Point Loma Sportfishing
1403 Scott Street
San Diego, CA 92106

Fisherman's Landing
2838 Garrison Street
San Diego, CA 92106

Oceanside Marina
5050 Maloney Avenue
Key West, FL 33040

First Key West Marina
U.S. Highway 1
Stock Island, FL 33040

Kona Charter Skippers Association
755663 Palani Road
Kailua-Kona, HI 96740

Breakaway Charters
Ocean Point Pier
East Boothbay, ME 04557

Captain Jack Clive Pool
P.O. Box 842
Camden, ME 04843

Frenchman's Bay Boating Company
West Street
Bar Harbor, ME 04609

Meet Chip, who hitchhiked to the cold north of Alaska from Colorado and took a ferry to Kodiak. He was told there was plenty of work here in the summer, and in fact, there was. He got hired at once by All Alaskan Seafood Cannery, with high wages and plenty of overtime. His job? Shoveling ice for eight to ten hours a day, while shivering in the freezer.

He saved money by sleeping in a tent, not far from his workplace. It took a while for him to get used to northern Alaska's summer daylight: at midnight it's still bright outside.

The cannery processes crab, pollock, and halibut, and the workers are allowed to take enough fish for full meals. Chip cooked his free dinners in front of his tent. The other workers were mostly young Filipinos with green cards. The pace was fast, and the summer unforgettable.

Work at a Cannery

You might want to try finding work at a cannery, where the pay is good and the work easier to come by.

A seafood cannery is a whole new world. In Alaskan canneries the company often provides accommodations for its workers, and employees are free to enjoy as much of the product as they can. I remember eating mountains of king crab legs for dinner for one whole week before the novelty wore off. Most jobs in these plants require little or no experience. And because the work is seasonal there is a high turnover.

For Further Information

Alaska Canneries:
Alaska Department of Fish & Game
Petersburg, AK 99833

Icicle Seafoods Company
Petersburg, AK 99833

Alyeska Seafoods
Unalaska, AK 99685

Pacific Pearl Seafoods
Unalaska, AK 99685

Blakes Canning
Cordova, AK 99574

Petersburg Fisheries
Cordova, AK 99574

Cook Inlet Processing
Kodiak, AK 99615

Sitka Seafood Producers
Sitka, AK 99835

Dominion Fisheries
Kodiak, AK 99615

Western Alaska Fisheries
Kodiak, AK 99615

E.C. Phillips Cannery
Ketchikan, AK 99901

Western Alaska Packers
Kodiak, AK 99615

East Point Seafood
Kodiak, AK 99615

California Canneries:
Bernard Food Industries, Inc.
P.O. Box 487
San Jose, CA 95103

Pan-Pacific Seafoods
338 Cannery Street
Terminal Island, CA 90731

Sportsman's Seafoods
1617 Quivira Road
San Diego, CA 92108

Star-Kist Foods, Inc.
582 Tuna Street
Terminal Island, CA 90731

Van Camp Sea Food Company
11555 Sorrento Valley Road
San Diego, CA 92121

Oregon Canneries:
Brandon Sea Pack, Inc.
5055 Boat Basin Drive
Charleston, OR 97420

Jack's Seafood Inc.
456 SW Bay Boulevard
Newport, OR 97365

Smith Pacific Shrimp
Mooring Basin Road
Garibaldi, OR 97118

Texas Canneries:
Clegg Shrimp Company, Inc.
Drawer C
Port Lavaca, TX 77979

Washington Canneries:
Alaska Fresh Seafood
4241 21st West
Seattle, WA 98109

All Alaskan Seafoods
130 Nickerson
Seattle, WA 98119

K Fisheries
4200 23d West
Seattle, WA 98111

Bumble Bee Seafoods
Bellingham, WA 98225

East Point Seafood
Fishermans Terminal Building
Seattle, WA 98119

Peter Pan Seafoods
2200 6th Avenue
Seattle, WA 98104

9

Working with Animals

If you "seek the quiet heart," as one Basque shepherd does, working with animals may be the summer job for you.

Be a horse wrangler for a *dude* or guest ranch in summer; hire on to a working livestock ranch as a "hand"; isolate yourself for a summer with a flock of sheep high in the western mountains; or jump into the rodeo circuit and compete in bull and bronco riding.

Work on a Dude Ranch

Shortly after dawn, Steve, the chief wrangler, and Karen, the "horse person," headed up the hill past the golden aspen trees to the Vista Verde Ranch pasture where the horses grazed. "Time for the corral!" Steve called to them as though the creatures could understand.

Later, with the horses saddled, the red-shirted dude ranch staff helped the guests to mount for a morning ride. To their surprise, this group of ten new arrivals had lots of riding experience. The wrangler trotted ahead, cantering along the winding trail. The western sky was perfectly blue and there was a smell of sage in the air. The Colorado mountains ascended gently toward deep forests. "Lucky you," one of the guests said to Steve. "Spending your summer up here! Getting paid for this!" The guest had a point.

It takes a special person to work as a seasonal wrangler at a private stable or a dude ranch. You need to love the outdoors, and accept a simple philosophy summed up by a cowboy prayer framed at many dude ranches. It reads:

May your horse never stumble
And your cinch never break.
May your belly never grumble
May your heart never ache.

Dude ranch work is one of the few remaining ways to get close to animals. Of course, you won't enjoy such a job unless you like horses and have been around them for part of your life. In fact, many of the young people who get these summer jobs—and there are hundreds of positions to be filled—first came to guest ranches with their folks as paying customers. Or they had a horse somewhere at home, trained horses, or came from a farm family.

You must be ready to start low on the ranch totem pole. "We send new people to the barn," says one ranch owner from Oklahoma. "We make beginners clean out the stables and sort saddles. We don't let them go out on a ride until they've been trained by us. And they must pay attention." The new future wrangler must therefore be willing to help out elsewhere on the ranch.

Most owners care about their employees, and the atmosphere is friendly. You might even consider the job a sort of working vacation. Applicants are often warned that the hours will be long. In fact, everyone in the business, including management, works about twelve hours a day at times.

Many ranch guests have never ridden before. They think that you can just climb on the horse and it will gallop off. In reality, it's thanks to the rider's guidance with reins and leg pressure that a horse will walk, trot, and canter (a slow gallop, also known as a "lope"). Galloping is rarely allowed at ranches. A wrangler must be able to teach a greenhorn, or first-timer, how to handle emergencies. If abused or startled, even a mild-mannered horse can buck and take off explosively. It's important that the rider know how to stay on throughout the ride.

Most dude ranches are located in Western states like Idaho, Montana, Arizona, Colorado, Wyoming, and California. The Peaceful Valley Ranch, one of Colorado's largest dude ranches, is typical for its employment details. The owner is looking for wranglers. "Lots of them . . . all summer long," he says. "Tell you what I don't need: Macho types; rodeo or trick riders." Like his colleagues, he also doesn't care much for "prima donnas." Wranglers must be prepared to clean the stables and do other chores. In short, the ranch owners need competent employees.

The Peaceful Valley runs 120 horses for about 120 guests at a time. With four decades of dude ranching behind him, the typical owner expects prospective wranglers to be able to instruct novice guests. If wranglers are not capable of teaching, they won't get hired.

The Peaceful Valley Ranch accepts application letters or phone calls and conducts interviews in the spring. There are usually about seven hundred applicants for the fifteen wrangler positions open every summer. Unlike other ranches, Peaceful Valley gives a one-week training course to employees.

The Vista Verde Ranch is another example of a typical ranch. Sitting at the end of a rugged road, thirty miles north of Steamboat Springs, Colorado, it's one of the best such vacation places in the state. The staff is warm, helpful, experienced, and eager to please. Apart from horseback riding, this dude ranch offers supervised hiking, cycling, fly-fishing, and even rock climbing instruction. Almost every Thursday, balloon rides lift the guests heavenward.

The summer staff consists of eighteen people who take care of the horses, keep house and clean rooms, run the office and kitchen, and serve as hiking guides. Much of the staff is versatile and interchangeable—the Vista Verde's bookkeeper, for instance, helps clean the rooms—

and the staff brings a diversity of backgrounds to the job. The typical wrangler knows how to shoe horses, treat the sick ones, and please the others. He or she also knows a dozen horse tricks.

Competition is keen for these outdoor jobs. Every year, the application letters cascade onto John Munn's desk. He gets from two hundred to three hundred applicants for the eighteen summer jobs. For best results, write to a ranch in January. Your résumé should include some relevant references (be aware that they'll probably be checked). In your letter, emphasize your experience with or interest in horses.

It might help if someone at the ranch knows you because you've been a guest there at some point. Always mention specialized experience, like having trained, bred, or shoed horses. A previous stint as a lifeguard or ski patroller helps, along with possession of a first aid card. John Munn hires his hands over the telephone after long interviews and reference checks. What does he look for? "The work ethic," he says. "The love of the outdoors. Real caring for the guests."

What You Need to Know

Participants You must be at least eighteen years old. Ideally, you should have a background in horses, though you can get around that. Bear in mind that there are hundreds of applicants for only a handful of openings (see descriptions for details). *Facilities* Dude ranches are basically rustic, with plain, Western-style furniture against a log cabin backdrop; the rooms often contain fur-covered sofas, rugged granite fireplaces, and antlers on the walls. There are some fairly primitive ranches, where employees sleep in cramped cabins with other hired hands. Vista Verde is small, compared to other such dude ranches. Employee accommodations include a log cabin-style bunk house for the men and a similar one for the women. On your day off at most ranches you can generally use the pool, go trout fishing in nearby rivers, join a hiking group, or take part in square-dancing at night, just like the paying guests. *Pay* The pay is adequate and you also get room and board. The modest wages are augmented by tips; the guests are often generous and tip money is usually pooled.

For Further Information

Any state tourist office has a complete list of dude ranches in its state. Here's a sampling of some employment leads:

Alisal Guest Ranch and Resort
1054 Alisal Road
Solvang, CA 93463

Averill's Flathead Lake
P.O. Box 2480W
Bigfork, MT 59911

Beartooth Ranch
Nye, MT 59061

Bill Cody's Ranch
Cody, WY 82414

Coffee Creek Ranch
HC2, P.O. Box 4940 Department OW
Trinity Center, CA 96091

Colorado Dude & Guest Ranch Association
P.O. Box 300
Tabernash, CO 80478

Eatons Ranch
Wolf, WY 82844

High Island Ranch
P.O. Box 81
Hamilton Dome, WY 82427

Lone Mountain Ranch
P.O. Box 69
Big Sky, MT 59716

Moose Creek Ranch
P.O. Box 350-OW
Victor, ID 83455

National Dude Ranchers Association
Tie Siding, WY 82084

Paradise Valley Guest Ranch
Scottsdale, AZ 85251

Peaceful Valley Ranch
Star Route, P.O. Box 2811
Lyons, CO 80540

Schively Ranch
1062 Road 15
Lovell, WY 82431

Star Meadows Ranch
P.O. Box G
Whitefish, MT 59937

Sweet Grass Ranch
Melville Route, P.O. Box 161
Big Timber, MT 59011

Rockin' R Ranch
P.O. Box 4610W
Sandy, UT 84091-0461

Tanque Verde Ranch
Tucson, AZ 85251

Vista Verde Ranch
P.O. Box 465
Steamboat Springs, CO 80477

Wild Horse Ranch
Tucson, AZ 85251

Wrangle a Pack Trip

Wrangling a horse pack trip or trail ride really helps you get away from
it all. Pack trips travel through wilderness areas where guests can ride
and fish. Hunting season is a prime time for pack trips. Following a
herd of elk and bringing home "the trophy" is a lot easier on horseback.

As a horse wrangler, your responsibilities include setting up camp
and handling heavy canvas tents, cots, sleeping bags, and foam pads.
You'll prepare and serve a hot breakfast and dinner, clean up, and pack
everything back on the animals to ride again.

Being tough is a main requirement of a trail wrangler: You are a
long way from a telephone if you need help. You'll also need good people skills, as well as horse sense: care of the horses or mules is of the
utmost importance.

Some outfits need employees for covered wagon trips, which are
slower trips. Guests sometimes ride horseback alongside the wagon
train. Accommodations are a bit more luxurious because the guests
and the wranglers get to sleep in the wagons, which provide shelter
from the elements.

The Box K Ranch in Wyoming has run the Jackson Hole Trail Ride
for over twenty-one years. Much of their five-day trip takes you high in

the forests of the Tetons. The 7W Guest Ranch heads out on horseback into the Flat Tops Wilderness in northwestern Colorado with two guides and six guests. The trail to the top of the plateau is steep and rocky. After three days of fishing and trail riding, the group comes back down the mountain on a steep and rocky trail that gets muddy and slick in the rain. One guest described the mood after three days of pouring rain, "The horses were nervous and wet; the guests were tired and wet. The guides still had to set up camp with wet gear and cook dinner. But after hot, hearty beef stew, coffee, and apple dumplings, the guests were still having a good time, thanks to the skill of the wranglers."

What You Need to Know

Participants Most outfits look for young men and women age seventeen and older, but if you know your way around horses and pack animals, age may not matter. *Duration* Expect to spend the entire summer on horseback. Individual trips last four to seven days. Sometimes you have a few days in between but be prepared to return from one trip, pack, and leave the next day for another. *Facilities* During your pack trips, you'll spend the night in a tent. Between outings, you may be put up in a bunkhouse or have to find an apartment in a nearby town. Depending on the outfitter, this might be included in your wages or may be an additional charge. Most outfitters provide all meals. *Pay* Generally minimum wage.

For Further Information

Some of the previously mentioned ranches also offer pack trips. In addition, consider the following leads:

Ken Sleight Pack Trips
Pack Creek Ranch
P.O. Box 1270
Moab, UT 84532

Schober's Pack Station
Route 2, P.O. Box 179
Bishop, CA 93514

Wagons West
P.O. Box 1156
Afton, WY 83110

Horseback Adventures
P.O. Box 73
Brule, AB, Canada TOE OCO

Wilderness Outfitters
3800 Rattlesnake Drive
Missoula, MT 59802

Join a Mule Skinner

The "mule skinners" of the Grand Canyon accompany ten to twenty people a day down the steep Bright Angel Trail on mules. From the south rim to the bottom, there is a drop of one long mile. The trail follows old deer paths. It is narrow, rutted, and treacherous. Some of the tourists hold on with their eyes shut—which is too bad, since this view is one of the most awesome in the world.

The Canyon's width and breadth cannot be taken for granted; nor can its colors. Even after several visits, you're still as deeply impressed with the shapes and colors as with the Canyon's six-thousand-feet depth. The mauve, blue, brown, and golden highlights of these geologic wonders stay with you a long time.

Despite the daunting trips, the mules remain calm and cautious. As large as horses, they have been used for centuries for pack and freight hauling. Mules don't spook as easily as horses. And they're not as stubborn as donkeys.

The employees' responsibilities are to groom and saddle the mules by dawn, assign each rider to an animal, and instruct them in riding techniques. Fortunately, the mules are used to the ride and aren't likely to go racing around anywhere, especially not off the trail.

The first stop is at Indian Springs, halfway down the Grand Canyon trail, which provides shade and water for riders and mules. They continue on down to Phantom Canyon Ranch where guests and their mules stay overnight, while the mule skinners saddle up and take back the people and mules who arrived the day before.

Seven days a week, weather permitting, the mule trains go in and out of the Grand Canyon. The mule skinner's job is to care for them. On days off, there is little to do. No pools or entertainment to offset the summer heat. But the majesty and grandeur of the Grand Canyon is more than enough for most.

The Molokai Mule Ride in Hawaii is another famous pack trip. Seven days a week, all year long, the mules clamber up and down switchback trails. The ride traverses rain forests with views of cliffs and the ocean below. Molokai is an island that feels remote, rural, and tranquil. Although it takes only twenty minutes to fly to the small island, it feels worlds away. There are no taxis here, no traffic lights, no fast food chains, or neon lights. Life on the island is slow.

And the Molokai Mule Ride is a big deal around here.

Can you get a job as a mule skinner? Generally, Hawaiians have preference. Openings are scarce. If you're determined to join the crew, bear in mind that, although the winter season is the busiest one, the Mule Ride operates all year long.

For Further Information

Superintendent
Grand Canyon National Park
P.O. Box 129
Grand Canyon, AZ 86023

Molokai Mule Rides
P.O. Box 200
Molokai, HI 96757

Work on a Cattle Ranch

The giant cattle ranches of the U.S. employ general ranch hands, fence builders and fixers, trench diggers, haying crews, cowhands, mechanics, and cooks. On smaller ranches, one or two persons may have to do all the chores, which include branding. In some cases, the ranchers' own sons and daughters can handle all the work, with no outsiders needed.

During the past decade, the entire cattle industry has changed. Now only the big livestock operators can succeed financially. As many as 200,000 head of cattle are fed huge amounts of alfalfa and corn at the giant grain elevators and compounds you see everywhere. Everything that goes on in the cattle pens, including veterinary shots, is honed to a fine science, complete with computers in the feedlot offices and annual reports.

There are fewer opportunities for beginners now than there were twenty years ago. For one thing, beef sales are not as good as they used to be. Many novice jobs were eliminated by the diminishing profits; other jobs by mechanization and new methods. Some cattlemen now use helicopters for roundups and practice highly sophisticated feeding and breeding methods. Yet a greenhorn can still participate in a cattle drive in spring or fall when the cowboys, complete with chaps and stirrups, drive the cattle to and from the high country grazing lands.

Cattlemen combine the best of the new with the best of the old: cows are fed newfangled nutritional diets, but motherless calves are still bottle-fed by hand.

Apart from pursuing work at a cattle ranch, which often needs temporary help when somebody gets sick or is on vacation, you should also consider the major feedlot operators. Some feedlots can be found in small unpolluted towns. You may join the sanitation crew that keeps the feedlot clean; or you can drive the truck that transports corn or other edibles to the animals. If you know enough about cattle, and have more than average horse skills, you might apply as a "pen rider," patrolling the stockyards on horseback, moving cattle around, and separating stock that is on its way to slaughter or is diseased. Stockyards in major metropolitan communities also employ such riders.

In bigger cities, at various times, replacements or seasonal workers are needed by packing houses. But this is a bloody business that doesn't suit many people. One thing is for sure: Packing houses won't appeal to vegetarians!

What You Need to Know

Participants You should be in good physical shape since the entry level jobs involve rough and dirty work. Most of the livestock people interviewed for this book kept saying that the cattle ranch "isn't for amateurs," so some experience helps. *Facilities* Lodging is usually provided, and some of the young cowboys may periodically get a side of beef and a pickup truck. *Pay* Employers emphasize the low pay: a new ranch hand earns less than the lowest-paid clerk in a city. *How to Apply* The best way to break in is to visit the farm specialist in a state employment agency or Job Service office. Or see a private employment agent who specializes in farm labor. The agent may have contacts to place farm and ranch labor, dairy employees, mechanics, foremen, and ranch superintendents.

For Further Information

Check with your local state employment agency or Job Service.

Ride in a Rodeo

The chute opens and a young Texas bareback rider holds on to the horse's riggings with one hand. He doesn't know this horse, never rode it before. He leans back, digging his spurs into the beast's neck. The horse rears wildly, hoofs in all directions, a bucking, pitching, twisting, snorting, wild-eyed rebel. The rider's hat flies high, landing in the dust.

He has been on the horse for five seconds now, and he still hangs on. He leans all the way back, ankles still spurring, his shoulder blades hitting the critter's spine. It's man against beast. Six seconds now . . . seven . . . eight.

The buzzer sounds. The rodeo rider jumps off the horse onto the ground. He stumbles to his knees, but picks himself up fast and avoids the one-thousand pounds of hoofed muscle close by. His forehead is bathed in sweat. Eight seconds of bareback riding can seem like eight hours. But he's earned eight hundred dollars this afternoon.

While the pros travel the circuit almost all year, turning up at dozens of the seven hundred sanctioned North American rodeos, you can also enter just an occasional rodeo. The horses are unpredictable, though, and so the winnings are unpredictable. If a horse refuses to buck, the rider will get nothing. If a horse tosses you off after two seconds, you get nothing. "They're the great American gamblers on horseback," says an announcer about rodeo cowboys. "And every day, they play with fire."

It takes nerve to tackle a furious, crowd-crazed animal, to look injury in the eye without flinching. You need stubbornness, the ability to keep your cool and to handle pressure . . . and intense concentration. Unlike many professional athletes who have sponsors and sell themselves for money, the majority of rodeo cowboys remain their own free agents. (Only a few get endorsements.) Saddle makers, horse breeders, even cigarette companies may contribute to the purses, but no one sponsors the majority of rodeo contestants.

And in addition to a financial outlay, you run the risk of the "crash and burn," a wreck or bad spill. A nervous horse can jerk back its head, smashing a cowboy's cheekbone. Most professionals wind up with broken arms, ribs, fingers, legs, or ankles at some point. In bareback riding, whiplash is common. The saddle bronc events can be still rougher; an unlucky rookie's ankles might still hang in the stirrups as the jumping, bucking bronc propels him to the ground. The angered creature drags him along the arena, suspended by an ankle, in a rack of pain.

Not all rodeo events are dangerous. Some of them merely demand skill, which is often acquired on a ranch. Take calf roping, for instance, which started in ranch work. Since the cows never stood still for branding or vaccinations, they had to be roped. Roping in a rodeo takes skill and a trained horse. The rider must be an expert in handling a lariat, or lasso. Competitors fight the clock to win. After lassoing the calf around the neck, the calf roper forces the animal to the ground and ties three legs together.

Remember that rodeos aren't just for men. One event women have always competed in is barrel racing. Riding a fast, spirited horse, the rider circles three barrels placed in the arena, in a cloverleaf pattern at frightening speeds. Galloping this fast, the horses seem suspended, almost parallel to the ground. Often, they lose their balance and collide with the barrel, rider and all. It's not a sport for the faint-hearted. Barrel-riding is pure speed. You must run that cloverleaf pattern as fast as possible. Most contestants own their own horse, because the bond between these high-strung animals and the rider must be strong. Expect to pay up to ten thousand dollars for a good horse. But don't expect your animal to be good for anything else: Once trained as a speed-crazy barrel horse, your horse will not be suited to pleasure riding.

Women also compete in bull and bronc competitions. They have their own association and circuit. Sometimes they compete against the men. The pay is low—the World Championship Woman Bull Rider only makes $2,260 in a typical year—and the life-style is gypsy-like, traveling from one rodeo to the next. But once the arena dust gets in your nostrils, it's like a drug. Once you feel the exhilaration of having two thousand pounds of angry bull under you, you want to come back for more. Riding a bull requires immense strength, dexterity, and agility.

The thrill of competition is what rodeo is all about. It's just you and the animal working with one another, like in the barrel races, or against each other, like in the bull rides. Injuries are common. The way most people get off a bronc or a bull is to fall or be thrown off. Expect broken bones and bruised muscles.

Most riders get started at a home town corral, often as small children, then graduate to small town rodeos. The rodeo circuit goes on in every small western town every weekend. Win enough and you go on to the big rodeos.

What You Need to Know

Participants You must be at least eighteen years old to ride, and you must be a member of the Professional Rodeo Cowboy's Association (see address). Ranch kids have an edge; they learn how to handle horses at an early age and know how to rope cattle. Many also learned to ride at collegiate rodeos. *Facilities* You'll pay your own way across the country. You must buy your own equipment, which is expensive: Some ropes cost as much as $50, the chaps $100. Even spurs are $50. *Pay* You can earn anywhere from $30 to $1,000 for just a few seconds atop a bucking animal. Contestants don't get an expense account; the rodeo cowboy draws no allowance, has no guaranteed annual wage. Your only income is what you can earn in a fiercely competitive sport; for you're competing not only against other cowboys, but against the rank animals. And you must pay for this privilege: entry fees run from $25 to $300 per rodeo.

For Further Information

Professional Rodeo Cowboys' Association
2929 West 19th Avenue
Denver, CO 80204

Women's Pro Rodeo Association
Route 5, P.O. Box 698
Blanchard, OK 73010

National Western Stock Show
4701 Marion Street
Denver, CO 80216

American Junior Rodeo Association
P.O. Box 481
Rankin, TX 79778

National High School Rodeo Association
11178 North Huron Street, #7
Denver, CO 80234

National Intercollegiate Rodeo Association
1815 Portland Street, Suite 3
Walla Walla, WA 99362

Find the Quiet Life of a Shepherd

The scene is about one hundred miles north of Boise, Idaho, over rounded mountains. No houses or villages for miles. It is early June, and the valley meadows are green. Higher up, among the massive fields of wildflowers, more than one thousand sheep are grazing. Every day they climb, following the receding snow line, only to come down again for good in October.

It will take you hours to reach the animals, but you can hear tinkling sounds of the bells on their necks far below. These bells help the shepherd find stray sheep. A few sheep make bleating sounds as the sheepdog moves them to higher pastures, to more wildflowers and tender grasses.

The shepherd walks slowly toward his camp wagon on a plateau. He smiles at you; he hasn't seen a human being in two days. His voice is hoarse, his speech awkward because he doesn't use it much. He's Basque and works as a seasonal shepherd. It's solitary work: one person surrounded by immense mountains. He must cope with the coyotes that attack sheep and with the fierce rainstorms that send him into his wagon for shelter. This wagon serves as his home for part of the year; it contains a stove, some food supplies, and a hard mattress for sleeping. But it's peaceful in those mountains.

Many of America's sheepherders are Basques. Australians are also drawn to this life, but very few Americans are. In recent years, according to the U.S. Department of Agriculture in Washington, the labor shortage in the sheep industry has become acute. During the late seventies, shepherds became so scarce that U.S. sheep production dropped by about ten percent each year. As you read this, there are only thirteen million head left.

The good news is that shepherding applicants have a good chance for summer employment because most ranchers say that they'll hire any young, strong American if he or she can stand the stress of being alone. Only on a few occasions will a rancher hire a second person, usually to do the cooking. "Most Americans can't stand the loneliness," says one Idaho sheep rancher. "Even the Basques get homesick and lonely and quit." To battle the loneliness, herders read, sing, and talk to the sheep.

Most of the jobs are in the Western sheep states of Idaho, California, Montana, Utah, and Wyoming. Herders are also sought in Colorado and Texas.

What You Need to Know

Duration The work is seasonal in nature. Officially, herders work a minimum of ten hours per day, but only a few months a year. In reality, the herder must look after his sheep from dawn to dusk—which amounts to more than ten hours each day. *Facilities* The rancher furnishes the food supplies plus the wagon and bedding. A herder can do all the fishing and hunting he wants to complement his diet. *Pay* The pay is low. Calculating the number of hours worked against the salary, the resulting average pay can be below the minimum hourly wage.

For Further Information

American Sheep Industry Association
6911 South Yosemite
Englewood, CO 80110

American Suffolk Sheep Society
52 North 1st East
Logan, UT 84321

Columbia Sheep Breeders Association
P.O. Box 272
Upper Sandusky, OH 43351

Be a Veterinarian Assistant

The chestnut stallion screamed and reared, pawing the air and throwing the woman holding his halter into the air like a piece of driftwood in a turbulent sea. The veterinarian caught the stallion's lead rope while his assistant picked herself up from the stable floor. This time they buckled and strapped the stallion's foreleg. He could only stand on three legs now. Then a long, thin, flexible rubber tube was gently threaded down the horse's throat and into his stomach. With a hand pump, thick white medicine was pumped in, a procedure that did not hurt the horse.

Veterinary assistant tasks range from vaccinating cattle, castrating pigs, and artificially inseminating dairy cows, to performing dental work on dogs, trimming a parakeet's claws, and helping set a cat's broken bone. As an assistant, you should be prepared to clean the stalls, kennels, and boxes of whatever animals are being cared for.

Medically caring for animals is very rewarding. The work itself is hard, physically and mentally. You poke and prod, investigating the mystery of what is wrong. You must cut, stitch, and clean wounds, and give shots. Be prepared for lots of blood.

And the risks are great. Working with horses, for instance, can result in being kicked, stepped on, slammed against a wall and even bitten. A horse bite is a painful injury. Trying to cure a horse is anything but glamorous, and working with large animals always carries the risk of being injured. Small creatures, too, can claw, scratch, and bite. But remember these "patients" are in pain and scared. If you have any desire to retaliate, this is not the job for you.

Pay generally starts at minimum wage. You could be working odd hours and sometimes even around the clock. You could be wading through a corral full of manure in sub-zero temperatures.

The best way to get a vet assistant job? Ask your own or a neighborhood vet. Be persistent: write letters and pay visits to the clinic. Show you care about animals and are willing to work. If your interests lie in eventually becoming a vet yourself, so much the better. Don't give up; your enthusiasm will be rewarded, even if only with a part-time summer job.

Board Horses this Summer

The smell of saddle leather, horses, and hay can be perfume to the true horse lover. If you're saving to buy a horse, or just want to work around horses this summer, try a job at a stable. Boarding stables can be found everywhere, even in New York City. Thousands of people who live in apartments and suburbs and own horses keep them in boarding stables and pay for their food and care.

Your tasks as a stablehand? Shoveling manure from stalls and corrals, changing the bedding used on the floor of each horse stall, pitching wet straw or wood shavings—at least you'll develop muscles doing this. Horses require a lot of clean water—and you're the one who will supply it. Each four-legged "guest" probably has its own special diet as well, so a different menu is prepared for each one. You'll also be the one leading the horses out to stretch their legs in a corral.

Boarding also sometimes includes grooming, which means you'll spend a large part of each day brushing the horses and carrying the different brushes and cloths (used for various parts of the animal) in a bucket. Generally, you're responsible for the horse's well-being while at the boarder. You must watch that it has not injured itself and is in good health. Bright eyes, interested manner, and good appetite generally mean good health.

One plus is that, because many of the people who board their steeds don't get to ride as often as they'd like, you may be able to ride for them. You'll get a chance to take a horse out when you are not scheduled to work in the stable.

Your income? Usually just minimum wage. If you work at an expensive stable some of the owners may tip you, but don't count on it.

To get a job in a stable, show up in person. Keep at it until you are hired. Most stable help turns over quickly. You just have to be there when someone quits.

10

Outdoor Work in the U.S.

Work in a National Park

How about a summer on a giant recreational playground? With a huge number of sports in a scenic setting beyond compare? Consider the magnificent Grand Teton National Park, Wyoming.

It is one thing to be a modest, part-time volunteer in one of the 359 national parks and monuments. The work is enjoyable, true, but volunteers are unpaid. (For details, see Chapter 2.) It is yet another thing to wear the smart uniform of the park ranger and to participate in such activities as lecturing to information-hungry, international groups at the Redwood National Park in California, or guiding the superb *National Geographic* photographers through the Grand Canyon, or serving as an expert on the flora and fauna of the Everglades in Florida.

Multiply these opportunities by the more than three hundred parks and you get an idea of the parks' diversity and the opportunities to administer and run these wonderful natural oases.

There is also a third group of park workers: the seasonal park employees. Almost every national park hires them in varying numbers.

Seasonal jobs are not easy to get. For one thing, the competition is fierce; there are at least ten—and sometimes one hundred!—applicants for every position. For another thing, preference is given to former volunteers (see Chapter 2) and to seasonal employees who have already worked for the park service during a previous summer and are known by the administrators. Thirdly, and most importantly, the seasonal people are generally college students (minimum age eighteen), who are studying biological or physical sciences, or have some experience in law enforcement, administration, or accounting. Other temporary folks are involved in giving lectures (you'll need a background in history or the sciences) and leading hikes (you should know something about botany). The seasonal employees also do mundane chores such as trail maintenance (removing rocks, for instance), restoration work (such as painting), and the like.

Of course, all is not sunshine in the parks. With 250 million visitors a year, the parks deal with tourists who trample flora to pick wildflowers, disturb protected wildlife, or commit crimes of various kinds. Too many campers behave like pigs. The hordes who invade the national parks each summer—three million in the Rocky Mountain National Park, for instance—leave plenty of litter and destruction. With funds tight, the National Park Service has a hard time coping. Their responsibilities also include rescuing rock climbers who get stuck on rock faces as high as one thousand meters and ferreting out vandals.

Nevertheless, working in the underfunded National Park Service is of great interest to people who truly love wild seashores and mountains, rare flowers and stately trees.

What You Need to Know

Participants You must be at least eighteen years old to be a seasonal employee. Seasonal employees always have special, demonstrable areas of interest, either in the sciences or parks and recreation or law enforcement fields. Other temporaries get hired for the summer because of their special skills. Many seasonal employees are college students majoring in biological or physical science. *Duration* The parks are very flexible as far as duration of employment during the summer season. *Facilities* You're on your own in most parks, though some furnish housing. *Pay* Although the application forms ask you to list your lowest acceptable salary, pay is generally commensurate with your educational background or skills. In any case, it's always higher than minimum wage. *How to Apply* The application for summer work must be in the National Park Service hands between September 1 and January 15, well before the summer months. You can get forms at the nearest park office (see list below), and send them to:

Seasonal Employment Unit
P.O. Box 37127
Washington, DC 20013-7127

For Further Information

You can either apply to your favorite park or send your application to the National Park Service in Washington:

National Park Service
P.O. Box 37127
Washington, DC 20013-7127

It can also be useful to talk to a person at one of the National Park Service regional offices:
Alaska Region:
National Park Service
2525 Gambell Street
Anchorage, AK 99503

Midwest Region:
National Park Service
1709 Jackson Street
Omaha, NE 68102

Western Region:
National Park Service
P.O. Box 36063
San Francisco, CA 94102

Southeast Region:
National Park Service
75 Spring Street, SW
Atlanta, GA 30303

Pacific Northwest Region:
National Park Service
83 South King Street
Seattle, WA 98104

Mid-Atlantic Region:
National Park Service
143 South Third Street
Philadelphia, PA 19106

Rocky Mountain Region:
National Park Service
12795 West Alameda Parkway
Denver, CO 80225

National Capital Region:
National Park Service
1100 Ohio Drive, SW
Washington, DC 20242

Southwest Region:
National Park Service
P.O. Box 728
Santa Fe, NM 87504

North Atlantic Region:
National Park Service
15 State Street
Boston, MA 02109

Help National Park Concessioners

Apart from actual national park summer employment, there are some openings with the commercial operators; the Yosemite Park and Curry Company is one example. Hotels, swimming pools, restaurants, cafes, and stables all create some summer jobs for a variety of employees.

The number of commercial enterprises varies, of course, from park to park. While some parks have no commercial operators, The Yellowstone Park Company, for instance, hires a staff of more than seventeen hundred employees every summer. The concessioner provides lodging, food, transportation, gift shops, vending, visitor services, boats, and horses in two-million acre Yellowstone National Park.

The season begins in late April with the opening of the historical and world-renowned Old Faithful Inn. Many thousands of visitors later, autumn frosts announce the October conclusion of the summer season. Most of the staff is comprised of young adults with a high percentage of college students from every region of the nation. Hospitality industry professionals are employed for positions of responsibility and authority. They also employ skilled tradespeople to perform numerous functions. A season spent working in this enormous wilderness enclave can be a most memorable and rewarding experience. And, in fact, many of the employees return year after year.

Actually, many of the national parks contain major hotels which grind into high gear during the summer tourist season. As a result, minimum wage vacancies pile up for those young people who don't mind working in the kitchens, the dining rooms (as hosts and hostesses), as housekeepers, as front desk help, or in other positions. While these offerings may not be as exciting as others in the national parks, they remain a wonderful opportunity for outdoors enthusiasts who enjoy hikes, climbs, botanical forays, horseback rides, wild animal viewing, and interesting lectures. These jobs generally pay minimum wage, but in most cases food and accommodations are provided.

For Further Information

Yellowstone Park Company
Personnel Division
Yellowstone National Park, WY 82190

Yosemite Park and Curry Company
Yosemite National Park, CA 95389

Grand Canyon National Park Lodges
P.O. Box 699
Grand Canyon, AZ 86023

Grand Teton National Park Lodges
Moran, WY 83013

Great Smoky Mountains National Park
Gatlinburg, TN 37738

See page 18 for more contacts in the national parks.

Find Work in America's Forests

What natural wealth America's forests offer us! Breathe deeply, drawing in their scents. Look at the beauty surrounding you at every turn. These beautiful lands provide seasonal work in tree farms, tree nurseries, and in reforestation. Some parts of the U.S., like Alaska, also offer many opportunities for would-be loggers.

The riches in our forests include 730 million acres, of which 500 million acres are considered "commercial" forest lands. This means that they can or do grow trees for harvesting. From these, about 9 billion board feet of lumber are cut and sold by the National Forest Service. The U.S. grows about 37 percent more timber than it harvests, and, according to the National Forest Products Association, is one of the few industrialized countries that does so.

Large timber firms also control a vast private conglomeration of wooded land. For example, the giant Weyerhaeuser Company owns 5.5 million acres of forest, including 1.5 million in Washington State alone. Weyerhaeuser employs almost 38,000 people in logging, newsprint mills, tree nurseries, saw mills, and other facilities. They continually replant trees after a harvest.

In areas like the Pacific Northwest, where timber used to make up a high percentage of the local business, and where jobs in logging went begging, environmental concerns and mechanization have reduced the number of summer jobs. But if you're considering going to Montana's Galatin Valley or to Idaho's Boise area, you'll still find lots of timber action. In fact, six out of ten railroad cars leaving the Oregon area still carry loads of lumber.

The U.S. exports tons of wood to various countries. And in this country, new housing, fencing, furniture, and telephone lines gobble up wood. Due to mechanization, our timberlands are also tapped by an increasing demand for paper, cardboard, insulation, chemicals, plastics, and a diversity of products you wouldn't associate with logging, like fertilizers, explosives, rayon, and turpentine. In fact, according to the U.S. Forest Service, timber demand will double by the year 2000.

Loggers are aware of the mystique of the deep forests. One industry expert who spent a decade in the Washington State timberlands, photographing and interviewing loggers, says that every logger is a dedicated outdoorsman. Loggers don't consider themselves special. "We're just doing our job," says one lifetime Idaho Panhandle sawyer. The helper he hired for the summer months loves the perfume of the pine needles underfoot and the challenge of hard, physical work. But he's also glad that his time in the forest is limited to only a couple of months. He's different from the old-time loggers; he sees himself as a free spirit.

The U.S. history of lumbering has its grim sides. As the country began its westward expansion in the nineteenth century, the need for wood products grew. There seemed to be an endless supply of trees, and since forest management methods were in a primitive stage, little attention was paid to future needs and reforestation. A general reck-lessness of the times led loggers to move from state to state, harvest-ing every tree in sight and then pushing on again to wherever the railroads and trails took them. Thus the timber capital of the U.S. was located at different times in Williamsport, Pennsylvania; St. Paul, Min-nesota; and Tacoma, Washington.

Greedy timber barons decimated the beautiful forests around Lake Tahoe, California, to supply the mines with lumber. Ruthless lumber-men denuded some of Colorado's finest woods. New England captains of industry filled their pockets with money. Montana's railroad owners "clear-cut" the forests. Conservation? No one knew the term.

It took years for the butchery to slow down; but today the loggers themselves want to practice less destructive ways. "Clear-cutting" is no longer popular. Yet ironically, logging is still necessary to keep the forests alive. For instance, as trees get older, they become subject to disease and high winds, and slopes can become littered with dead wood, which is a fire hazard. Damage is caused by fires, insects, diseases, winds, and floods. If you log the timber early, new healthy trees can grow back. Much dead or dying timber is thus salvaged for commercial use.

Forest rangers explain two other reasons for logging: "Selection cutting" involves the removal of mature trees either singly or in small groups at intervals. And "intermediate cutting" affects trees that must be removed periodically for commercial use during the life of a stand. This is done to reduce crowding and stimulate growth (by thinning an overgrown area), and to improve the quality of the remaining stand (called "improvement cutting").

The U.S. Forest Service harvests and sells timber (a controversial issue), handles grazing permits, and administers 3,300 miles of rivers, 115,000 miles of hiking trails, and 33 million acres of precious wilderness. They also hire some one thousand people for part-time work each summer.

Timber Harvests

"We drove over twenty miles on ever-worsening roads," reported one young summertime logging assistant volunteer. "It was quite an experience to be out in Alaska. Challenges are everywhere, and the work utilized nearly every muscle. I walked through the forest tangle each morning with a fifty-pound coil of haywire slung over my shoulder, being careful to leap across fallen logs; my legs would ache from handling the jumbled obstacle courses. It was the hardest I'd ever worked in my life, but I built up my stamina and strength."

The Alaskan forests have a legendary quality about them. Like the massive woods of the Pacific Northwest, the Alaskan scene is laden with mist and moisture. Not much light penetrates through the stately trees, and it rains often in summer.

Ketchikan, Alaska is similar to Norway's Fjord country: The trees extend from the mountain tops to the waterline and deeply wooded islands look across to the steeply ascending peaks. Southeast Alaska is richly forested with tall Sitka spruce and Western hemlock, and from a plane you can see endless conifers bordering the Cook Inlet and the areas surrounding the town of Ketchikan.

From Ketchikan, loggers travel in buses through belts of fog. The buses strain up the steep inclines and across rugged roads to the work sites. Inside the bus, some of the old-timers chew tobacco; others drink raw whiskey. The forest is a milky green world of sweet-smelling tree sap and soft rain and wet bark. It is a world with touches of Paul Bunyan, of cussing and isolation.

Tree harvesting has become highly mechanized. A six-foot tree can now be cut in two minutes by a chain saw. The harvester is designed to fell and delimb about a thousand trees per day. Hydraulic equipment often replaces human muscle for loading timber. The hydraulic log loader achieves more in minutes than three men in an hour. All-terrain vehicles and noisy tractors shatter the forest stillness. But this mechanization has not replaced loggers. For one thing, compared to equipment costs, the novice lumberjack's wages seem modest.

Several positions are considered entry level in logging. It helps if a greenhorn knows the logging language and is informed about the duties of various people. The most commonly available slot on the tree felling crew is that of *chokesetter*. The chokesetter attaches the cable to a log so that it can be moved. When the logs get to the loading area the *chaser* unhooks the choker cable. The *hooktender* is the boss of the rigging or yarding crew. Under his direction the rigging *slinger* picks logs for loading, installs and removes rigging, and coordinates the choker crew and the yarder engineer's activities. The *toploader* or *head loader* is the person in charge of loading operations. The *faller* and *bucker* cut down the trees, clean the branches off, and saw them into specified lengths. Fallers use power chain saws and may work alone or in two-man teams. The *bull buck* is a cutting crew supervisor who decides where to put each faller and estimates how much timber needs to be cut. He keeps records of each man's *scale*, the amount of timber he has cut, and keeps an inventory of the total downed timber. There are various ways to transport or *yard* the felled logs to the loading site for shipment to the mill. Most require some type of rigging system. A mechanical hoist device called a *madil tower* or *skagit* is erected at the yarding site. This tall metal tower supports the blocks and rigging hung from the top. It gives lift to the pull of the cable.

Be careful, since newcomers often forget about the real dangers of logging. "You must cope with frequent injury," advised one first-timer. "Today it was my right thumb. Last week my left knee. A lot of guys injure their shoulders. Several workers wound up in the hospital. Logging teaches respect—you're almost at war with the forest. The wilderness can wreak its revenge upon an unwary logger, snap him in half like a pretzel stick." Remember, too, that because soil conditions must be moist for trees to grow, you can assume that any area where a forest grows gets some bad weather. There are other dangers, too: you can be hit by sliding logs and by falling trees; a chain saw can slip out of your hands. A Washington State logger warns, "Chain saw blades can come apart. Tree branches can fall on you. One false step can cause a plunge down a ravine."

Accident figures bear out these statements. In a single year and a single state (Oregon), there were almost three hundred lost days due to accidents. And each Washington State season usually produces more than a hundred disabilities, some of them permanent. Hence logging operations search for "experienced" workers who come properly equipped. The lumberjacks' most important items are a pair of boots with studs to bite into the bark of fallen trees, a hard hat, and thick gloves.

Fortunately, there are many other jobs in logging that are not so dangerous, and that require little or no experience. Summer work can often be found as a road-building crewman, cook or bunkhouse flunky, dishwasher, kitchen helper, mechanic's helper, oiler, or general maintenance laborer. If there are no such vacancies, you might be able to find work temporarily in a nearby lumber mill or pulp mill. Or you might try a licensed tree-planter contractor. Tree planters employ crews of seasonal workers to help fulfill their contracts with private timber companies and with the state and federal forest service.

What You Need to Know

Participants Timber firms estimate that there are about three thousand jobs in Alaska, to name one state. Logging work demands physical strength, good health, great stamina, and a love of nature. The minimum age for paid U.S. Forest Service "temporary employees" for summer work (from May through September) or longer, is eighteen; if you're younger, you need written permission from a guardian. U.S. citizenship is essential, too. Minorities are sought for openings from coast to coast. In addition to the temporaries, a special "cooperative program" has been successful to attract a multi-ethnic group. This "cooperative program" targets inner-city young people (high-school age or older) for introduction to career opportunities. Participants receive hands-on experience in a variety of forest service jobs for seven weeks each summer. Preference is given to any applicant whose parent or sibling works for the forest service. Experience counts, of course. The bosses dread a clumsy novice who gums up the works and slows down production. If a worker doesn't do his or her job, the bosses won't hide their irritation. Too many mistakes can cause disabling accidents. In some cases, however, you can still wangle a job without lumberjack experience. You only need a degree in forestry if you'll be working as a forester. If you want to be a logger, you need no specific educational background. It's important that you be in excellent physical condition, though. *Duration* The job is so hard that nationwide only one person in a hundred sticks it out for more than one month. Lumbering is seasonal, mostly from April or May through September. Winters can be harsh; in some Alaska areas, the thermometer will plummet to fifty degrees below zero. Logging shuts down in such cold conditions. *Facilities* Live-in logging camps, once the main accommodation for loggers, are scarcer than they ever were. Most loggers live in towns like Petersburg, Ketchikan, and Sitka, Alaska; Aberdeen and Raymond, Washington; Medford, Roseburg, and Eugene, Oregon; Dubois, Wyoming; and Belgrade, Montana. *Pay* Your wages will vary, depending on where you work. For instance, in Alaska, you'll get one of the best hourly pays (but bear in mind that prices are much higher there than in other states). The wages in the Pacific Northwest are lower, and it's more difficult to find work. You'll earn the least in America's southern states. And when you think about the income of the timber barons and the stockholders of the giant lumber companies, it seems even lower. The hours can be long, but an experienced, fast logger can earn as much as $200 in a day. Some loggers prefer to get paid by the amount of lumber they cut (or "piece"). But piecework has its disadvantages. "Sometimes you have to dig for hours before you can start to cut. You only get paid for timber, and not for shoveling snow," says one piecework logger from Wyoming. *How to Apply* You can apply for work to the district ranger in charge of the nearest national forest. Or you can apply at the nearest job service or state employment office. If you're a student you can ask to be put in touch with the regional cooperative education coordinator at the nearest forest service office. Students in the areas of forestry, range management, soil science, wildlife biology, engineering, landscape architecture, hydrology, and business administration have the best placement potential. Other disciplines will be hired as needed. Otherwise you can apply in person to a logging company. Don't bother writing a letter. An employer will want to see you in person to judge how strong you are. *Other* The available work is varied. You may get hired as an assistant to record tree heights or width or to chart the contents of rain gauges. Some part-timers thin young timber stands; others work with surveyors, carrying equipment and assisting with calculations.

For Further Information

The following leads should help in your job search:

The Employment Security Division
Alaska State Department of Labor
Juneau, AK 99801

Anchorage Job Service
3301 Eagle
Anchorage, AK 99501

Alaska Loggers Association
Crazy Horse Drive
Juneau, AK 99801

Department of Labor
Anchorage Regional Office
3301 Eagle
Anchorage, AK 99510

Department of Labor
1111 West Eight
Juneau, AK 99811

Department of Labor
675 7th Avenue
Fairbanks, AK 99701

Ketchikan Pulp Company
Ketchikan, AK 99901

Ketchikan State Employment Service
Sea Level Drive
Ketchikan, AK 99901

Sitka Job Service
Cathedral Apartment Building
Sitka, AK 99835

Petersburg Employment Center
Petersburg, AK 99833

Wrangell Forest Products
Wrangell, AK 99929

Whitestone Logging
Hoonah, AK 99828

American Forest Council
1250 Connecticut Avenue, NW, Suite 320
Washington, DC 20036

Louisiana Pacific Logging Company
Breckenridge, CO 80424

Baumgartner Logging
P.O. Box 88
Eatonville, WA 98328

Manke Lumber Company, Inc.
1717 Marine View Drive, NE
Tacoma, WA 98422

Boise Cascade
Jefferson Square
Boise, ID 83702

Plum Creek Timber
Belgrade, MT 59714

Boise Cascade
P.O. Box 62
Boise, ID 83707-0062

If you're interested in logging you should know that logging is a dirty word in some quarters. The giant Wilderness Society and Sierra Club lobbies fight tree cutting, and it can sometimes get dangerous. Extremists have been known to pound nails and screws into trees in the dark of the night, causing chain saws to explode; they have poured sawdust into the gas tanks of the logging trucks, and have even pulled the spark plugs of a forklift. But these radical fanatics are the extreme. You should, however, expect demonstrations.

Washington Contract Logger's Association
P.O. Box 2168
Olympia, WA 98507-2168

Boise Cascade Lumber Company
1351 East 66th Avenue
Denver, CO 80229

Weyerhaeuser
Tacoma, WA 98477

Holbrook Inc.
Everett, WA 98201

In addition, because of the Endangered Species Act, logging has been reduced in more than eight million acres of national forests and on private lands. These cutbacks have caused other industries, including retail stores and towns near logging sites whose economy depends on the timber harvest, to suffer as well.

The controversy rages....

Zack's Forest Products
5101 228th Avenue, NE
Redmond, WA 98052

Johnson Logging
18335 SE Covington-Sawyer Road
Kent, WA 98042

Logging Information Booklet:
"Log Rules and Other Useful Information"
Northeastern Logger's Association
P.O. Box 69
Old Forge, NY 13420

Join a Tree Planting Operation

While logging doesn't supply as many jobs as in the old days, especially in the states of Washington and Oregon, the tree planting business continues to boom. Debby Price, the recruiter for the thirty-thousand-employee Weyerhaeuser Company headquartered in Tacoma, Washington, reminds job seekers that opportunities abound in the Puget Sound area. Weyerhaeuser's four Pacific Northwest tree nurseries plant some twenty million trees each year. "We replant within one year of harvesting," says Price. "This work is particularly well-suited to the person seeking adventure and exercise." Seedlings go in by machine or by hand; either way, expect to work hard.

What You Need to Know

Duration Start looking when the snow melts: usually late spring in the Pacific Northwest. Tree planting in Alaska accelerates in June and July. *Pay* Newcomers should not hold out for high wages; accept whatever you're offered. Work closely with the old-timers on the crews, and they'll guide you to more money. *How to Apply* Don't expect a response to any correspondence; it's best to show up in person.

For Further Information

Sylvia Reforestation, Inc.
P.O. Box 11228
Tacoma, WA 98411

Mineral Creek Foresters
P.O. Box 235
Mineral, WA 98355

Timberline Silvics, Inc.
P.O. Box 542
Snoqualmie, WA 98065

Newaukem Valley Tree Company, Ltd.
396 Byrd
Centralia, WA 98531

C & V Reforestation
177 Vista Road
Chehalis, WA 98532

Help Control Fires in the National Forests

"Fire! Fire!" the lookout screamed over his radio to forest headquarters. The dispatcher on duty immediately plotted the location of the raging flames. Mobilizing as though for war, people and materials were instantly moved to the fire line by truck, bus, and helicopter.

Battling forest fires requires lookouts, smoke jumpers, and firefighters. The job title, "fire lookout," says it all; you watch for forest fires and notify the firefighting team. Fire lookouts are employed by the U.S. Forest Service. Living conditions can be primitive and pay is minimal, but tending a forest makes the solitude and rugged conditions endurable.

Smoke jumpers are the first line of defense in battling forest fires. Smoke jumpers are dropped into the threatened areas from the air, and some are brought to the fire by motorized vehicle. They rotate jumps, parachuting out of the plane eight at a time, landing with a slam to the ground or a jerk back into the air if the chute catches on a tree. Leaping from small propeller planes, smoke jumpers take great risks and often suffer broken ankles.

Being a firefighter means sawing down trees and digging trench lines. You are wearing a high-collared, fire-resistant jumpsuit, ten-inch-high boots, and a helmet with a mesh grill face cover.

After the fire is out, the hard part begins. You may have to hike out over twenty miles of rough terrain, breaking trail as you go back to camp or out of the wilderness.

The hours are long, the pay is fair, and you need to love solitude. In the famous blaze of Yellowstone, over ten thousand firefighters battled the sky-high flames in roaring winds and searing heat. These jobs sure pack plenty of excitement.

What You Need to Know

Participants Most firefighters are young, aged eighteen to twenty-eight, and have had experience fighting fires with volunteer groups or in the military. *Duration* The fire season runs May through October. *Facilities* Living arrangements vary from primitive to rugged. One firefighter pays $1.75 per day to live in a Quonset hut built by other jumpers in the 1940s. This is home four months a year, unless he's on the fire line sleeping next to a tree. *Pay* A firefighter earns about $7.50 an hour, plus $1.87 per hour more for overtime and hazardous duty. *Other* Most of the jobs are west of the Mississippi. Write to the U.S. Forest Service and request a list of forests that need lookouts. If you know the name of the nearest district ranger, it will help to expedite your application. All fifty states have agreements with the U.S. Forest Service in the Cooperative Forest Control Program, which provides financial and technical assistance to the states.

For Further Information

Headquarters:
U.S. Department of Agriculture
14th and Independence Avenue, SW
South Agriculture Building
Washington, DC 20250

Regional Offices:
Northern Region:
Federal Building
Missoula, MT 59807

Rocky Mountain Region:
11177 West 8th Avenue
P.O. Box 25127
Lakewood, CO 80225

Southwestern Region:
517 Gold Avenue, SW
Albuquerque, NM 87102

Intermountain Region:
324 25th Street
Ogden, UT 84401

California Region:
630 Sansome Street
San Francisco, CA 94111

Pacific Northwest Region:
319 SW Pine Street
P.O. Box 3623
Portland, OR 97208

Southern Region:
1720 Peachtree Road, NW
Atlanta, GA 30367

Eastern Region:
310 West Wisconsin Avenue
Milwaukee, WI 53203

For information about smoke jumpers, write to:
National Interagency Fire Center
3905 Vista Avenue
Boise, ID 83705

*The National Contingent of Smoke Jumpers is maintained by
the Department of the Interior's Bureau of Land Management.*

Smoke Jumping Job Leads:
Bureau of Land Management
Department of the Interior
Washington, DC 20240

McCall Smoke Jumpers Base
P.O. Box 1026
McCall, ID 83638

Firefighter Job Leads:
U.S. Forest Service
Department of the Interior
Rocky Mountain Region
11177 West 8th Avenue
Lakewood, CO 80225

North Eastern Forest Division
P.O. Box 6775
Radnor, PA 19087-4585

Forest Lookout Job Leads:
U.S. Forest Service
South Building
12th Street & Independence Avenue, SW
Washington, DC 20240

11

Cashing in on Tourism

Go Wild at Club Med

Hey there, Monsieur, Mademoiselle: Do you speak French fluently? Have you ever been involved in the international vacation industry as a guide, a culinary-school-trained cook, a bartender? *Oui?* With a little extra experience as a stand-up comedian (especially a bilingual one), a juggler, or a nightclub deejay, you may have a chance with Club Med, the super-successful French vacation club spread over four continents. Of course, you've heard of this "antidote for civilization" which hosts almost one and a half million vacationers a year and employs twenty-three thousand versatile people in 110 "villages" or resorts.

For the guests, known here as G.M.s or *gentils membres* (gentle members), Club Med offers an abundance of diversions. You name it and they probably provide it: waterskiing, windsurfing, scuba diving, sailing, snorkeling, kayaking, archery, tennis, Ping-Pong, horseback riding, aerobics classes, volleyball, rock climbing, arts and crafts, supervised jogging, even a circus workshop. You get out of breath just thinking of so many activities.

For the staff, here known as G.O.s or *gentils organizateurs* (gentle organizers), all these sports signify jobs, especially in summer, when Americans, Canadians, Europeans, and Asians go on vacation. Club Med also needs housekeepers, hotel registration clerks, dance instructors, computer teachers, and basketball referees, all of whom must be flexible enough to handle other jobs as well. There's a rah-rah cheeriness about the Club's atmosphere because of the rapport between the G.M.s and G.O.s. G.O.s mingle with the gentils membres in sports, at mealtime, and at night in the discos or the fast-paced cabarets. And after one week of reveling, a fresh bunch of guests arrive, to be instructed and entertained anew.

For the guests, Club Med is convenient enough, what with the sports, recreation, entertainment, and the socializing being included in one tariff. But the tariff is exorbitantly high, and corners are cut (for instance, most beds are singles, and singles must have roommates, or are charged extra). The food can be outstanding but it can also be lousy; often the buffet stands in the blazing sun for many hours.

The G.O.s always have their hands full, teaching some activity, arranging competitions and then at night doubling as magicians, jugglers, singers, dancers, and the like. In short, you need to be adaptable and you need plenty of stamina to be a G.O. What's more, the French-owned Club Med requires that you *parles Français,* and if possible, several other languages.

The "villages" occupy some of the planet's most idyllic spots: Tahiti (where members run around in sarongs); Guadeloupe's Caravelle; Paradise Island in the Bahamas; Sandpiper in Florida; Ixtapa, Playa Blanca, and Cancun in Mexico; and many more.

Applicants would be wise to study the "Profile Evaluation Form" which reveals all except the salary; the latter is Club Med's closely-guarded secret. But what a way to spend a summer!

What You Need to Know

Participants The G.M.s are all ages; in recent years, the Club has even encouraged children to participate. As for employment (as G.O.s or

Profile Evaluation Form

The following checklist will help us better evaluate your qualifications to work as a Club Med G.O. Please check all applicable boxes.

❏ I speak French fluently	❏ have over 1 year culinary school or work experience	❏ over 3 years tennis instruction experience
❏ I speak Spanish fluently	❏ have over 1 year baking school/work experience	❏ have organized tennis tournaments
❏ I speak Italian fluently	❏ have over 1 year pastry school/work experience	❏ over 3 years sailing instruction experience
❏ I speak German fluently	❏ have over 2 years food & beverage management school/work experience	❏ have over 2 years restaurant management school/work experience
❏ I speak Japanese fluently	❏ over 3 years waterski instruction experience	❏ have performed in waterski shows
❏ I have more than 3 years retail experience	❏ over 2 years plumbing work experience	❏ over 3 years horseback riding instruction experience
❏ I am able to work a cash register	❏ over 2 years electrical work experience	❏ can ride Western style
❏ I have more than 1 year of bank cashier experience	❏ over 2 years carpentry work experience	❏ can ride English style
❏ I have current infant CPR certification	❏ over 2 years air conditioning repair work experience	❏ have over 1 year dressage/jumping experience
❏ I have current lifeguard certification	❏ over 2 years industrial/hotel landscaping work experience	❏ PSIA certified snowski instructor
❏ I have minimum 1 year nursery care experience	❏ over 2 years industrial/ hotel housekeeping work experience	❏ over 4 years snowski instructor experience
❏ if R.N., I have at least 2 years E.R. experience	❏ over 2 years of Lotus 1,2,3 or other spreadsheet software experience	❏ extensive basketball officiating experience
❏ I have more than 1 year trilingual tourguide experience (French/English/Spanish)	❏ over 2 years of Wordperfect or other word processing software experience	❏ extensive volleyball officiating experience
❏ I have more than 2 years bartending experience	❏ over 1 year bilingual secretary (French/English experience)	❏ extensive softball officiating experience
❏ over 1 year flying and/or catching on a trapeze	❏ over 1 year travel agency related experience	❏ over 3 years windsurfing instruction experience
❏ over 1 year converting foreign currency experience	❏ over 1 year of front desk hotel reception experience	❏ currently certified as PADI or NAUI open-water diver
❏ over 1 year full time theatre lighting	❏ current aerobic instructor certification	❏ currently certified as PADI divemaster
❏ over 1 year full time theatre set design	❏ over 1 year night club DJ experience	❏ currently certified as PADI SCUBA instructor
❏ over 1 year full time theatre sound	❏ over 1 year mobile DJ experience	❏ certified massage therapist
❏ over 1 year full time theatre costume design	❏ over 1 year radio DJ experience	❏ over 2 years masseur/euse experience
❏ able to design and sew clothes	❏ over 1 year of stand-up comedy experience	❏ over 1 year of clowning experience/training
❏ over 2 years choreographing experience	❏ over 3 years ballet dance classes	❏ over 3 years jazz classes
❏ over 2 years modeling experience	❏ over 2 years varsity cheerleading experience	❏ able to work in United States (US Citizen or have Green Card)
❏ I have served in the Armed Forces	❏ I can play a musical instrument instrument: _____	❏ I have vacationed at Club Med

otherwise), the Club lists no minimum age requirement, though the youngest tend to be seventeen or eighteen years old. Of course, you must have an outgoing personality, and it helps if, apart from French, you speak another foreign language. *Duration* Since it takes a while to get to the faraway villages, the gentils organizateurs should try to stay for at least one month; most stay for an entire summer. Winter jobs are available in the Caribbean, Pacific, and in Colorado, if you have free time. *Facilities* Most employees share rooms with single beds. Meals are included and plentiful. *Pay* Though Club Med won't release their salary figures, they're not known for paying generously. On the other hand, they provide their employees with great quantities of food, wine, sports, and social activities.

For Further Information

Club Med
3 East 54th Street
New York, NY 10022

Club Med
106-110 Brompton Road
London SW3 1JJ

Ride the Disney Scene

People either love or hate the famous, folksy Disney theme parks, Mickey Mouse, Goofy, Donald Duck, and all. If you think that Disneyland and Disney World are just a lot of artificiality, with a touch of kitsch or ineffective make-believe for little kids, then read no further. Otherwise, you might consider a summer at one of these wonderlands.

Since the Parks stay open from 8:00 A.M. to 1:00 A.M., they require a big staff. Some thirty thousand summer jobs are available at the two Disneys for the asking. To become one of the employees you'll have to come in to the "casting office" (personnel office) for a personal interview. And the Disney CIA will know right quick whether you're sincere.

Walt Disney World near Orlando, Florida is a twenty-nine-hundred-acre complex with umpteen hotels, almost fifty bars, scads of night-clubs, discos, rides (known there as "adventures"), shops and more shops, plus a ninety million dollar aquarium with four thousand sea creatures. All the attractions require clean-cut employees who are eager to work long hours with a smile.

Disneyland in California is smaller but employs eight thousand people including many college students (sorry, no high school students here). They get sixteen thousand applications for the eight thousand jobs. Some folks work full-time in the summer; others, in turn, are hired only part-time; still others toil the year-round for Disney. Whatever your desire, many employment slots are interchangeable; you may be parking cars one week, working as a ticket seller the next, and running around in a sweaty, zany Disney costume the next. Young people also help in the public relations office and with the rides, sell popcorn in the snack bars, and work an endless assortment of other jobs. There are even more possibilities at Disney World, with its Epcot Center-Pleasure Island where about thirty thousand are gainfully employed. Although the basic pay there is modest, perks include meal discounts, free tickets on your day off, and sometimes lodging.

One former employee described it to me as "like being in the Army, with rules and more rules."

What's a Disney staffer, known as a "cast member," really like? Who gets hired? Who gets fired? The Disney people let it be known officially that they like enthusiastic, energetic, neat, positive, friendly young people who must, repeat, *must* be "clean-cut." Naturally, employees have to be believers in the Disney product.

Disneyland and Disney World also offer a "college relations" program for students who live too far away to apply in person. The program travels throughout the U.S. offering interviews at colleges and universities. For a summer working at Disneyland or Disney World, you are provided with subsidized housing and an opportunity for college credit. Write to Disneyland and request the school visitation schedule.

Euro Disneyland is controversial; the French press love to hate it. But it's still a great source for summer employment. Euro Disney employs twenty thousand people. Like Disneyland, Disney World, and Epcot Center, a personal visit may be necessary to get a job there. They are looking for the same characteristics as the other Disneys: clean-cut students with good people skills, and students majoring in recreation, communication, or hotel management. But unless you are fluent in French, can prove previous Disney experience, and have solid references, it's unlikely you can get on the Euro Disney payroll.

What You Need to Know

Participants Disney's staff is made up of enthusiastic, clean-cut college students with high energy and a good attitude. *Duration* The hiring of Disney's seasonal employees is done year-round. Full-time and part-time employment are available. *Facilities* "Cast members" get discounted employee meals, free costume and uniform laundering, a free subscription to the employee publication, access to the parking shuttle, and a locker. Employees can take advantage of a flexible scheduling policy. Those in the college relations program also get subsidized housing. All employees are admitted to the parks for free on their days off and can purchase reduced admissions guest passes. Membership is available in an employee credit union, and all can take advantage of a flexible job transfer policy. *Other* Credits are available to students participating in co-op education.

For Further Information

Disneyland
Anaheim, CA 92803

Euro Disneyland
Marne-la Vallee, France

Walt Disney World
P.O. Box 10000
Lake Buena Vista, FL 32830-1000

Walt Disney World College Relations Department
P.O. Box 10090
Lake Buena Vista, FL 32830-0090

Set Sail as the Member of a Cruise Ship Staff

Sea of Cortes on a beautiful day: You're on deck, under the incredibly blue Mexican sky. Moving at about twenty knots, you can see the golden beaches drawing past. The captain steers closer to the shore now. You're just two miles away from the coast. Yesterday, you put into Mazatlan. Tonight it will be Cabo San Lucas.

On Monday, you sail to Acapulco, then to Puerto Vallarta. During some weeks, you're in the Caribbean. Or maybe all summer long, you steam through scenic Alaskan waters or explore Scandinavia. As assistant purser, you handle the nuts and bolts for passengers from behind a comfortable desk, somewhat like the front desk of a hotel. The ship is a floating resort. And while your cabin is small, the food in the special staff dining room is excellent.

Wherever they go, cruise vessels travel at a moderate speed to avoid pitching and rolling. Moreover, the entire cruise industry is based on selecting ports in good weather zones; this way you get the maximum sunshine.

The hours are longer than if you worked at a hotel. You're on duty seven days a week. Twelve-hour shifts are common at sea. On the other hand, you're going home on vacation after several months and you get a land-based furlough; in fact, the cruise line pays for your flight home.

Nowadays the crew on a ship is a mini-United Nations. Take the *Sagafjord*, for example. The ship's captain, the officers on the bridge, and the technical staff are all Norwegian. Of the 350-person crew, Austrians rank first in number with forty-four people, including the cruise ship's superb chefs and cooks. They hail from Vienna or Graz or Salzburg.

Another thirty-five—mostly waiters—are Germans. The wine stewards are French and Belgian. The casino personnel are Americans who last worked in Las Vegas. Your cabin is being cleaned and restocked by Swedish, Danish, and Dutch women.

This internationalization is a trend that demands attention. On the twenty-four-thousand-ton Cunard ship, an all-Polish, six-man orchestra plays for the passengers' dancing pleasure, and at the afternoon tea hour the dance instructors have thick French accents. The Golden Door Spa is an import from California; two American women teach aerobics in the ship's gym. What a remarkable mix! What a babble of languages! Nowadays, most ships are like this.

The international approach to hiring prevails on other vessels as well. The fast *QE 2* was built by Swedish shipwrights. Its officers are British while the crew come from some two dozen nations including Honduras, the Philippines, Spain—and the U.S. Other cruise lines, often for practical reasons, ask recruiters to pick the staff to match some of the passengers' nationalities. The Dutch liners, for example, employ Dutch pursers; the P&O lines get many British passengers and use a British crew.

The *Sagafjord*, *Vistafjord*, and other Cunard vessels merrily sail the seven seas. You can cruise to such exotic ports as Pago Pago, Tonga, Bali, and Bangkok; for people who prefer to sail "closer to home," there is the popular Alaska Inside Passage.

In general, musicians, dance instructors, disk jockeys, beauty parlor staff, and cruise directors are Americans; ditto for the various lecturers (who speak on investments, handwriting analysis, and the like), and bridge and other card game instructors. Ships that sail under the American flag naturally offer the best opportunities for Americans. On such vessels, American unions may be involved; they have their own quirks, of course. In general, the pay is modest but you get free travel, lots of adventure, plus room and board.

Most cruise ship companies do not advertise for employees, so it's up to you to present yourself and your qualifications in a convincing manner. The majority of experts also point out that you need resourcefulness and perseverance. Which jobs are the easiest to get? Most ships have a good turnover, and therefore have room for entertainers of all kinds, beauty parlor personnel, casino staff, shipboard boutique sales-women, aerobics instructors, and professional photographers.

Begin by drawing up an impressive résumé that aims at one of the above slots. Call on the personnel departments of the cruise lines. Try to get an interview. Keep trying. And be ready to sail on a moment's notice. . . .

For Further Information

Admiral Cruises/Royal Caribbean Cruises
903 South America Way
Miami, FL 33132

American Hawaii Cruises
550 Kearny Street
San Francisco, CA 94108

Chandris/Celebrity Cruises
900 Third Avenue
New York, NY 10022

Classical Cruises
132 East 70th Street
New York, NY 10021

Commodore Cruise Line
800 Douglas Road, Suite 600
Coral Gables, FL 33134

Costa Cruises
World Trade Center
P.O. Box 019614
Miami, FL 33101-9865

Crown Cruise Line
Crown Courtesy
P.O. Box 10265
Riviera Beach, FL 33419

Crystal Cruises
2121 Avenue of the Stars, Suite 200
Los Angeles, CA 90067

Cunard Line
28-21 Jackson Avenue
Long Island City, NY 10011

Delta Queen Steamboat Company
30 Robin Street Wharf
New Orleans, LA 70130

Dolphin Cruise Line
Passenger Service
1007 North America Way, Suite 114
Miami, FL 33132

Epirotiki Lines
551 Fifth Avenue, Room 605
New York, NY 10176

Holland America Line Westours
300 Elliot Avenue West
Seattle, WA 98119

Norwegian Cruise Line
95 Merrick Way
Coral Gables, FL 33134

Royal Viking Cruise Line
95 Merrick Way
Coral Gables, FL 33134

Ocean Cruise Lines/Pearl Cruises
1510 SE 17th Street
Fort Lauderdale, FL 33316

Paquet French Cruise Lines
1510 SE 17th Street
Fort Lauderdale, FL 33316

Premier Cruise Lines
P.O. Box 573
Cape Canaveral, FL 32920

Princess Cruises
10100 Santa Monica Boulevard
Los Angeles, CA 90067-4189

Regency Cruises
260 Madison Avenue, 15th Floor
New York, NY 10016

Royal Cruise Line
Passenger Service
One Maritime Plaza, Suite 1400
San Francisco, CA 94111

Seabourn Cruise Line
55 Francisco Street, Suite 710
San Francisco, CA 94133

Seafarer's International Union
636 Cook Street
Honolulu, HI 96813

Sun Line Cruises
1 Rockefeller Plaza, Suite 315
New York, NY 10020

World Explorer Cruises
555 Montgomery Street, Suite 1001
San Francisco, CA 94111

Join a Sailing Schooner Adventure

The brochures are seductive: "How can we describe a Maine wind-jammer vacation? It is the sun sparkling off the waves, the smell of bacon cooking in the morning, the eerie sound of a bell buoy in the fog, the warm scent of fir trees coming over the water, a hot deck under your feet, salt on your lips, endless stars in a clear sky, a hot mug of coffee on deck in the early morning, the easy motion of the schooner as she scuds along on a broad reach, the rattle of the anchor chain, the tingle of windburn after a stiff day's sail, the warmth and companionship in the main cabin on a cool evening, a heap of steaming lobster on the shore, jokes told on the after deck, that first cold dip in the ocean, exhilaration, total relaxation."

One ship, the *Roseway* is described in equally romantic terms: "Come aboard a proud vessel that has sailed the seas for most of this century. Stand on her solid decks with a good breeze abeam, and you'll understand the thrill of cruising on a true Tall Ship. Even if you've never sailed before, you'll love it."

The sailing ships are indeed magnificent and far different from regular cruise ships with their hundreds—often thousands—of people. Schooners take on ten to a hundred passengers at the most, in addition to the very busy crew. And while normal cruise vessels, say the *QE2*, are enormous, with lots of deck and adequate cabin space, sailing schooners are claustrophobic, often small rooms with only a shared shower down the hall (there are no private facilities). "Windjamming" makes for laid-back, non-dressy type of cruising; people often sleep right on the beautiful wooden decks, the sails flapping overhead.

The voyages usually last three days, a week, or a couple of weeks, after which new passengers come aboard. There is never a boring moment for the crew.

The schooners employ one or two crew members to serve as cook, kitchen helper, deckhand, meal server, cabin cleaner, and bartender. Most of the time, the captain acts as personnel manager; find out the skipper's name and send him or her a good résumé.

What You Need to Know

Participants Schooners are looking for workers with "an outgoing personality," a lot of energy, and a good appearance. The passengers, usually in their thirties, are slightly older than the crew, some of whom just completed high school, or are junior college or college students. *Duration* Some of the selections are made in early spring and you need to be available from May through at least October. *Facilities* There are no private facilities—you'll share a cabin and a shower. You'll also get all the food you can eat. Dress is casual, and the atmosphere is laid back. *Pay* Pay is usually minimum wage, plus tips.

For Further Information

Maine Windjammer Association
P.O. Box 317
Rockport, ME 04856

Maine Windjammer Cruises
P.O. Box 617
Camden, ME 04843

Rockport Schooner Cruises
P.O. Box 247
Rockport, ME 04856

Windjammer Barefoot Cruises
P.O. Box 120
Miami Beach, FL 33119-9983

Windstar Sail Cruises
7415 NW 19th Street
Miami, FL 33126

Spend a Summer on the Beach

"Boundless, endless and sublime," wrote Byron about the sea, "thou glorious mirror...."

"I must go to the seas again, for the call of the running tide is a wild call that may not be denied," said Poet John Masefield.

Some lifeguards get so absorbed by the constantly changing seashore, by the fluctuating moods and colors of the ocean, that their day passes quickly. The sand line stretches or narrows with the tides. Surfers, beachcombers, scuba instructors, swimming teachers, and sailing instructors are all continually drawn to the water.

The U.S. has twenty thousand miles of beaches. Not all ocean people view the Pacific, Atlantic, or Gulf of Mexico as an irresistible magnet. To some people, the beach is just a nice place to earn a little cash in summer. Some perceive it as a place to meditate, to be alone. Others, conversely, see the sands as a place to meet for romance.

What does a lifeguard (or "beach guard") do all day? A Clearwater, Florida supervisor explains: "Beach guard responsibilities are diverse on Clearwater Beach. First and foremost is watching the water and trying to spot danger areas in an attempt to prevent accidents from occur-

Clive Cussler, author of the bestselling novel Raise the Titanic, was in his twenties when he chucked a promising career as a West Coast adman to take a job in a beachside diving gear store at a salary of a few hundred dollars a month.

His mind was so freed by the new environment that he started to write in earnest, and created novels that made him a millionaire.

ring. Also, beach guards must constantly 'keep the peace' on the beach, find lost kids, find lost parents, answer questions, train daily, move equipment and much, much more. Last year there were approximately thirty-five swim rescues on Clearwater Beach. Of those, probably close to a dozen incidents were potentially life threatening."

Seaside jobs are among the healthiest summer job options. A lifeguard runs or jogs every day. A swimming instructor also gets plenty of exercise. The person who takes care of surfboards for a hotel can probably find time to surf.

The lifeguard, also known as a Water Safety Officer or a Beach Guard, is the most common beach job. Of course, they work not only on beaches but at swimming pools as well. The American Red Cross, which certifies the lifeguards by testing their first aid knowledge and swimming ability, offers no exact figures on summer employment, though one American Red Cross official claims "Thousands!"

Your employer can be a major seaside hotel, a city recreation department, a parks department, a private beach club, a state agency, even a federal agency in charge of a national seashore. In Florida, the local community or county does the lifeguard recruitment. In Hawaii, the parks and recreation departments hire.

Apart from hotels with swimming pools, lifeguards can also apply to YMCAs, health clubs, and country clubs. Many people prefer the ocean, however. And certain U.S. beaches enjoy a perennial popularity. The bigger the crowds, the more lifeguards needed.

The trick is to show up long before the season, to get acquainted with the other paid ocean watchers, and to ask the employed lifeguards about the beach scene. In some areas, you should apply in January for a June position. Remember there are beaches that are so desirable that the same individuals return year after year. One typical example: Hawaii. According to Betty Krauss, a travel expert on the islands, it takes great luck to find lifeguard employment in Hawaii. Beaches in the South and New England are more likely places for this kind of seasonal work.

According to Joe Lain, the water safety supervisor of Clearwater, Florida, "The procedure for becoming a beach guard on Clearwater

Beach is as follows. First, candidates must provide the City of Clearwater Human Resources Office copies of current American Red Cross Lifeguard Training, Standard First Aid, and CPR cards. After that, candidates complete a standard job application and are put on a 'referral list.' At this point I begin contacting each candidate and try and set up a time for our water test." The various American Red Cross papers are a requirement all over the U.S.

It's also a given that you take a specialized physical fitness test. A typical one was described by Joe Lain: "The test consists of a 220-yard open water swim followed by a five-minute rest. Next is a dismount from a beach lifeguard tower and a swim out to a buoy a hundred yards offshore followed by a five-minute rest. Next, a mile run. Last, candidates are asked to perform a simulated rescue. All events are timed and notes are taken with emphasis on candidates' skills, knowledge of currents, general conditioning and so forth. At this point, if candidates have passed our 'water test,' they are interviewed and we choose those best-suited to our overall program."

If this doesn't work out, you may consider working at a surf shop or as a cabana helper (giving out towels, renting cabins, helping with chairs, etc.); someone also has to be in charge of the marinas and keep track of rental sailboats or motorboats.

If nothing else works, you can always wander along beaches after sundown to gather the coins, books, combs, and other trinkets that people left behind.

What You Need to Know

Participants With minor differences, the requirements around the country are similar. You must be a good swimmer; if you've taken part in competitive meets, so much the better. You may have to take a fitness test. You should take the complete American Red Cross Basic Water Safety, Basic Rescue, lifesaving courses, and of course, CPR. Most of this will be covered in the classes for certification as a WSI (Water Safety Instructor). Check the phone book in the nearest city for the American Red Cross address. In general, you must have at least nine hours of the Basic First Aid Course or better still, the Advanced First Aid and Emergency certificate. Advanced lifesaving courses will result in the Red Cross Advanced Lifesaving Certificate and better chances for the better jobs. Your vision must be at least 20/40. In addition, there's usually a residence requirement; you need to live in the area where you want to be employed, so if you don't live in Hawaii, for instance, you shouldn't even apply. *Pay* The pay differs from coast to coast, depending on budgets. Your check can vary from minimum wage to $1,700 per month for full-time people.

For Further Information

Some Major U.S. Beaches:

Huntington Beach, California

Laguna Beach, California

La Jolla Cove Park, San Diego, California

Malibu Beach, California

Point Reyes NH Seashore, California

Cocoa Beach, Florida

Miami Beach, Florida

Poipu Beach, Kauai, Hawaii

Ocean City, Maryland

National Seashore, Cape Cod, Massachusetts

Hampton Beach, New Hampshire

Asbury Park, New Jersey

Atlantic Beach, Long Island, New York

Lido Beach, Long Island, New York

Jones Beach, Long Island, New York

South Padre Island, Texas

Galveston, Texas

Virginia Beach, Virginia

Some Major Hotels with Beaches and Pools:
The Tides Inn & Lodge
Irvington, VA 22480

The Colony Beach & Tennis Resort
Sarasota, FL 33578

Sonesta Beach Hotel
Key Biscayne, FL 33149

Marco Beach Hotel & Villas
Marco Island, FL 33937

Holiday Inn Hilton Head Racquet Club
Hilton Head, SC 29928

The Breakers
Palm Beach, FL 33480

Sea Pines Plantation
Hilton Head Island, SC 29948

Grand Hotel
Point Clear, AL 36564

Mauna Kea Beach Hotel
Kamuela, HI 96743

Coco Palms Resort
Wailua Beach, Kauai, HI 96791

Be a Tour Guide or Tour Escort

The bus roars down Interstate 70, catching the sun, gleaming as it starts its climb toward Berthoud Pass, Grand Lake, and the Rocky Mountain National Park. Shiny modern tour buses visit Cape Cod, Vermont, and Quebec. You've seen the buses all over the U.S. and perhaps wondered, what is it like to accompany such a tour? Could you possibly get a job as a tour escort? Or be a local guide on a sightseeing bus?

Both are possible for outgoing, well-groomed, knowledgeable men and women who are twenty-one years old or older. Tour escorts need to know the areas they operate in well; they must have poise and leadership qualities. After all, the escorts (also known as tour managers) handle all the nuts and bolts and emergencies for a group.

This seasonal employment offers all kinds of opportunities for calm, well-organized local folks who can get along with the bus passengers. Good health, stamina, and genuine friendliness are other desirable traits. And knowing a foreign language, especially Japanese, German, French, or Spanish, gives you an edge over other applicants.

Bigtime tour operators like American Express hire as many as six hundred tour escorts worldwide every summer. In addition, local guides are often utilized: These guides come aboard to talk about the museums, monuments, churches, and fountains of a city.

The guides are versed in history and art and often have college degrees in these fields. The escort is responsible for the guides showing up, as well as for the luggage and the overall schedule. I remember a long German bus tour where our escort personally knocked on our hotel door at 6:00 or, at the latest, 7:00 every morning to get us up for the day's trip.

Despite being on call for practically twenty-four hours a day, the life of the tour manager (another term for tour guide) isn't all bad: like the clients, the escorts stay at spiffy hotels, eat first-class meals, receive an adequate salary and lots of tips. They travel a lot; one career tour escort told me that he's accompanied buses through most of the European countries dozens and dozens of times. He retired at age seventy, with comfortable savings. And he worked only in the summer.

For an American citizen, it's not too difficult to get hired as an escort or guide in the U.S. It just takes a well-worded résumé, good looks, and enough persistence.

It is much harder to be taken on as tour manager or city guide in Europe, unless you've been in the particular country for a long time, know several languages, and are familiar with all the local attractions. In most foreign cities, American-born managers are kept out by a special tour guides' association, and the big companies—like American Express—all have long lists of native applicants for the European routes.

Still, there's room for the resourceful lone operator. Some eager Americans have found themselves an automobile load of tourists or students, homemakers, or even dentists, and they drive merrily back and forth between places like New York and Mexico City or Paris and the Riviera.

One long-time world traveler claims that he met entrepreneurs in Africa, Asia, and South America who take clients on tours in Volkswagen buses or larger vehicles. These freelancers find their customers by advertising in student newspapers and in foreign centers like Istanbul, Kathmandu, Nairobi, and Cuzco, Peru. And in Switzerland, an American operator leads hikers through the Alps all summer. He does this on a freelance basis, charges an arm and a leg for a six-day outing, and even gets Swissair to distribute brochures for him.

Tour escorts find as much pleasure in the human relations part of the job as in the travel itself. "It's fascinating to observe what happens in a group," observes a retired American tour escort in England. "By sharing an experience for the first time, passengers who were perfect strangers at the beginning become friends by the end of the trip. And they get close to the manager. I still correspond with many people who've been on tours with me."

What You Need to Know

Participants The minimum age is between eighteen and twenty, depending on the company. Applicants must have good looks and a pleasant personality. Knowledge of other languages is a plus, even in the U.S. (because there are a lot of foreign tourists). *Duration* Work lasts all summer long (this is known as the high season). *Facilities* Free accommodations plus meals at good hotels. *Pay* You'll earn $500 to $1,500 a month, plus tips. But the hours are long and the responsibilities great.

For Further Information

Alaska Nature Tours
P.O. Box 491
Haines, AK 99827

American Express
65 Broadway
New York, NY 10006

American Express
19-20 Berners Street
London W1P 3DD England

Cross Cultural Adventures
P.O. Box 3285
Arlington, VA 22203

Five Star Touring
60 East 42d Street, Suite 612
New York, NY 10165

Globus Tours
727 West 7th Street
Los Angeles, CA 90017

Perillo Tours
Woodcliff Lake, NJ 07675

Work for a Hotel or Resort

While tourists shell out up to two thousand dollars per week to vacation, *you* could spend the whole summer in holiday land, being paid while enjoying luxury hotels.

The resort may well be the ideal place for young people looking for summer work. Tourism is one typical industry that relies on seasonal labor during the summer months. Do you have experience waiting tables, house cleaning, or in retail sales? Even if you're inexperienced, you can easily get a job.

Students flock by the thousands to summer resorts like Cape Cod, Massachusetts; Atlantic City, New Jersey; and the newly legalized low-stakes gambling casino cities in Colorado, small-scale copies of Reno, Nevada. These areas hire young people who are eighteen years old to do a multitude of odd jobs such as cooking, waiting and busing tables in restaurants, changing sheets, and vacuuming hotel rooms. Young waitpersons serve lunches to guests in hotels and Bed and Breakfasts (B&Bs). They work at reservation desks in resort hotels, meeting interesting people. They sell swimsuits and bikinis at beachside boutiques, and much, much more. And don't forget the large ski areas—Stowe, Vermont; and Aspen and Vail, Colorado—which also go into high gear during the summer season; cumulatively, they provide thousands of jobs.

You can be employed with other youth in the most desirable regions of the country: along the nation's seashores, in mountains, along scenic highways. What does it take? A pleasant personality, a healthy body, and a willingness to please and take care of tourists. You may toil long odd hours, following typical tourists' schedules: late breakfast, late lunch, late dinner. Employee housing is sometimes provided by the resorts themselves, but the key to the job—and a factor in its desirability—is securing housing ahead of time. One-season resorts like Cape Cod have major bed shortages during the summer months.

Mackinac Island

Visitors in the 1880s raved about "the place where heaven and earth glow with light and color"; the pristine lake waters inspired early poets, and travelers praised the "Eden-fresh air."

Mackinac Island (pronounced Mackinaw), the object of such rapture, sits at the juncture of Lake Michigan and Lake Huron. But its remoteness makes you think of Nova Scotia or perhaps Nantucket. Mackinac's harbor meanwhile reminds one of picturesque Rockport, Massachusetts. The Michigan island has also been compared to Martha's Vineyard, upscale Hilton Head, South Carolina, and elegant Newport, Rhode Island. All of these maritime getaways hire for the summer.

There is one major difference, though. Mackinac Island allows no cars. This makes it unique; you awaken to the *clop-clop* of hoofs as draft-horses pull hotel carriages, or "taxis," supplies, and excursion surveys. Six hundred horses do their duty here in summer. This means job openings if you like horses.

There is much to see on this eight-mile long, 2,200-acre isle, with a resident population of six hundred. Some travelers rent their own horse and buggy or saddle horses from the local stables. (This again requires staff.) The most popular touring is by bicycle. Some twenty miles of good Michigan roads—all carless—cross assorted cedar, spruce, fir, and birch forests; luckily, most of the island is a state park and the state here believes in preservation, which means no camping, hunting, or flower picking. There are healthy walks under chestnut trees or along the lakeshores on boardwalks.

Now more than a century old, the Grand Hotel appeals to an older clientele. It is dressy; suit and tie are required at night. Overlooking a hillside, the hotel sits among magnificent floral gardens of twenty thousand tulips and five thousand geraniums, roses, daffodils, and begonias. This means employment for gardeners.

Most of the twelve hundred or so hotel rooms overlook the beautiful Great Lakes. The white Victorian buildings, most dating back to 1780 or 1875, have been meticulously kept up. The summer cottages, the private houses, and the bed and breakfasts couldn't be prettier.

The 311-room Grand Hotel remains not only Mackinac Island's largest but also its most spectacular, glamorous, and charismatic hostelry. The white pine facade and the enormous white Grecian columns yielding the world's longest porch are indeed impressive. The hotel employs at least two hundred people in summer.

The Grand's public rooms, with their rare etchings, original paintings, and objets d'art—not to mention the music of harpists and pianists—add a touch of elegant nostalgia. Bellhops are sought in June, July, and August to carry luggage. The food is good; every summer, the hotel recruits dining room waiters by the dozen.

Like most of the hotels, the Grand closes in early November and re-opens in late May. The fresh air, the blue tranquil lakes, the varied accommodations, and the healthful activities make Michigan's Mackinac Island an ideal place to work. The absence of cars gives it a special, unforgettable character.

Other Areas

Beyond Mackinac, the resort and convention areas of Waikiki Beach, Honolulu; Ft. Lauderdale, Florida; Estes Park, Colorado; Las Vegas, Nevada; New York City and the Catskills, New York; or hotels like the Wentworth-by-the-Sea, New Hampshire; the Beverly Wilshire, California; The Broadmoor, Colorado Springs all gobble up staff in summer. The choice is yours as to what job to apply for and which area is most tempting for you.

If you know a city and a resort thoroughly, you might consider applying as a concierge; this position has become more and more popular at five-star hotels and resorts. Concierges give guests local information, arrange for sports outings, get tickets to musical events, local theater, and other entertainment. They must know details about local restaurants. The salary is sufficient, and tips can be excellent. Large resort hotels also scout for personnel clerks, human resource secretaries, food and beverage people, computer programmers, electricians, plumber's helpers, desk clerks, cashiers, bartenders, barmaids, locksmiths, security guards, telephone operators, and dish-washers.

Always apply early; April is a good time to start. Write to the local tourist office, ask for brochures, then contact or visit the individual establishments.

For Further Information

The following are a few well-known summer resorts that can be contacted by mail:

West:
Central City/Black Hawk
Central City, CO 80427

Telluride Resort
Telluride, CO 81435

Aspen
Aspen, CO 81612

Keystone
Keystone, CO 80435

Steamboat Springs
Steamboat Springs, CO 80487

Vail
Vail, CO 81658

Alta
Alta, UT 84092

Deer Valley
Park City, UT 84060

Park City
Park City, UT 84060

Sun Valley
Sun Valley, ID 83353

Taos Ski Valley
Taos Ski Valley, NM 87525

Jackson Hole
Teton Village, WY 83025

Heavenly Valley
South Lake Tahoe, CA 95705

Mammoth Mountain
Mammoth Lakes, CA 93546

Northstar/Tahoe
Truckee, CA 96160

Squaw Valley
Olympic Valley, CA 95730

Mt. Bachelor
Bend, OR 97709

East:
Sugarloaf
Kingfield, ME 04947

Killington
Killington, VT 05751

Stowe (Mt. Mansfield)
Stowe, VT 05672

Cape Cod
Hyannis, MA 02601

Atlantic City
Atlantic City, NJ 08401

Bolton Valley Resort
VT 05477

Stratton Mountain
VT 05155

Sugarbush Valley
VT 05674

Lake Placid
NY 12946

Waterville Valley
NH 03223

Cape Cod
Hyannis, MA 02686

Midwest:
Boyne Mountain
MI 49713

Mackinac Island
MI 49757

South:

Hilton Head Island
SC 29928

South Padre Island
TX 78597

Innisbrook Resort
Tarpon Springs, FL 34286

Virginia Beach
VA 23450

Palm Beach
Florida 33480

Meet New People as You Wait Tables

The scene has a postcard prettiness: light blue sky with a tiny flock of clouds over the calm green-blue ocean lapping the beaches of Cape Cod. A magnificent lodge where guests pay $250 a night. The colonial-style, three-story building, impeccably white, is freshly painted each spring for summer use.

And in the bright dining room, with white tablecloths and sparkling silver, the guests dine on crab cakes or baby lobsters, sometimes washed down by California wines.

The waiters and waitresses work for a few weeks in summer. The job is easy to learn: the dining room manager shows the new people where to place forks, knives, and spoons, how to fold the linen napkins, and from which side to serve.

The lodge-hotel charges customers a fifteen percent service charge but the wait persons also get tips from generous luncheon and dinner guests: a second basket of fresh French bread, a second platter of butter rosettes, or advice on what to order can do tipping wonders.

Should you consider a summer waiting on tables? Opportunities fairly jump at you at many restaurants and summer vacation resorts; in certain states, especially Colorado, Wyoming, and Montana, wait staff is much needed. Personality, an eager smile, and a pleasing demeanor help to secure the job; in many cases employee housing is furnished.

Here's how to proceed: in spring (by the end of March), write to the three tourist offices (listed below), requesting their lists of hotels, then contact the hotels directly with a brief typed letter. Describe your skills and send a photo of yourself. Be sure to include your phone number.

Many hotels close on Labor Day, which is an ideal setup for a student. Income is adequate. But the adventure also has to do with the customers: fascinating and wealthy men and women, sometimes from other countries, make the experience interesting. Many foreigners are interested in practicing their English language skills, and the Americans are often friendly; some seek to get acquainted with the staff, if only to find out about the best places to go in the area. Friendships also develop among the young waitpersons.

For Further Information

Colorado Tourism Board
1625 Broadway, Suite 1700
Denver, CO 80202

Montana Promotion Division
Department of Commerce
1424 Ninth Avenue
Helena, MT 59620-0411

Wyoming Travel Commission
Frank Norris Jr. Travel Center
I-25 & College Drive
Cheyenne, WY 82002-0660

Be an Au Pair Overseas

Being an au pair is certainly one route to a foreign country for a few months. Ads appear regularly in the *International Herald Tribune* which is published in Paris and available all over Europe and in major U.S. cities and libraries.

Most au pairs are female and there is such a lack of household and child care help in Europe nowadays that almost any young woman (eighteen and over) could cross the ocean in summer and be sure of a warm reception as an au pair, especially in the Scandinavian countries, in France, the British Isles, Germany, Italy, and Switzerland. You'll always get your own room, but are expected to do more than an American baby-sitter does.

"Au pair" is defined in Merriam Webster Dictionary as "a girl who does domestic work for a family in return for room and board and the opportunity to learn the family's language." The Random House College Dictionary translates au pair into "exchanging services as a governess, companion or the like for board and room, usually by a student."

Your child care services may be coupled with some light housework, but aren't always, since the truly wealthy employ housemaids and cleaning women as well. What's great is that such wealthy families take you traveling as well, allowing you to enjoy the seacoast or the mountains; a villa on the French Riviera, perhaps; a chalet in beautiful Switzerland; a vast, stately apartment in Vienna, Austria; or even a small castle overlooking the Rhine River in Germany. In addition to your lodging and good food there's a small salary, say four hundred to six hundred dollars a month, sometimes more.

In general, you work about five hours a day, plus frequent baby-sitting in the evening. You're off one to two days a week. Needless to say, you must love children almost as much as Julie Andrews did in *The Sound of Music.*

One final point and a caveat: You might land a job more quickly by going through one of the many au pair agencies. They charge a fee, however, so make sure to know the financial details before you sign a contract. The fee could be minimal (thirty dollars, for instance) or it can run into several hundred dollars, which you might not want to pay. To be sure, you don't have to pay a fee if you ferret out the newspaper ads placed by would-be employers. Employers will take care of the work permit, if one is needed.

For Further Information

Amies de la Jeune Fille
Bureau de Placement
2 rue du Simplon
1005 Lausanne, Switzerland

Amies de la Jeune Fille
Bureau de Placement
9 Avenue de Ste-Clothilde
1205 Geneve, Switzerland

Au Pairs Italy
46 The Rise Sevenoaks
Kent TN13 1RJ England

Au Pairs Referrals
Beckenhofstrasse 16
8001 Zurich, Switzerland

Edgeware Au Pair Agency
19 Manor Park Crescent
Edgeware
Middlesex HA 8 7NH England

International Au Pair
Via S. Stefano, 32
40125 Bologna
Italy

L'Acceuil Familial
23 Rue du Cherche Midi
Paris 75006, France
One of the oldest and best known.

Pro Filia
14B Avenue Mail
1205 Geneve, Switzerland

Solihull Au Pair & Nanny Agency
87 Warwick Road
Olton, Solihull
West Midlands
B92 7HP England

Verein der Freundinnen Junger Mädchen
Zäringerstrasse 36
8001 Zurich, Switzerland

12

Sports with Pay

Hit the Tennis Scene

It is noon on the outskirts of sporty, upscale Scottsdale, Arizona. Time for lunch? Not yet. The guests at the Gardiner Tennis Ranch are still at school until 12:30, leaping and bounding, hitting thousands of tennis balls. The Ranch is a lovely place to combine a hard physical workout with a vacation. Gardiner's two dozen tennis courts, assorted swimming pools, and *casitas,* or bungalows, are scattered among the russet hillsides and orange trees of Camelback Mountain.

The instructor puts the guests through their paces; a machine shoots balls at the players—industrialists, bankers, wealthy oilmen, corporate attorneys, executives, and college professors. The fifteen or so classes are kept small, three to four people in each. Every thirty minutes, the students are sent to a different court where one more teacher makes them run, polish backhands, forehands, lobs, and volleys.

John Gardiner originated the concept of a week-long tennis clinic, planning each minute of the program. Nowadays there are a number of such programs. More than two dozen top-notch instructors are kept busy at the luxurious, scenic Gardiner complex in Scottsdale; Gardiner's second school is in Carmel Valley, California.

Similarly, Dennis Van der Meer's well-attended classes in Hilton Head, South Carolina, utilize the talents of some sixty instructors every summer at the Van der Meer Tennis University.

What does it take to teach tennis at one of the better known schools or at a big resort hotel? "Instructors must be knowledgeable and presentable," explains Van der Meer. "Friendliness is another important trait." Many tennis directors (who supervise the instructors) also list good communication skills, solid playing ability, enthusiasm, charisma, dynamism, and of course the ability to demonstrate the strokes.

A professional instructor has to be able to explain the complexities of the various grips and the subtleties of service technique; the instructor needs to know how to work the ball machines and the video equipment, answer tennis questions, and most of all, get along with people. Enjoyment of tennis is essential, of course. Pros often spend extra hours in special tennis clinics or playing other pros. Any young person with enough tennis experience and some teaching knowledge can apply for an instructor's job.

At the Gardiner Ranches in Arizona and Northern California the students are kept in constant motion. On one court, the drill uses three thousand tennis balls; on the next, two instructors fling hundreds of volleys at the guests. Elsewhere, the recruits line up to practice their serves. Gardiner times serving speed with a radar gun; the tennis balls fly like bullets.

In general, tennis instructors enjoy the perks of meeting interesting and often wealthy people. There's always a chance for promotion to head pro. Directors of tennis and their assistants are on a salary, which can be generous. The teachers themselves operate on an hourly basis and often remain on standby, depending on the number of students to be taught. At Gardiner's idyllic outposts, staff lunches and pro uniforms are included.

The Gardiner Tennis Ranches never advertise. Yet according to Jeff Stewart, the Carmel Valley head pro, they get at least a hundred summer applications from all over the U.S. "The applicant's background is important," says Stewart.

Gardiner's Scottsdale clinics can always count on lots of celebrities like actor Robin Williams, NBC's Tom Brokaw, tennis enthusiast Johnny Carson, and many others, some of whom are excellent players. Leading tennis schools, therefore, select the most technically competent instructors with a proven talent for teaching. Before making an offer, the Head Pros personally test each applicant. Before approaching the pro, find out his or her hours and request a testing session on a court. Then simply ask for a job.

Instructors with a few years of teaching and competition may go on to a coaching job at a high school or college or a position as a resident pro at a tennis club, country club, or resort hotel. Many resorts employ a tennis host who arranges games for hotel guests, keeps track of courts, and perhaps spends time running the tennis shop as well.

People who prefer to be self-employed can place an ad in the Sunday paper saying, "Tennis instructor available for private lessons." In such tennis-happy communities as San Diego, Santa Barbara, Denver, Reno, Palm Springs, Hilton Head, Palm Beach, and many others, the telephone should start ringing.

For Further Information
South:
The Breakers Hotel
Palm Beach, FL 33480

The Cloister
Sea Island, GA 31562

The Colony Beach & Tennis Club
Sarasota, FL 33578

Doral Country Club & Hotel
4833 Collins Avenue
Miami Beach, FL 33140

Saddlebrook Golf & Tennis Resort
Tampa (Wesley Chapel), FL 34249

Van der Meer Tennis Center
Hilton Head, SC 29938

Midwest:
French Lick-Sheraton Hotel & Country Club
French Lick, IN 47432

Grand Hotel
Mackinac Island, MI 49757

East:
Bolton Valley
Bolton, VT 05477

East River Tennis Club
44-02 Vernon Boulevard
Long Island City, NY 11101

The Mount Washington Hotel
Bretton Woods, NH 03575

Stratton Mountain, VT 05155

Woodstock Inn
Woodstock, VT 05091

West and Southwest:
The Bishop's Lodge
P.O. Box 2367
Santa Fe, NM 87504-2367

Boynton Canyon
P.O. Box 2549
Sedona, AZ 86336

John Gardiner's Tennis Ranch on Camelback
5700 East McDonald Drive
Scottsdale, AZ 85253

John Gardiner's Tennis Ranch
Carmel Valley, CA 93924

Lakeside Tennis Club
955 Tahoe Boulevard
Incline Village, NV 89450

Quail Ridge Inn Resort
Taos, NM 87571

Teton Village, WY 83025

Sun Valley Company
Sun Valley, ID 83353

Be a Golf Caddy

Sea Island, Georgia, is a golfer's paradise, with fairways in all directions and three nine-hole courses with names like Tall Pines and Great Oaks scattered across eight hundred green acres. The first thing you notice here are the tall, wide-shouldered trees—native cedar, palmetto palms, magnolias, pines, and moss-draped oak. As the golfers play on one of the South's most interesting courses, they're flanked by lagoons and lakes, ponds and rivers.

You'll see pelicans, herons, egrets, hear the calls of terns and herring gulls. Thanks to the sea breezes, the resorts are never too hot in summer; the area is pleasant enough for Canadian "snowbirds" who travel south in winter.

And best of all, the Island's resort hotels employ several dozen golf caddies. So do the dozens of other luxury hotels across the country, including the handsome white Broadmoor Hotel Golf Club in Colorado Springs. There the caddies are already fanning out over one of the several eighteen-hole golf courses by breakfast time. The area rolls uphill toward the steeply ascending Cheyenne Mountain. Paths curve up to conifer forests. The links flow and undulate in the sunlight which bathes the grass in deep green colors. The scenery is beautiful.

The caddies at this hotel, and others like it, know the rules of golf, and most enjoy playing it as well. Some golf courses provide uniforms for caddies. Training classes are required and each employee must report to the caddy master, their manager for the season. The younger caddies get a real kick out of the job, especially driving the carts and even carrying the players' bags of clubs which weigh at least twenty pounds.

In addition to the plenty of fresh air and exercise this outdoor job allows, it also provides an opportunity to improve your own golf game. Being around good golfers and pros, carrying bags at various tournaments (which allows you to be up close to the action), and having the chance to play frequently, all add to your knowledge of the game.

Some of the country's older pros—the famous names like Palmer, Nicklaus, or Trevino, for instance—sometimes fly their own caddies to the tournaments, whether these take place at hotels or clubs. But on occasion, local talent is used. The best perk is front row seats to the event.

What's the etiquette on the greens? What should a would-be caddy watch out for? A Colorado club pro makes these few suggestions:

1. Dress properly. This means no torn Levi's, no bare chests, no halter tops for female caddies, and no cutoffs.
2. Adjust your pace to the players. Don't walk too fast or too slow.

Let the player choose the club and don't touch the club unless he
or she asks for it.

3. Give no advice—even if you think you're better than the pro.

Golf courses at resort hotels—and naturally those at country clubs, as
well—require many kinds of additional personnel. How about applying early in the season for a greenskeeper job? It involves fertilizing,
mowing, aerating and watering the extensive lawns on golf properties.
The installation of new lawns and lawn maintenance on golf courses
and elsewhere requires a large labor force, too.

What You Need to Know

Participants Most of the caddies at the Broadmoor are under twenty
years old. The Broadmoor's minimum age is fourteen. Of fifty young-
sters employed for the summer, only three or four are girls. (Most of
the applicants are male.) The minimum age for the greenskeeper job
is usually seventeen. *Pay* The pay isn't very high, even including tips.
Depending on experience, a caddy at the Broadmoor will be paid $15
to $20 per round of golf. Tips range from $5 to $10 per round also. An
early bird caddy can usually fit two rounds of golf into one day. There
are no benefits because the caddies are not on the hotel's payroll. *How
to Apply* Don't bother looking in the newspaper or writing for an application; you're best off talking to a friend or relative who golfs and asking them to introduce you to the head pro where they play. If that's
impossible, become familiar with the local fairways and ask to see the
person in charge. Then just ask for work.

For Further Information

Grossinger Hotel
Grossinger, NY 12734

The Homestead
Hot Springs, VA 24445

The Greenbrier
White Sulphur Springs, WV 24986

Sea Palms
St. Simons Island, GA 31522

French Lick
French Lick, IN 47432

The Cloister Resort
Sea Island, GA 31561

The Broadmoor
Colorado Springs, CO 80901

The Sun Valley Resort
Sun Valley, ID 83353

The Arizona Biltmore Hotel
Phoenix, AZ 85002

Canyon Hotel Golf Resort
Palm Canyon Drive
Palm Springs, CA 92262

The La Costa Resort and Spa
Rancho La Costa, CA 92008

Give Sailing Lessons

If you love the open water and want to share that love with others, you might consider teaching sailing at one of the many fine sailing schools in the U.S. (You might also want to take lessons; see Chapter 3.)

The Offshore Sailing School in Fort Myers, Florida, places job ads in various sailing magazines, and is always looking for help, especially experienced sailors who are personable, good communicators, and above all, "have patience and humility." Skill at ocean-going "Keel" boat maintenance is a plus, too. Offshore gets about 150 to 200 employment inquiries a year, of which only about sixty applicants have enough experience. About twelve to fifteen are finally hired as new recruits for the summer. The job lasts from April through September; there are both full- and part-time positions available. Minimum age for teachers is twenty-one.

As an instructor you work about forty hours a week. Each day consists of two hours in the classroom and one four-hour sailing stint. Each instructor teaches a group of four to five adults on a twenty-seven-foot Solling Class boat. Salaries run from sixteen thousand to eighteen thousand dollars per year, prorated. And instructors work up a sweat for the money.

For Further Information

See addresses and contacts on p. 168.

Raft the Great Rivers

White water rafting is the essence of thrilling adventure. The guides and oarspeople might battle with the rapids of the Colorado River in Arizona, the Salmon River in Idaho, or Oregon's Snake River. The waters splash high, wetting crew and passengers; the river explodes in your face, thunders against your lifejacket. Your rubber boat rolls and lurches as you race along in a blur, or drifts gently along the flat stretches as eagles soar overhead.

As a river guide, you come to know portions of a river intimately; you learn how to avoid colliding with the rocks and how to negotiate the roiling waters. You learn the difference between the inflatable boats, the dories, and the big motor rafts for different journeys. Some trips last two full weeks, with improvised campsites and campfires every night; others involve a few exploratory days in the stunning Grand Canyon on oar-powered rubber boats; still others offer a full-day or half-day river rafting sampler.

"Outfitters," the companies that run river rafting adventures, use any number of boatmen and boatwomen. In addition to guiding the boats, these people are responsible for the clients and they serve as nature guides, explaining and interpreting the scenery and the geology. The guides know how to give commands to the passengers (most for the latter's own good) without offending them. Experienced guides prevent the flipping, or capsizing, of their craft. "A good boatman must know when to act, when to react, and when to rest," explains one expert.

Jodi Johnson, a recruiter for the American Adventure Expeditions, says they employ about fifty people in summer. She looks for the following qualities in hiring river guides: calmness, maturity, first aid and CPR experience, professionalism, good appearance, and communication skills. In addition, river guides must be nonsmokers and meet training requirements. The River Rafting Division of the American Adventure Expeditions is located in Buena Vista, Colorado.

Peter Ambrose, staffing director of Brunswick, Maine's Unicorn Expeditions, hires guides for white water rafting the Penobscot River in Maine and the Moose River in Upper New York State, among others. Unicorn has a ten-day training program. Their float trips take from one to six days. Some of their guides play the guitar or tell stories about the area. Like most outfitters, Unicorn also hires drivers for the shuttle vans. The excitement of the river, and the beauty of the landscape, are breathtaking.

What You Should Know

Participants You should be eighteen or over but young and outdoorsy. Most outfitters require first aid and CPR experience. They also look for maturity, calmness, professionalism, and good communication skills. Drivers need commercial licenses. *Pay* Pay starts with minimum wage and goes up all the way to $60 per day, depending on experience and responsibilities.

For Further Information

American Adventure Expeditions
P.O. Box 1549
Buena Vista, CO 81211

Arizona Raft Adventure
4050 East Huntington Drive
Flagstaff, AZ 86001

Canyoneers
P.O. Box 2997
Flagstaff, AZ 86003

Epley's Whitewater Adventures
P.O. Box 987
McCall, ID 83638

Expeditions, Inc.
625 North Beaver Street
Flagstaff, AZ 86001

Falcon Floats
HC61, P.O. Box 411
Tahlequah, OK 74464

Grand Canyon River Reservations
P.O. Box 581
Angels Camp, CA 95222

Hells Canyon Adventures
P.O. Box 159
Oxbow, OR 97840

High Country River Rafters
P.O. Box 709
Golden, CO 80402

Impulse Rafting & Kayaking, Inc.
P.O. Box 4121
Vail, CO 81658

Mountain Waters
P.O. Box 2681
Durango, CO 81302

National Outdoor Leadership School
P.O. Box AA
Lander, WY 82520-0579

North American River Runners, Inc.
P.O. Box 81
Hico, WV 25854

Rocky Mountain River Tours
P.O. Box 2552-BP
Boise, ID 83701

Unicorn Rafting Expeditions
P.O. Box T
Brunswick, ME 04011

Warren River Expeditions
P.O. Box 1375
Salmon, ID 83467-1375

Western River Expeditions
7258 Racquet Club Drive
Salt Lake City, UT 84121

Western Whitewater Association, Inc.
P.O. Box 8922
Boise, ID 83707

Hike as a Mountain Guide

The summer hikes are gentle at the low altitudes of the Swiss Alps, with the trails crossing meadows of deepest green. Wildflowers grow profusely: gentian, columbines, yarrow, daisies, wild orchids and tiny strawberries. Brown cows roam among clover, cowbells ringing. The air is alive with the healthy smells of animals, tall grasses, raspberry bushes, and peach orchards that border Lake Lucerne. This is central Switzerland's largest and perhaps most beautiful lake; mountain slopes climb on all sides of the blue *Vierwaldstättersee*.

Higher up, the conifers and glades with chalets give way to a ring of glaciers, reaching up into the sky. Mountain guides lead hikes in all directions. Wanderings around the lake can be short and flat, or longer and a bit steeper, as one wishes. Paved or cobbled footpaths meander off all over the area, with benches inviting you to rest.

Brightly painted passenger ships connect the villages: from Brunnen (only thirteen hundred feet above sea level) to the Bay of Lucerne (where Richard Wagner lived and composed from 1866 to 1872) to Altdorf (where William Tell had to demonstrate his archery skill in 1307 by shooting an apple from his son's head).

The communities of Sisikon, Rütli, Treib, and Küssnacht have historical significance and all can be reached on foot. Trail heads are linked not only by ship but also by a network of cogwheel trains, cable cars, gondolas, and chair lifts.

For many years, an adventurous American hiking guide named Fred Jacobson, of Jacobson Alpine Trails, has led ten-day to two-week summer hikes with other American leaders around the magnificent Swiss mountainscapes in the pristine Kandersteg region, up toward the Matterhorn Pyramid from Zermatt, in the cheese-making Appenzell area, around Pontresina, and many more places. Jacobson, an entrepreneur of the first order, knows the Swiss peaks well from his own experience; he now employs several other congenial guides who ascend the mountains around the cozy little villages of Mürren and Grindelwald, each with about fifteen American tourists in tow.

Could *you* be a hiking leader or mountain guide?

Do you love mountains enough to face the blistering sun at high altitudes? To keep going after hours of rain? Can you name the peaks and flowers? Would you know what to do if one of your hikers sprained an ankle? Are you strong enough to carry fifty pounds of weight for your guests?

Paid mountain guides are employed not only by private entrepreneurs but also by tour operators, YMCAs, YWCAs, travel agents, national parks, mountain clubs, chambers of commerce, and sports shops. (A sampling of leads appears on page 261.)

You need not necessarily live in the high country; Jacobson, for instance, is a New York City dweller during most of the year. But most hiking guide positions can be found in mountainous states like Vermont, Colorado, Montana, Wyoming, Washington State, and Oregon. Write an intelligent letter to the person who does the hiring (see list to follow), or ask someone to introduce you.

Some organizations run a big business catering to outdoor enthusiasts. One of the big outfits is Vermont Hiking Holidays. It employs scores of guides and tour leaders for its outings of various lengths to such pretty Vermont places as the Berkshires, the Mad River valley, Stowe, Sugarbush, and many others.

Naturally, the tour leaders partake in these civilized joys. Generally tour leaders are in their mid-twenties or younger, charismatic, and experienced. The age range isn't ironclad, however; if you're mature and energetic, you have a shot at almost any age.

Not far away from Bristol, Vermont—headquarters for Vermont Hiking Holidays—a very successful competitor called New England Hiking Holidays also sells vacation outings to the public from North Conway, New Hampshire. Organizer Kurt Grabher and his wife Clare

The Vermont Hiking Holidays director describes a typical five-day vacation:

"We begin our sojourn at the elegant Inn at Montpelier, situated in the nation's smallest capital city, where deer roam the forested hill behind the state house. The town is quaint, uncrowded, and fascinating to explore. Soon we are headed for the quiet 'Northeast Kingdom.' Here we hike down country lanes, to glacially scoured lakes (such as dramatic three-hundred-foot-deep Lake Willoughby) and up mountain peaks where spectacular views await us. One day we ramble along a trail aptly called the Sea of Ferns. In picturesque Craftsbury we will stay at the beautifully restored adjoining inns, Finchingfield and The Brassknocker. You will find our consecutive nights at the Wildflower Inn in Lyndonville memorable for the expansive country setting, hot tub, sauna, and cuisine."

have been at it for a decade. They explain the program:

"We have sought out the best trails, both long and short, challenging and gentle. We have chosen some of the finest country inns in each area.

"We always have two guides per trip and this together with the great diversity of hiking, allows us to accommodate both slower and faster walkers and to appeal to the casual but enthusiastic walker as well as the experienced hiker. Our groups are small and personal (never more than sixteen people per trip) and our experienced guides are always eager to share their love and knowledge of the natural world."

The guides of the New England Hiking Holidays are in their thirties. But, if you're mature, charismatic, energetic, and in your twenties, it's worth applying for a job. These hiking groups do not tolerate guns, cigarette smokers, or drug users.

Young people who crave fresh air, exercise, and a chance to see large chunks of country might be interested in Trek America: Adventure Camping Tours for 18-38's. Knowledge of U.S. wilderness areas and national parks is helpful for these jobs. Specifically, a Trek America tour leader is responsible for the organization, safe transport, and overall welfare of a group of thirteen foreign adults ages eighteen to thirty-eight, on tours lasting three, six, and nine weeks. This involves planning each day's activities, finding campsites, sightseeing, entertainment, and more. The trek leader is also responsible for all the driving—covering approximately five thousand miles in every three week period—and the daily maintenance and troubleshooting of the group's van. The traveling season will be both enjoyable and rewarding, provided it is approached with the right attitude: a freedom to travel and experience adventure with a desire to show the U.S.

Gussie Motter, of Wilderness Southeast, sums up the jobs this way: "Our leaders are folks comfortable in the wilderness and practitioners of minimal-impact camping. All of our field leaders have current Red Cross certification in CPR and Advanced First Aid and must be able to teach natural history and ecology to children and adults."

What You Need to Know

Specifics vary with each program, but in general:

Participants You should be mature and charismatic. You must have some wilderness experience and be able to walk long miles with heavy gear. Many groups require that you have Red Cross or first aid certification. *Duration* Tours vary from a few days to several weeks. *Pay* The pay is not great, but since living expenses are minimal, tour leaders generally can save a large portion of their allowance.

For Further Information

Alpine Trails, Ltd.
141 East 89th Street
New York, NY 10128

Appalachian Mountain Club
Pinkham Notch
P.O. Box 2098
Gorham, NH 03815

Idaho Outfitters & Guides Association
P.O. Box 95
Boise, ID 83701

Idaho Travel Council
Statehouse Mall
Boise, ID 83720

Montana Wilderness Association
P.O. Box 635
Helena, MT 59624

National Park Service
P.O. Box 37127
Washington, DC 20013-7127

New England Hiking Holidays
P.O. Box 1648
North Conway, NH 03860

TREKAMERICA
P.O. Box 470
Blairstown, NJ 07825

Swiss National Tourist Office
222 North Sepulveda Boulevard, Ste. 1570
El Segundo, CA 90245

Be a Rock Climbing Instructor

It is still early when the jeep pulls into Yosemite National Park, swishes across an oiled road, and then comes to a stop. The four passengers are eager to spend the weekend climbing two thousand feet.

The challenge could be the Cathedral Rocks, Sentinal Dome, or the sheer El Capitan. This time, it's one of the smaller, nameless rock structures in Yosemite. From the road, you can see the granite pillar slicing the lightening sky. The climbers shoulder their heavy packs. Winding their way through trees, they reach the steep slope that leads to the base of the cliff. They rope in silently, purposefully.

By afternoon, they have made the top: A total gain of eight hundred vertical feet. The climbers feel a great sense of achievement.

It would have been difficult without the professional mountain guide.

There's a special mystique about rock climbing and an excitement rarely matched by other sports. For some, mountaineering is exploration. You become an adventurer, never knowing what is around the next corner. Scale the sheer cliffs of the Hudson River valley in New York State, and you might find yourself face to face with two young owls. When climbers first struggle up the enormous reddish rocks of the Mesa Verde National Park, they are likely to gasp: This is the site of the cliff dwellings of a civilization dating back to the year 1000. Wyoming's Teton guides have stepped on ancient Indian arrows, necklaces, and artifacts. In Idaho, you and your climbing students may come upon the nest of a hawk, or suddenly look into the eyes of mountain sheep. When a party of young climbers went to sleep near a forlorn mountain creek in Wyoming, they awoke to find themselves surrounded by a dozen porcupines. And the higher you go, the more mysterious it becomes.

Rock climbing has become an art form, a delicate vertical ballet choreographed by the peculiarities of the rock itself.

Many of today's climbers are in their early twenties, although a few children are seen in some of the canyons, too. While the sport has a macho image and is still dominated by men, women are often found leading on some of the most difficult routes. Good judgment and finesse are a match for brute strength. Of course, it takes also good health and stamina, coordination, will power, and patience. You need plenty of experience to lead.

An inadequate leader is often dictatorial, and won't tolerate any questions from his group. Such a leader plays god, or plays the ruffian who doesn't check whether the crew can maintain the pace. Bad leaders refuse to give up. Incompetent leaders can also be recognized quickly when they break basic mountaineering rules. One of the cardinal rules: You must check with forest service or national park or other authorities before you begin a climb and the leader must register.

Vertical adventures can be found all over the mountains of the U.S. The quickest way to becoming a full-fledged leader is to enroll in one of the many climbing schools in the nation (see Chapter 1 for leads). Or if you already have experience, you can apply for a job. Contact the director of the mountaineering organization nearest you (see list below). Offer to come along on a typical climb. This will give you a chance to demonstrate your climbing technique and get acquainted with the leader. Then simply ask for work.

Climbing is perhaps the most exhilarating of sports invented by humans. The ascent brings not only a conquest of the mountain but a conquest of the self. You push yourself to the farthest physical and emotional limits during the climb. You learn more about yourself in those intense moments than in a lifetime of flatland existence.

American climbing schools vary enormously in scope and costs. Many are designed for the pure novice, others cater to the experienced individual looking for an intense expedition. Still others are known for training veteran climbers in the art and science of teaching others to climb and survive in the wilderness. Apply for a job or brush up your skills at one of the following schools, listed in the approximate order of their importance and popularity:

Jackson Hole Mountain Guides, P.O. Box 7477, WY 83001. A professional climbing instruction school and guide service. Internationally authorized concession to the Grand Teton National Park and also remote areas in the Wind River mountain range. You'll explain and demonstrate most of the fundamentals of mountaineering, which the climber will later execute. The school includes the instruction in uses of the rope, knots, climbing posture, tempo, climbing order, belaying, the use of pitons and caribiners, and rappelling.

Rainier Mountaineering, Inc., 535 Dock Street, Tacoma, WA 98402 or Mt. Rainier National Park, Paradise, WA 98402 (summer only). Known for summer snow- and ice-climbing techniques.

Sierra Club, 730 Polk Street, San Francisco, CA 94109. Extremely active nationwide. All age groups.

Colorado Outward Bound School, 945 Pennsylvania Street, Denver, CO 80203. Known for youth programs and special scholarships. Programs designed to increase or create self-reliance and teamwork.

National Outdoor Leadership School (NOLS), P.O. Box AA, Lander, WY 82520. NOLS is not just another climbing school. NOLS's instructors teach wilderness survival to the teachers of Outward Bound schools. One student recalls how they climbed three days on a three-thousand-foot granite face in Wind River Range, Wyoming, only to return with nothing to eat but rancid cheese for the two-day hike out from the remote location. Knowledge of the outdoors and of self is the reward.

The Iowa Mountaineers, P.O. Box 163, Iowa City, Iowa 52240. You'll train novices in various phases of safe and enjoyable mountaineering.

Colorado Mountain School, P.O. Box 2062, Estes Park, CO 80517. Provides one- to eleven-day lessons and expeditions for intermediate and advanced students. Estes Park is near many high-alpine climbs in Rocky Mountain National Park.

Bob Culp Climbing School, 1335 Broadway, Boulder, CO 80302. Culp specializes in day trips around Boulder and Rocky Mountain National Park. Instructors follow a systematic skill-based program in four ability categories (novice to extreme) that is ideal for beginners.

International Alpine School, P.O. Box 3037, Eldorado Springs, CO 80025. This is an international outfit based in Colorado, sponsoring expeditions as far away as South America. Known for climbing instructors who are famous for first ascents and daring feats, the school generally caters to elite climbers who want to push themselves even further. Ice climbing and mountaineering techniques also taught.

InnerQuest, Inc., Route 1, P.O. Box 271 C, Purcellville, VA 22132. Special one- to three-week adventure programs for boys and girls ages ten to eighteen are conducted by East-Coast-based InnerQuest, Inc. The programs feature rock climbing, caving, and multiday mountain trekking expeditions.

Chamber of Commerce, P.O. Box E, Jackson, WY 83000. They may know of new schools who're expanding and need more guides.

Join the Outward Bound Staff

One of the largest, best-organized outdoor adventure outfits is also one of the big employers of assorted instructors. Known as Outward Bound Schools, this amazing organization teaches teenagers and adults about survival in the great outdoors. The experience is rugged but safe and well planned. (see page 11 for a complete description).

Outward Bound receives about fifteen hundred applications for instructors annually. They employ about that number of instructors per year, but only have about two hundred job openings because of returning employees.

It takes up to five years of outdoor experience and training to qualify for a staff position and you must be at least twenty-two years old. Get experience in Outward Bound's regular programs first. Sign up for some summer action, and then volunteer the following year to help with logistics and transportation. Learn advanced first aid, obtain the Red Cross Advanced Certificate, and continue to volunteer for back-country expeditions.

One young school instructor qualified by taking the initial courses with Outward Bound, got a Bachelor's Degree in Recreational Science, continued to volunteer, and after four years was rewarded with a year-round position as admissions counselor and field instructor.

People with community experience or a counseling background have a good chance of getting hired. Salaries range from about four hundred to one thousand dollars per month.

Outward Bound has this to say about what it looks for in job applicants:

Each individual who has the ultimate responsibility for instruction and safety of an Outward Bound course will be qualified as an instructor according to the following criteria:

The candidate must:
- have competence in teaching, counseling and guiding;
- be at least 22 years old;
- have first aid competence equivalent to advanced American Red Cross, plus specialized training in wilderness emergency care;
- have Senior Red Cross lifesaving or equivalent training run by the school (for courses that are primarily water based);
- relate well to others and work effectively with a variety of people;
- have competence in the primary outdoor activity for the given program;
- demonstrate proficiency in managing all "risk" activities as demanded by the terrain and weather;

- demonstrate the ability to anticipate and manage potential hazards, both physical and emotional;
- demonstrate sound judgment and the ability to handle a group effectively under stressful conditions;
- demonstrate an understanding of and commitment to the methodologies and philosophy of Outward Bound;
- be competent in navigation, search and rescue;
- be proficient in environmentally acceptable practices for "wilderness" living;
- demonstrate competence in teaching the above 7 items to students and to apprentice instructors;
- demonstrate the ability to implement through effective teaching the procedures and curriculum as outlined in the Instructors' handbooks;
- demonstrate an ability to provide appropriate structure, perspective, and guidance in the process of managing an Outward Bound course;
- be sufficiently fit to lead all activities in the course and maintain ample energy, strength and clarity to assist students with physical and emotional obstacles;
- have attended a staff training or equivalent program orientation;
- have a working knowledge of the course terrain to be used.
- Instructors are chosen mainly because they're adventurers in their own right.

For Further Information

Addresses for employment information and applications are listed on pages 13–14.

Ride the Trails as a Bicycle Tour Guide

Ride the Slick Rock Trail in Moab, Utah. Tour the California Napa Valley wine country. Pedal through the colors of Provence, France, where Van Gogh painted.

Bicycle tour guides are needed by many companies that specialize in fully-supported bicycle touring. On these trips, vans carry the cyclists' luggage and also carry gourmet meals, repair equipment, and extra bikes, and are available for a cyclist to ride in if they can't complete part of the planned ride. Bike repairs, flat tires, fatigue, minor accidents, and nasty weather can affect the people in your charge. As a guide, you should have better-than-average people skills to manage your group.

For foreign touring, language skills may be required. You'll probably share the burden with one other tour guide, so you'll have time to ride along with your group and get to know them.

Depending on the employer, you may stay in lodgings or campgrounds. If camping, you will be chief cook and bottle-washer, and will be in charge of setting up and taking down tents. The pay is minimal, but travel experiences and room and board make up for low wages.

In addition to guides and leaders, bike touring companies offer positions as van drivers and assistants. Minimum age is usually twenty-one, and you may have to have a valid driver's license and be eligible for a Tour Bus Certificate or commercial driver's license.

One tour operator who specializes in European bicycling vacations is enthralled with travel on two wheels. "It's hard to describe how much fun this kind of travel can be, other than to say it is romantic and stimulating exercise. You're pedaling slow enough so that you can still smell the flowers. Not rushing through the world, you get a chance to absorb the sights, sounds, and smells of the countryside."

Although applications number into the thousands, finalists are usually invited to a training weekend where the best ones are selected for the available jobs. The applicants come from all backgrounds, and might be lawyers, architects, students, and college professors. For foreign travel, these applicants must know the language, geography, culture, history, and the folk of the area they guide tours in.

Because mountain bikes are becoming so popular, many tour companies specialize in areas of the country that lend themselves to off-road riding. Some of these are: Mt. Tamalpais in Marin County, California; Crested Butte area in Colorado; The Big Island, Hawaii; Maplewood State Park, Minnesota; Pisgah and Nantahala National Forests in North Carolina; Great Smoky Mountains National Park in Tennessee; Big Bend National Park in Texas; Northeast Kingdom Area in Vermont; New River Trail State Park, Virginia; The Birkie Trail, Wisconsin; Canyonlands National Park, Utah; and Red Desert in Wyoming.

What You Need to Know

Participants Tour operators are looking mostly for people with good communication skills and managerial ability. The paying guests on a bicycle tour might get tired and irritable. The tour leader has to be able to cope with this behavior. An up-to-date Red Cross First Aid Certification is required and additional training is suggested. Repair skills are a must, as is some background in outdoor leadership. This could take the form of scouting, camping, recreational school groups, or previous employment. You must be twenty-one and have a valid driver's license.

For Further Information

American Youth Hostels Association (AYHA)
World Adventures Program
P.O. Box 37613, Department 811
Washington, DC 20013-7613

Far West Tours International
4551 Glencoe Avenue, Suite 205
Marina del Rey, CA 90292

Forum Travel International
91 Gregory Lane, Suite 21
Pleasant Hill, CA 94523

Arrow to the Sun
P.O. Box 115
Taylorsville, CA 95983

Gerhard's Bicycle Odysseys
4949 SW Macadam
Portland, OR 97201

Backroads Bicycle Touring
1516 Fifth Street
Berkeley, CA 94710-1713

International Bicycle Tours
12 Mid Place
Chappaqua, NY 10514

Bicycle Africa
International Bicycle Fund
4247 135th Place, SE
Bellevue, WA 98006

Paradise Pedallers
P.O. Box 32352
Charlotte, NC 28232

Bikecentennial
P.O. Box 8308
Missoula, MT 59801

Progressive Travels
1932 First Avenue, Suite 1100
Seattle, WA 98101

Bike Vermont
P.O. Box 207 AH
Woodstock, VT 05091

Rocky Mountain Cycle Tours
P.O. Box 1978
Canmore, ALB, Canada TOL OMO

The Biking Expedition
P.O. Box 547
10 Maple Street
Henniker, NH 03242

Sierra Club
730 Polk Street
San Francisco, CA 94109

Butterfield & Robinson
70 Bond Street
Toronto, ONT, Canada M5B 1X3

Timberline Bicycle Tours
7975 East Harvard, Unit J
Denver, CO 80231

Chateaux Bike Tours
P.O. Box 5706
Denver, CO 80217

Vermont Bicycle Touring
P.O. Box 711
Bristol, VT 05443

China Passage/Asia Passage
168 State Street
Teaneck, NJ 07666

Vermont Country Cyclers
P.O. Box 145
Waterbury Center, VT 05677

Classic Nepal, Ltd.
33 Metro Avenue
Newton, Derbyshire DE55 5UF England

Euro-Bike Tours
P.O. Box 40
Dekalb, IL 60115

Country Cycling Tours
140 West 83d Street
New York, NY 10024

Part III

Travel
Adventures

13

Great Escapes Abroad

The best is left for the end. The great escape: World travel.
In Sweden, a college student from Georgia finds total solace as
a musician; a young girl from Kansas City sends home rave letters about
her temporary physical education job in Brisbane, Australia. Every summer, thousands of students enjoy visits to Canada, France, England,
and Italy. Their travels are for the joy and adventure of exploring.

One traveler who spent July in Milan explains the charms of the
countryside: "You're bound to fall in love with Lake Como and its little ancient towns, their red roofs, their ochre walls and russet balconies.
All around this lake, even in medieval Como itself, you have a sense of
living on another planet. Perhaps it is the absence of commercialism:
little forgotten churches, old shuttered villas, and flowing hillsides,
sprinkled with far-apart houses, with friendly places like Moltrasio,
Varenna, and Tremezzo."

Naturally, there are also fascinating guided trips to remote areas
like Antarctica; summer skiing in Morocco; rafting the Bio-Bio River in
Chile; and lots more.

At a few of the escapes, you get paid, sometimes enough for room and board; at the majority, though, you dig into your savings and pay for the flight to the far-flung outpost and for the tour.

Some of the trips and brief stays are expensive, yet others represent good values. But the eye-opening foreign summer may change your life.

Read on, and take your choice.

Bicycle Down Under

There are many options for international bike travel. Here's an example of two trips offered by Backroads.

Lush northern Queensland, Australia boasts white sand beaches, the Great Barrier Reef, and an inland tropical rain forest renowned for rare plant and wild animal life. The famed sugarcane fields of Australia are here, in open valleys between mountainous jungles like the Atherton Tablelands and Daintree National Park.

A mountain bike trip starts you up through the valleys of the tablelands, past spectacular scenery, dark gorges, and crashing waterfalls. Then on through the rain forest, riding off-road, you circle Lake Tinaroo. Under the canopy of trees, you are surrounded by chirping birds and other creatures that may be taken by surprise as your nearly silent mountain bike rolls through their world.

Out of the rain forest, the valleys open up to the lush agricultural fields of farmers and ranchers. Sometimes on horseback, always (it seems) with dogs, these friendly people will stop their work to wave and talk to you.

A rest day by the Mossman River provides free time to swim, canoe, and walk in the rain forest by the coast. Then on to Cape Tribulation and across the Daintree River. Close to the warm Pacific Ocean, you are faced with recreation choices. There's swimming, snorkeling, windsurfing, diving, or taking a guided nature walk in the rain forest. Hop aboard a catamaran to the Great Barrier Reef for a day of diving with the living color and motion of exotic reef fish.

On an eight-day trip, you have the choice of riding up to six days, with rest days interspersed. Each night your accommodations are in luxurious resorts and hotels. You only rough it on your bike, and even then, a shuttle van is available if you decide not to go the distance that day.

If road riding is more to your liking, take a sixteen-day trip around New Zealand's South Island. With an average of thirty miles per day (you can ride more), you cover miles of spectacular green scenery through rolling terrain. Cyclists will enjoy the many short hills, some longer grades and once in a while a steep climb.

From the pine forests near Marlborough Sound, the route passes through the Rai Valley and Whangomoa Scenic Reserve. Private home hosts welcome traveler-cyclists in Nelson, New Zealand's sunniest city. Then you bike south through wine and apple country where the sweet aroma of fruit surrounds you. The beech forests of Nelson Lakes National Park welcome you to Lake Rotoiti. A rest day here means time for rafting, horseback riding, fishing, or *tramping* (New Zealand hiking).

Through Buller Gorge, you reach the sea, then on to the once prosperous gold-mining area and the rural township of Hari Hari. From this primitive coastal region, the peaks of the Southern Alps soar to the east. West, the shores of the Tasman Sea are wind-and-water-sculpted rock structures. Your route takes you into Westland National Park, past the Fox and Franz Joseph Glaciers.

Ride across the Southern Alps following the Haast River, then climb Haast Pass. Relax at Lake Wanaka for two nights. Cruise Milford Sound or take a ski-plane flight over the Southern Alps. The final leg of the ride goes through Kawarau Gorge to Queenstown, and then come the fond farewells.

You need a valid and generous credit card for the Australia or New Zealand adventure.

What You Need to Know

Participants Many special student trips are available for people ages fourteen to eighteen. Open trips have a minimum age of eighteen, with a mix of all ages. The average group size is from twenty to twenty-four people. *Duration and Cost* Tours differ from company to company and range from a $1465, five-day, four-night tour through Italy to a nine-day, eight-night road tour through the Loire Valley of France, for $2,798. *Facilities* All meals are provided. All you have to do is ride and enjoy. Bring your own bike or rent one from the company, helmet included. A list of recommended clothing and gear will be provided when you decide which adventure is for you. *Other* If you don't ride much, don't worry. Each day has different mileage options. If you feel like you need a rest, the support van will give you a lift as far as you like.

For Further Information

Backroads, Inc.
1516 Fifth Street, Suite RS
Berkeley, CA 94710-1740

Trek the Himalayas

Here's the ultimate high: If you have time, money, and an adventurous spirit, you can hike to the bases of the Himalayas and even climb some of them.

Thousands of people visit this "Roof of the World" every year. They're stunned by the tier upon tier of lofty mountain ranges: The thirty peaks rise more than 25,000 feet or 7,620 meters. The names are easily recognized: Everest, Annapurna, Kachenjunga.

In the Himalayas, literally "Home of the Snows," travelers undergo a change in spirit. The immense grandeur and snowpacked beauty of the highest mountains in the world make the most weighted cares of visitors seem inconsequential.

As you trek between remote villages or head off to ascend a major peak, you'll walk upon trails that have been used for centuries to traverse the high passes and deep cut valleys. Passing ancient Buddhist monasteries and pastoral herdsmen and farmers, you may think you have stepped back in time. The Nepalese people are relaxed and friend-ly and follow rhythms of a way of life that stretches back thousands of years.

Solo trekking is not recommended; the distances, the complexi-ty of the visas, and the remote locales make a guided tour mandatory.

But there are scores of reliable companies that organize Himalayan expeditions. Some of the tours are easy; others are physically very demanding. The National Outdoor Leadership School (NOLS) (see page 14 for description) even has a mountaineering course (age eigh-teen minimum). The objective of this thirty-five-day course is to learn the snow and ice climbing techniques and expedition skills necessary for a Himalayan expedition. Participants will attempt at least one peak over eighteen thousand feet in the Garhwal region of northeastern India during the course.

The expedition begins with a four-day trek through green jungle and small villages into base camp. The Garhwal area has few western visitors compared to more well known Himalayan peaks; and in this remote wilderness region, outside help is days away. NOLS is known for the rugged nature of its Himalayan expeditions.

The Garhwal offers a good environment for learning snow climb-ing, ice climbing, and glacier travel in the post-monsoon season. You will also learn firsthand what is involved in planning and organizing an expedition to the Himalayan region.

The Colorado Outward Bound School (also known as COBS) has a solid reputation for its long, action-packed Nepalese treks. One of the leaders describes a typical trek: "Sometimes the trails are wide, stair-stepped stone promenades; sometimes they are narrow tracks. Trails are commonly steep, making up- or downhill progress a slow and steady affair. Daily elevation gains can be as much as five thousand ver-tical feet. The mileage maximum is ten miles per day."

COBS offers both trekking and the even hardier high-altitude mountaineering in Nepal; participants must move at elevations of twen-ty thousand feet. Compared with the highest peaks in Colorado (low-er than fifteen thousand feet), that's some trip!

Some twenty-day outings pay atten-tion to cultural, artistic, and region-al attractions; the COBS brochure describes the highlights of one typi-cal trip as follows:

"Early in the trek you leave the tra-ditional approach route to Everest to traverse the Pike Danda (13,100-feet high). This offers panoramic views of the Everest region and of the Lumd-ing Himal, the sacred mountains of the Solu Sherpas. The terminus of this trek will be the village of Junebesi, location of a Hillary School and a monastery known for the intricate wood block carvings produced by its resident monks.

"The central highlight of the trip will be three days and nights spent at the Trakshindu Monastery and the vil-lage of Chuleumo, the home of the Outward Bound Sherpa staff."

Whichever tour you join, your preparations have to be extensive. It can take four months, for example, to secure a visa. You need to get a passport, too, of course. Ask for a clothing list and find out if you need any shots. Prepare for the heat of the valleys, the cold of the mountains, and days without showers.

In the end, though, a Sanskrit proverb says it best:

"A hundred divine epochs would not suffice to describe all the marvels of the Himalayas."

For Further Information

Here are some of the better tour and expedition companies, some of which were mentioned in these pages:

National Outdoor Leadership School
288 Main Street
Lander, WY 82520-0579

Colorado Outward Bound School
945 Pennsylvania
Denver, CO 80203-3198
(303) 837-0880

Sierra Club
730 Polk Street
San Francisco, CA 94109

Himalaya
1900 Eight Street
Berkeley, CA 94710

Wilderness Travel
801 Allston Way
Berkeley, CA 94710

InnerAsia Expeditions
2627 Lombard Street
San Francisco, CA 94123

Mountain Travel/Sobek
6420 Fairmount Avenue
El Cerrito, CA 94530

Join the Great Antarctic Explorers

The peninsula of Antarctica has been made famous by great explorers
like Richard Byrd, Roald Amundsen, R. F. Scott, and others. How exciting to traverse this remote and little-traveled part of the globe!

There are a variety of ways to approach the South Pole and travel
to Antarctica. Nature photographers, for instance, can join well-known
professionals on a photographic expedition. Final transportation is on
Twin Otter planes. On location, you stay in tents and learn all about nature
photography from the likes of Galen Rowell, author of many books and
articles (address follows).

An enormous array of expeditions are offered by Mountain Trav-
el/Sobek (MT/S) which has been leading expeditions and tours all over
the world since the 1960s. On its Antarctic destinations, MT/S grades its
trips as "Easy," "Moderate," or "Strenuous." All the tours include a stop
in the Falkland Islands, where there are penguins, seals, and other wildlife.

Another firm, Adventure Network International (ANI), flies you to
Antarctica and the South Pole; from there you travel via (air lifted) snow-
mobiles. Other ANI tours focus on mountaineering. All of this takes
ruggedness.

Antarctica's highest peak, the Vinson Massif (Mt. Vinson), remains
one of the world's ultimate climbing destinations. It is estimated that
fewer than 130 persons have reached the top of Mt. Vinson, the most
remote of the Seven Summits.

Climbing Mt. Vinson is a strenuous and expensive quest. Even though the mountain is not terribly steep—there is a moderate glacier ramp most of the way up—many top climbers consider Mt. Vinson to be a tougher summit than Alaska's Mt. McKinley, due to the rugged Antarctic environment. The weather is unpredictable and incredibly harsh when it turns bad—one hundred mph winds and temperatures as low as forty degrees below zero are possible even in the Antarctic's "good" season.

Lastly, one of the most comfortable and luxurious ways to explore Antarctica is to fly to Santiago, Chile, and then sail by small cruise ship toward your destination. To get still closer to the ice, you board a fleet of Cousteau-designed, inflatable boats that take you from ship to shore— to cormorant nesting areas, to rocky beaches where only seals have been before, and to dense penguin rookeries. Witness the *calving*, or splitting, of glaciers and visit scientific research stations.

The nature spectacle reminds one of the much-cruised Inside Passage of Alaska and Canada, with large ships everywhere taking visitors to view the icebergs and high mountains. But Antarctica is much larger than the Inside Passage.

For Further Information

Adventure Network International
200-1676 Druanleau Street
Vancouver, BC, Canada V6H 3S5 2627

Galen Rowell
c/o InnerAsia Expeditions
2627 Lombard Street
San Francisco, CA 94123

Mountain Travel/Sobek
6420 Fairmount Avenue
El Cerrito, CA 94530

Society Expeditions
723 Broadway East
Seattle, WA 98102

Discover the Flora and Fauna of the Galapagos Islands

Here's a world of birds you cannot find anywhere else, of giant turtles that weigh five-hundred pounds, of four-foot-long lizards, of herons and rare crabs. You're 650 miles west of South America, astride the equator, visiting the Galapagos Islands, once known as the Enchanted Isles.

Although first discovered in 1535, the islands were barely known to the world until Charles Darwin visited them aboard the H.M.S. *Beagle* in 1835. Darwin was so impressed with his findings there that he was inspired to develop his renowned theory of evolution.

Today you too can discover these fascinating islands with their rich variety of landscape, interesting lava formations, vast sand beaches, remarkably tame animals, and untouched natural beauty. You can visit the Galapagos Islands aboard one of the small vessels that carry ten to twenty passengers and offer weekly departures. The small number of passengers allows for a flexible itinerary and personalized natural experiences not available on the larger ships. All excursions on shore are accompanied by a licensed naturalist guide who explains the unique flora and fauna.

For Further Information

All Adventure Travel, Inc.
P.O. Box 4307
Boulder, CO 80306

National Audubon Society
Expedition Institute
Northeast Audubon Center
Sharon, CT 06069

Climb Mt. Kilimanjaro

In the valleys, you see herds of antelope and wildebeest, gazelles and impala. The amazing Tanzanian National Parks are one great reason to travel to Africa. For truly active, hardy people, though, there are many more. How about climbing Africa's highest mountain? With a summit of 19,340 feet, it is certainly challenging; even the tour operators call it demanding. The trek usually begins at about six thousand feet, where it's very hot; you climb about three thousand feet every day, camping in special huts on the mountain at night until you reach the lofty, chilly summit. Porters carry your gear and there's always a guide along. Afterward, you can safari (without guns) through Africa's most spectacular parks with outstanding wildlife in legendary Ngorongoro Crater, Serengeti, and Lake Manyara Parks, tenting under starry African skies at night.

Some adventurers want to see gorillas and chimpanzees and plan to photograph other rare wildlife. And they often can. Just ask your travel agent for a tour. There are tours aplenty.

For Further Information

Natural Expeditions International
P.O. Box 11496
Eugene, OR 97440

Overseas Adventure Travel
349 Broadway
Cambridge, MA 02139

Questers Worldwide Nature Tours
257 Park Avenue South
New York, NY 10010

Voyagers International
P.O. Box 915
Ithaca, NY 14851

Wilderness Travel
801 Allston Way
Berkeley, CA 94710

Explore the Altiplano

Bolivia is a country of superlatives. Landlocked in the western part of South America, it sprawls over 424,165 square miles (1,098,580 square kilometers) and shares borders with Peru to the northwest, Brazil to the north and east, Paraguay to the southeast, Argentina to the south and Chile on the west. It is a country that claims the highest navigable lake in the world, the highest airport, the highest golf course, the highest ski run, the highest capital, one of the newest and wildest frontiers, one of the oldest ruins, and what is said to be the highest concentration of cosmic rays on earth.

Bolivia is also a nation of contrasts, which led a French explorer-scientist to call it the "microcosm of our planet." It has every type of geologically classified land, flora, fauna, minerals, and tropical products.

The country's population, now 6.4 million, is indigenous, with a relatively small admixture of Spaniards. Bolivians take pride in their heritage from a noble race, and they live among the remnants of the ancient civilization.

Bolivia lies wholly in the tropical zone, yet temperatures vary from the heat of its equatorial low lands to the cold of the Andes. To focus on Bolivia's diverse land, most tours start with the inland sea of Lake Titicaca (12,600 feet) and work east.

The animal life on the Altiplano includes wool-bearing sheep, llama, alpaca, and vicuna, along with fur-bearing chinchilla and red fox. The fabled vicuna, a rare and very delicate animal, still roams the high regions of the Altiplano, but articles made from its scarce fleece are hard to find because the government strictly prohibits its sale. You can, however, easily obtain rugs, ponchos, and a number of other articles made from llama and alpaca wool.

From the high plain, the land spills down into lush, semitropical valleys to the north and east. These valleys, called *yungas*, are drained by the Beni River System, which then empties into the Amazon River. This land of present beauty and future development begins three hours out of La Paz. The soil of the Altiplano washes into the basins of the region, where citrus fruits, cattle, and other products are raised, many of them eventually making their way to La Paz.

Outward Bound offers a twenty-six-day expedition during which you get to know Bolivia's communities, as well as the Altiplano and the Cordillera Real, the Andes mountain range. The school supplies all the climbing and camping gear.

NOLS also offers a yearly trip, this one to Chile and Patagonia. It involves hiking, visiting the local farmers, observing local wildlife, backpacking, and sea kayaking.

Wildland Adventures also sponsors an excellent outdoor tour of Venezuela.

For Further Information

Colorado Outward Bound School
945 Pennsylvania Street
Denver, CO 80203-3198

The National Outdoor Leadership School (NOLS)
288 Main Street
Lander, WY 82520-0579

Wildland Adventures
3516 NE 155th Street
Seattle, WA 98155

Hike the Costa Rican Rain Forests

Ask any longtime traveler or any savvy journalist. They'll agree that Costa Rica is a democratic, peace-loving country with friendly natives,

warm welcomes everywhere, splendid beaches, lovely tropical water-
ways, and thunderous waterfalls. And most of all, unforgettable, lush
rain forest where you can hike, photograph rare white monkeys and
other animals, go rafting and kayaking, and enjoy spectacular bird-
watching.

According to the authoritative National Audubon Society, Costa
Rica's rain forests provide the perfect backdrop for the study of birds
and tropical plants. In fact, Costa Rica harbors some twelve thousand
known species of plants and at least eight hundred kinds of birds.

The National Audubon Society organizes well-run tours into Costa Rica's National Parks, with stops to observe bird life. Among others,
they promise "fiery-throated and cerise hummingbirds, slate flower-
piercer and long-tailed silky-fly-catcher. Other birding stops as we continue downslope will likely reveal colorful tanagers (bay-headed, emerald,
black-and-yellow), hummingbirds (black-crested coquette, green thorn-
tail, and purple-crowned fairy) along with immaculate antbird, rufous-
browed tyrannulet, and black hawk-eagle."

Another reliable Costa Rica-bound group, Wilderness Southeast,
paints a tempting picture in its travel literature: "The remote rain forest preserve of Rara Avis is on the Atlantic slopes of the central mountains. We will hike through the lush virgin rain forest surrounding our
lodge to observe the amazing diversity of tropical plants and learn about
the complex relationships between the jungle flora and rain forest animals. Especially impressive is the riot of epiphytic growth here: thick
lianas, strangler figs, giant philodendron vines, orchids and bromeli-
ads. We will swim at the base of a pristine waterfall that tumbles down
the jungly slopes. En route to our second site we will stop to take a
short hike to one of Costa Rica's exciting active volcanoes. We will then
explore the tropical dry forests of Palo Verde National Park. In stark
contrast to the rain forests of Rara Avis, this area experiences a distinct
dry season when many trees drop their leaves and produce colorful
blossoms. Here we can see the wildlife so hidden from us in more lux-
uriant rain forests. We will likely see such tropical animals as monkeys,
peccaries, huge iguanas and troops of playful coatis. We will also observe

many colorful birds including parrots, motmots, trogons, and the endangered jabiru stork."

How could a nature lover resist descriptions like these? Wilderness Southeast also offers Jungle Backpack trips whose "participants must have a strong sense of adventure and an interest in tropical ecology."

Still one more travel provider, Berkeley, California-based Backroads, not only arranges the usual hikes, but offers bicycle tours as well (see above), which include travel on ferries, excursion boats, sea kayaking, and busing.

For Further Information

Backroads
1516 Fifth Street, Suite RP
Berkeley, CA 94710-1740

Costa Rica National Tourist Office
2112 S Street, NW
Washington, DC 20008

Explore Costa Rica
P.O. Box 818-1200 Pavas
San Jose, Costa Rica

National Audubon Society
613 Riversville Road
Greenwich, CT 06831

Wilderness Southeast
Savannah, GA 31410-1019

Wildland Adventures
3516 NE 155th Street
Seattle, WA 98155

Experience the Ultimate in Summer Skiing: The Parsenn

Davos, Switzerland. To ski here is to dream of the ultimate experience, which, at least in Switzerland, has to be at a year-round mountain range and ski complex known as the Parsenn. It is the area the Swiss are proudest of; the runs attract hordes of Germans. Even Austrians, who claim that the Alberg region is the mightiest, travel to the more prestigious Parsenn. Every serious European skier wants to try the famous runs at least once in a lifetime.

Why the magnetic pull? For one thing, Davos is easy to reach from Zürich and equally easy from Austria and Germany. For another thing, the Parsenn is not only scenically compelling with all that treeless Alpine terrain, but there simply is more of it. The region has 160 ski runs (amounting to 192 miles) plus a whopping fifty-five aerial trams, gondolas, chairlifts, T-bars, and mountain trains.

Even the length of the runs seems remarkable: it is some twelve miles from the 2844-meter Weissfluh summit down to Klosters (only the upper part is open in summer). The average skier will need at least one hour for that trip, providing that he or she isn't tempted by the many restaurants on the way down. Most of the terrain is intermediate and ego-building, but the mountain remains one of the most famous and prestigious around.

The Parsenn first turned up in the Swiss history books as "Parsenna," which translates into "something special." Of course, the farm historians of 1883 were actually referring to the excellent regional hay! Ski races were held here in 1907 when a German official described the Parsenn as the "Olympus of the winter gods." The local red train first beckoned to enthusiasts in 1933.

There are few identifying signs on the runs, and ski patrollers or ski guides (who answer questions as they do at many large North American resorts) are rare. Compared to Vail and Jackson Hole, which employ at least a hundred such free guides between them, it's surprising. On the other hand, the Parsenn runs are well-maintained; large crews, some with heavy equipment, manage to spread the white stuff where it is most needed during the winter season.

Davos, population fifteen hundred, has grown tremendously and hectically during the past decade. The atmosphere here is mostly impersonal. To accommodate the throngs there are 13,700 beds in condos, plus another 7,500 hotel beds in and around Davos, a huge convention center, several hundred restaurants, forty-seven miles of cross-country trails, and toboggan runs. The much smaller Klosters features excellent hiking paths (for year-round use), skating, curling, indoor swimming, and saunas. Parsenn lift tickets are now computerized; a machine checks on the validity.

European skiers zoom downhill at a faster clip than North Americans. "Defensive skiing" therefore makes sense.

The nearest Swiss National Tourist office can sell you a practical (and inexpensive) Swiss Pass for all railroad and bus travel. These offices—or your travel agent—can also arrange accommodations close to the famous Parsenn. It *is* something special and you'll quickly know why when you ski it.

For Further Information

Swiss National Tourist Office
608 Fifth Avenue
New York, NY 10020

Swiss National Tourist Office
222 North Sepulveda Boulevard, Suite 1570
El Segundo, CA 900245

Swissair
The Swiss Center
608 Fifth Avenue
New York, NY 10020

Roam through Italy

Italy can be an adventure, too.

If you're at all sensitive to the colors of a medieval roof, an ochre palace, the Mediterranean sky, a rocky shoreline, or a flower market; if the stately shape of a cypress tree enthralls you; if architecture and historic streets matter more than having a lot of money—then Italy, the *Bel Paese,* must be your choice. Italy has no peers visually. Stand at the Piazza Navona in Rome and you seem to stand before a painting. Baroque fountains, artists showing their canvasses, and the cafés all around beckon to you.

In every age, artists and poets have succumbed to the poetry of Rome and come to live in this city. Great artists drew inspiration for their work from the surroundings of the balustrade that surmounts the Spanish steps; among them, Berlioz, Goethe, Byron, Keats, Shelley, Dickens, Ruskin, Gogol, and Hawthorne. Looking at Rome, Chateaubriand sighed: *"Quelle ville pour y mourir."*—"What a town to die in!"

One of the advantages of living anywhere in Italy is the mild climate. In the north the Alps protect Italy from extremes of winter weather; on all other sides the mild Mediterranean Sea moderates the climate of the peninsula, making all seasons comfortable.

Italy has a fascinating history involving art, beautiful music, and opera. The gastronomic joys are as great as the lovely hills that produce Italy's wines, fruit, and cheeses. Gentle hills give way to sharp-peaked mountains that stretch toward a sandy ocean. Many Americans who work here succumb to the *dolce far niente,* the "sweet do nothing." And all foreigners, if they have a musical ear, fall in love with the Italian language. The atmosphere is cosmopolitan in the larger Italian cities. The country is full of kind people. In fact, one good reason for deciding to visit Italy might well be the Italians themselves; they are among the most interesting, fascinating, captivating people of Europe.

For Further Information

Italian Government Travel Office
630 Fifth Avenue
New York, NY 10111

Alitalia
666 Fifth Avenue
New York, NY 10103

Index